Susanne Everett
Introduction by John Keegan

Hamlyn

London · New York · Sydney · Toronto

A Bison Book

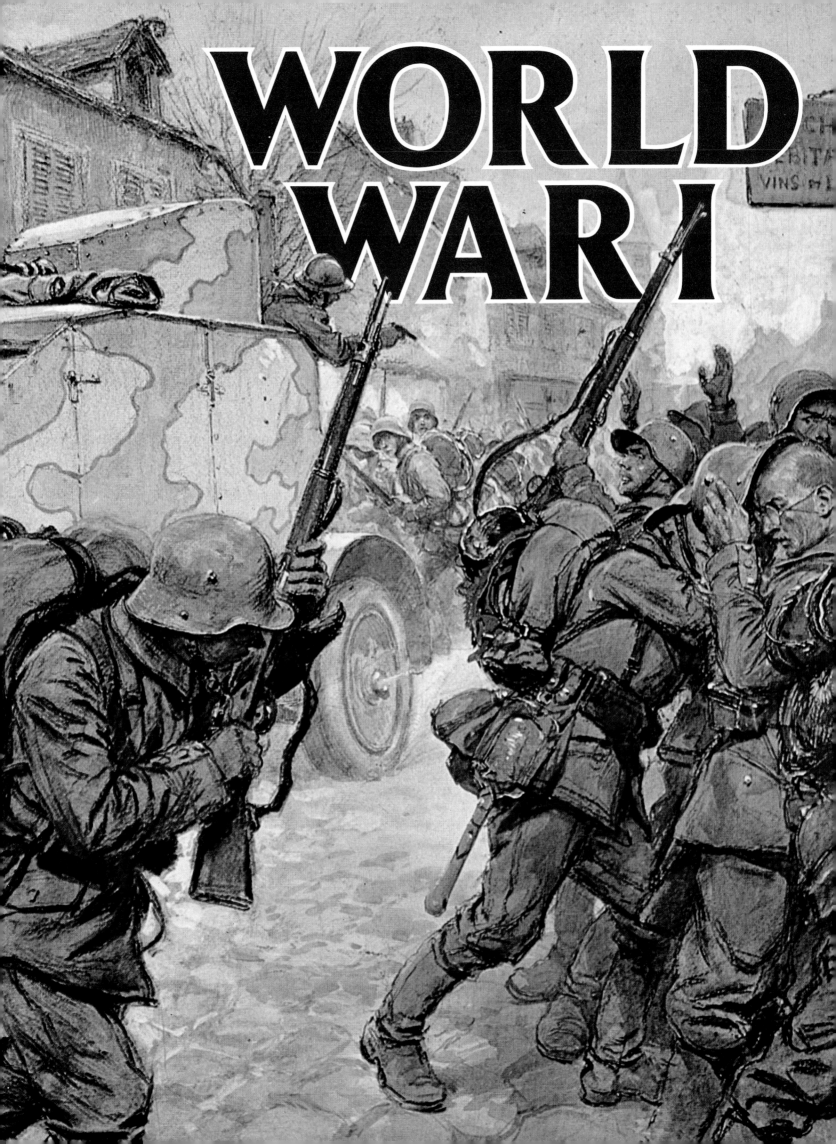

WORLD WAR I

Published by
The Hamlyn Publishing Group Limited
London · New York · Sydney · Toronto
Astronaut House, Feltham
Middlesex, England

© Copyright Bison Books Limited 1980

Produced by
Bison Books Limited
4 Cromwell Place
London SW7

ISBN 0 600 39480 8

Printed in Hong Kong

Contents

p 1: A lonely tommy on lookout duty in a trench in 1917.
p 2–3: A French armored truck spreads confusion among German infantry men, who are trying to retreat.
p 4–5: An anti-aircraft gun in action outside Saint Jean, during the Third Battle of Ypres, October 1917.

Introduction by John Keegan

The First World War stole upon Europe by surprise. There had been two small Balkan conflicts in 1911–12, but neither had looked to involve the armies of the Great Powers. Before that, one had to go as far back as 1871 to find a time when international peace was sundered by fighting. The European 19th century has indeed come to appear in retrospect as an era of almost miraculous tranquility for, though we can count half a dozen sizeable conflicts between the abdication of Napoleon in 1815 and the assassination of the Archduke Ferdinand in 1914, none was protracted or very costly in life. This appearance seemed valid also to contemporaries. Peace had become a habit of mind as well as a condition of life and was expected to persist, whatever the sums spent upon armament and even though they rose year by year.

Yet we are now able to see, as Europeans of the last century were not, that there were special and local reasons restraining the Powers from waging major war against each other. Most important was the enormous expansion in the availability of resources, in Europe and beyond, which for the first time in human history not only relieved populations of the ever present fear of famine and privation, but actually offered them the prospect of better times. The hardships to which the industrial revolution condemned the new manufacturing classes have been made notorious. What is forgotten is that manufacturing provided continuous year-round work, and created a steady demand for agricultural produce, thus transforming the conditions of life both in town and countryside. Even when the exploitation of the new lands in America and Australia provoked an agricultural slump in the second half of the century, it also provided a way of escape from the consequences at home, via the open door of emigration. It is therefore perhaps the 19th rather than the 20th which deserves to be called 'the century of the common man,' since it was in those 100 years that the real transformation of his conditions and expectations occurred.

This 'peaceful progress,' which was the ideal of 19th-century liberalism, by definition precludes war. There were other factors at work to distract the peoples of Europe from hostility toward their neighbors. The most important turned on the belief that people of the same language should share a common statehood. That belief could lead to war, as between Austria and Savoy in 1848 and 1859 and Austria and Prussia in 1866. Since these conflicts were normally between states of unequal strength, none persisted enough to become general. They were emotionally important enough, however, to the parties concerned to nullify quarrels with neighbors of a different language group. Nationalism therefore served, for a time at least, to overlay the danger of quarrels between neighbors speaking different languages.

In the case of three of the powers – Britain, France and Russia – there were the attractions and rewards of imperialism to draw their military efforts away from a European focus. Britain's rise to great empire in the

19th century is a familiar story. It is less well-remembered that France acquired enormous colonial possessions in the same period, in the Far East and in North and West Africa. Russia, whose pioneers had carried the outposts of Czarist power to the shores of the Pacific in the 18th century, turned southward thereafter, and subjected the Muslim kingdoms and khanates of Central Asia to her control. Thus distracted, the states of greatest war potential had little energy left to waste in struggles within the European heartland, and indeed little motive. It was only when their imperial ambitions conflicted, as they did over the future of the

Above: A colorful example of British 'war art' in the decoration of an artillery piece during the Battle of the Somme, 1916.

Below: Casualties after a hand-to-hand skirmish.

enfeebled Turkish Empire in 1854, that they found cause to fight each other. Then their geographical locations, at the periphery of Europe, ensured that they fight at arm's length, without the means to do each other serious or lasting harm.

These invisible and beneficent influences had run their course by 1914. The imperial powers had completed their expansion; there were indeed few new lands to conquer by that date. The new states of Europe were also complete. Italy had thrown off the power of foreign rulers and united under the House of Savoy. Germany had ceased to be a cluster of small kingdoms, under the thrall of more important powers, and become an entity, with the King of Prussia at its head. The enormous expansion of the European economy had also lost its first wind. Cheap resources were harder to come by, easy markets more difficult to find. Economic competition took on a new edge, sharpened by the military powers of those states which felt threatened most keenly by the new commercial climate. Britain was

the first to suffer. Though in dimensions of empire by far the greatest power in 1914, she had already ceased to be the most productive manufacturing country, and was losing her status as the world's leading merchant and carrier. France too felt economically disadvantaged. Her start in the industrial revolution had been slow and her industry did not compete well in foreign markets. These were increasingly dominated by the Germans, who had the inventiveness, energy and discipline to make and sell at a price and in volumes which the older industrial powers could not match.

Trade war had therefore become a condition of life in the European world of 1914. Peace might have survived that development. What fatally threatened it was the transplantation of nationalist urges from the large peoples to the small, those whose weakness and backwardness had left them within the boundaries of the empires which the large peoples had created or preserved. The Poles of Russia and Germany felt a bitter sense of deprivation. They were an isolated case which could be contained. That of the peoples of the Austro-

Hungarian empire could not, for they formed a majority which could be deprived only by the artificial super-ordination of two of them — Austro-Germans and Hungarians — over the rest. Yet the maintenance of that superordination was essential: internally, because to give autonomy to the 'nationalities' would leave Austria and Hungary as tiny rumps; externally, because the liberation of the 'nationalities' would provoke instability elsewhere, notably inside the German Empire itself.

Germany was therefore compelled to defend Austria-Hungary against any danger of dissolution, even to the point of going to war, but she had other reasons for thinking the risk of war bearable. The disparity between her economic power, which was great, and her overseas possessions, which were small, was a constant source of national discontent, heightened by the traditional powers' determination to treat her as a new-comer to their table and to exclude her from it as much as possible. Hence her indulgence in state investments which were not really necessary to her well-being, like the enormous High Seas Fleet, built to remind Britain of the fragility of her naval supremacy. That fleet, by 1914, was almost large enough to proffer the chance of

Below: New Zealanders in a switch trench near the Somme, 15 September 1916.

victory at sea. The German army, in efficiency if not in size, was a force which made the prospect of victory on land highly realizable. Discontent, ambition and new-found strength therefore combined to turn Germany into a warlike power by 1914, and worked on the fears of her neighbors to generate a complementary motivation. It needed only one incident, at the wrong place and time, to set these motivations into action.

The Sarajevo assassination was that incident. Its immediate outcome had been foreseen. Its long-term consequences had not. Men of power, military as well as civilian, held it as a dogma that any large European war must be short, with victory going quickly to the side which could best mobilize its resources. They were nearly right. Germany did almost win in August 1914, because she brought to the battlefronts, east and west, a better army than her neighbors could find in the time. The mistake the men of power had made was in their definition of 'mobilization.' They had grossly under-estimated the resources, material, human and spiritual, of the societies at the head of which they stood. The campaigns of 1914 devastated the armies which fought them. However, such were the reserves of manpower, so deep the resources, so flexible the economies, so fervent and obedient the populations of Britain, France, Germany and even Russia, that their governments found themselves able to create new armies for the next round, to which the logic of circumstances bound them without opportunity of escape.

A war of quick victory was thus transformed, against all expectation, into a struggle of attrition, of which the lives of millions of young men were to be the raw material. 'World war' it became, because the imperial states carried the fighting to wherever their colonial possessions impinged; 'world war' because the clients and allies of the European powers — Turkey foremost among them — were bribed or compelled to join in; 'world war' because in the penultimate year, America judged it her duty and necessity to intervene. The strangeness of the war, and its best-known, most-reviled quality, was its narrow geographical confinement. Its only great sea battle, Jutland, was fought within a few miles of the British and German coasts. Its great land battles were fixed within even narrower limits. All the fighting on the Eastern Front was played out in a belt 100 miles wide north and south of the Carpathians, or on the crests of the Caucasus. Gallipoli, where the Turks defeated the British and French attempt to destroy their power at a blow, was a pocket handkerchief battlefield. The Italian Front, which opened up in 1915, clung to a few strategic peaks in the Tyrol and the Julian Alps. In the west, parts of the front fixed in 1914 did not move a yard throughout four years of offense and defense. It was in these narrow strips, defined by the range of the artilleries of the two sides, and so never more than 10 miles wide at any one time, that 'attrition' did its work. The results remain for all to see. They reside in the great war cemeteries which cluster together along the trace of the old Western Front in France and Belgium. In them lie buried nearly a million British, over a million German and nearly two million French soldiers. Nearly a million Germans lie buried elsewhere, in less solemn surroundings, and with them millions of Russians, Turks and soldiers of the Habsburg armies. A majority of the victims of the war probably have no known grave.

They demand a memorial. Their deaths require an explanation. The best memorials have come from the pens of the survivors, in whose lives their months or years at the front remained overwhelmingly the most important event. The best explanations paradoxically tend to emerge with the passage of time, as passions cool and the tragedy which the war was find its place among all the other tragedies which civilized men obstinately visit on themselves. This book is an attempt at an explanation. It looks for it particularly in the nature and quality of the fighting which, like the ascent of a mountain of small gradient, offered those who took part a succession of illusions, a replacement of one false crest of conquest with another, toward which the dwindling band of survivors constantly struggled forward in the belief that victory lay just beyond it. That illusion was one of which the soldiers of the war were themselves bitterly conscious and yet from which, being human, they could not liberate themselves. Unable to believe that next day, next week, next month would not reward their efforts with success, they soldiered on. Some of them, in the end, won a sort of victory. We all live with the defeat which they inflicted on the world of the hundred year peace.

French *poilus* are cheered on the way to the front at the beginning of the war, August 1914.

1 Europe Blunders to War

The Ancients believed that wars were made in heaven. World War I was made on earth and, in particular, in the dangerous triangle of central Europe where, in 1914, three empires met. Eastward stretched the great empire of the Czar of all the Russias; west and north lay the empire of the German Kaiser; south along the Danube ran the hereditary lands of the Archduke of Austria, inhabited not only by Germans but by Hungarians, Rumanians, Poles, Czechs, Slovaks, Slovenes, Ruthenians, Croats and Serbs. The two other empires had their minorities — Poles in Germany, Finns, Letts, Estonians and more Poles in Russia, not to mention the myriad Asiatic tribes and mountain peoples of her deep interior. Both were states unmistakably founded upon a majority. Austria was not. It was an empire of factions, some major, some minor, some enthusiastic over their standing in society, and a few outrightly dissatisfied. Foremost among the last were the Austrian Serbs, who wished above all to be united with their independent brethren inside the borders of the kingdom of Serbia.

The government of the Austro-Hungarian Empire was, however, adamantly opposed to releasing them. Not only would the cession of the territory inhabited by the Austrian Serbs diminish that of the empire in a place of great military vulnerability; not only would it add greatly to the power and pretensions of the Serbian kingdom, itself a potential ally of Russia rather than Austria; but it would fan the flames of nationalist and separatist ambitions burning inside every one of the other communities of which the empire was composed. Austria was caught in a vice. Although in the grip of a domestic organization both cumbersome and illogical she was nevertheless obliged to maintain the status quo, in the fear that any attempt to improve the situation would merely heighten problems for which the empire, however inadequately, provided a solution. Vienna and Budapest, twin capitals of the Dual Monarchy, could only hope that by refusing to move in any

way to meet nationalist demands the whole gigantic artifice of empire could be held immobile against a day of reckoning that might, with luck, never come.

The worm in the apple of their hopes was the impatience of the most fervent of the Serb nationalists. Like others before and since, their thoughts had turned to terrorism for they felt it was only through violence that their dreams of a day of liberation could be realized. It was by no means an easy task. Not only were such practical idealists few and far between, they were inexperienced and, more important, lacked opportunities for a dramatic gesture to promote their cause. By 1914 the ancient emperor, Francis Joseph, barely travelled beyond his palaces, and, in any case, his immense popularity made his assassination unthinkable even to the most fanatical of nationalists. A more promising target presented itself in the form of the Emperor's nephew and heir, the Archduke Franz Ferdinand, who was out of favor with his uncle due to an ill-judged marriage and universally disliked throughout the empire. On 28 June 1914, together with his wife, he was to visit Sarajevo, capital of the formerly Turkish province of Bosnia, the disputed area, scene of many uprisings, which had been administered by Austria-Hungary since 1898 and annexed in 1908. A fraternity of adolescent Serb patriots led by a schoolboy, Gavrilo Princip, decided that the moment had come to take action, and resolved to make an attempt on the Archduke's life. Their first efforts were not promising. As the royal pair drove into the city two of the young conspirators faced with the 'enemy' could not bring themselves to shoot him, a third threw a bomb and missed. Princip, presented with a second chance thanks to the imperial chauffeur's mishandling of the Archduke's car, took it with determination. Three shots killed Franz Ferdinand and, probably unintentionally, his wife. Princip was arrested alive and taken for trial — the empire he hated so much proved to be no tyranny. The Austrian intelligence service, however, had clearly decided that its counterpart in the Kingdom of Serbia lay behind the outrage, and the Austrian government accordingly decided to punish its neighbor so severely that it would not in future foment disorder within the imperial borders.

The punishment was not to be military but moral; Serbia was to be obliged to apologize for the assassination, to give guarantees of good behavior in the future and to permit representatives of the Austrian police to enter Serbian territory in order to track down the conspirators still at large. If she accepted these terms, Serbia would, in effect surrender an important part of her sovereignty to her great neighbor. If she refused, she would give Austria the pretext for justifiable military action against her. Austria would, in fact, have been content with either outcome, but in anticipation of refusal had, before issuing her ultimatum to Serbia, taken the precaution of extracting from Germany an assurance of her support should an Austro-Serbian military confrontation threaten to develop into something wider.

That such a development was threatened was made highly probable by the prevailing pattern of European alliances. For Austria was not the only state in Europe to enjoy the protection of a stronger neighbor. So, too, did Serbia itself — that of Russia, which, in turn, was linked by treaty to France. This state of affairs, the so-called 'interlocking pattern of alliances,' had come about in the past 20 years and in the following fashion.

Germany, under the Chancellorship of the great Otto von Bismarck, had always been careful to avoid enmities on both her frontiers,

Bottom: The aging Kaiser Franz Joseph of Austria in the Hofburg grounds. His heir apparent was Franz Ferdinand.

Below: The Royal couple pass through Sarajevo prior to their fatal meeting with Princip.

Below: Archduke Franz Ferdinand of Austria and his wife arrive in Sarajevo on 28 June 1914 followed by General Oskar Potiorek, who was military governor of Bosnia. He met the fated couple at the station and travelled with them in an open sports car.

Right: Gavrilo Princip, assassin of the Archduke and his wife. His actions on 28 June 1914 led the world to war.

Far right: Czar Nicholas II and Czarina Alexandra of Russia.

Below right: The Archduke and Archduchess lie in state in Sarajevo after their assassination.

eastern and western. Enmity on her southern frontier, with Austria, might have seemed unavoidable after the War of 1866. The two German-speaking courts had too natural an affinity and their empires too many common interests for the aftermath of that quarrel not to be quickly forgotten. The rancor of France, defeated in 1870 and stripped of her frontier provinces of Alsace-Lorraine, could not be so easily dissipated. It had, therefore, seemed essential to Bismarck that Germany should always be on good terms with Russia, thus avoiding any prospect of the Czar and the French President co-ordinating plans for military action against Germany of an offensive, or even a mutually defensive, nature. Bismarck, however, had been removed from office in 1888 by the young Kaiser, who had subsequently failed to renew Bismarck's 'reinsurance' treaty with Russia. The failure had not been an oversight, but a deliberate omission, designed to increase Germany's diplomatic freedom of maneuver, from which Wilhelm II hoped to reap wide benefits on the world, rather than the nearby European scene.

The immediate effect of the Treaty's lapse had, however, been to excite Russian fears of isolation in European affairs and to turn her toward exactly that reinforcement of her strategic position which Bismarck had most dreaded: an alliance with France. Tentative negotiations between the two countries fared well and in 1894 they consolidated their understanding. It had remained intact throughout Russia's war with Japan in 1904–1905, which had, in one way or another, soured her relations with the rest of the great power community, and it had been renewed and refreshed since. Germany was thus confronted on her eastern and western frontiers with powers each of which, Berlin had reason to suspect, would react to a German attack by assisting the other.

However Germany's diplomatic predicament did not end there. More recently Great Britain had been drawn into the system of military precautions against Germany. No formal undertaking had been arranged, but since 1910 British officers had been conducting staff talks with their French opposite numbers and had agreed on a plan to integrate the deployment of a British Expeditionary Force (BEF) with the French field army if both should be called upon to resist a German invasion of France.

Politicians and diplomats in France and Britain remained remarkably ignorant of the details of these discussions, though aware that they were in progress. The isolation of soldiers from politicians was however a feature of public life at the time. It was even more marked in Germany, where control of the armed forces rested not with the Minister of War or the Reichstag but with the Kaiser. His chief military servant was the Chief of the Great General Staff, who was answerable to him directly. The war plans of the German army, which the Chief drew up, were not, therefore, necessarily known in all their details to the Chancellor, who was head of government. As things stood in Germany in 1914, the current war plan had not been drawn up by the then Chief of Staff, General Graf Helmuth Johannes von Moltke (the Younger) but by his predecessor, Graf Alfred von Schlieffen, and its details had remained almost unaltered since his retirement in 1906. Chosen by the Kaiser for his name (his great uncle was the victor of 1870) rather than for his qualities of command, which were slender, Moltke was a reluctant Chief of Staff. He had not wanted the job, and he filled his post badly, entirely failing to convey to Chancellor Theobald von Bethmann-Hollweg a proper understanding of the consequences of a German mobilization. Perhaps, as one historian has suggested, he did not understand them fully himself.

They were dramatic enough. Schlieffen had lived during his long tenure of office (1891–1906) with the nightmare of the 'war on two fronts,' which he feared the Kaiser's new foreign policy might bring about. He feared Russia – whose vast spaces and great reserves of man-power would, he thought, engulf any German army which marched eastward – more than he feared France, but only in the longer term. In the short term his fears were exactly reversed. His solution of the military predicament was, therefore, to engage Germany's main force first against France rather than against Russia and to pit the German army against the latter only after the former had been defeated. But how was this to be achieved? France, defeated by an attack across the common frontier in 1870, had since spent large sums on frontier fortification, filling the gap between southern Belgium and Switzerland with a dense belt of forts and obstacles. A passage in the middle – the so-called 'Trouée de Charmes' – had been left open, but only with the idea of funnelling any German invading force into a space so constricted that it would emerge through it helplessly exposed to decapitating thrusts by mobile French flanking forces. He was determined to avoid this deliberate trap. But what other approach was there? He could not contemplate a seaborne invasion. He dared not risk a move through Switzerland, whose mountainous terrain was the best guarantee of her diplomatic status as a permanently neutral state. He therefore had to look at Belgium.

What he saw was another inconveniently neutral country with the additional problem that her neutrality was guaranteed not only by Britain and France but, as the inheritor of the obligations of the Kingdom of Prussia, by Germany also. This diplomatic conundrum was originally sidestepped by Schlieffen when he first put his mind to it in 1891. Only a small violation of Belgian neutrality, 'no more than was necessary to outflank the French line of forts in Lorraine' would, he considered, be needed. Such a limited move, he felt, would not only be acceptable to the international community but, even more important, would not provoke Britain into rallying to the defense of her small ally. However, further deliberations drew Schlieffen to the awkward conclusion that a small violation would not be enough to answer Germany's military needs – he felt he had to place at least two armies, each of 150,000

men, on the left flank of the French, and that required the use of a plentiful road network on a wide front. Southern Belgium was hilly, wooded and badly provided with communications. Any violation would therefore have to be executed in the northern Belgian plains. On the principle that he might as well be hanged for a sheep as a lamb, Schlieffen decided to make the whole of Belgium the scene of his outflanking maneuver, and to commit the greater part of the German army to it.

By 1906, when ill health forced his retirement, the plan was complete. Such was Schlieffen's prestige that his successor did not dare to question its logic or tamper with its details and it therefore remained the blueprint for Germany's part in a European war in 1914. Its full implications, however, had even then not been grasped. It was a recipe for dealing with a combined offensive against Germany by France and Russia united, either through an instantaneous response or by what today would be called a 'pre-emptive attack.' It left Germany with no plan for fighting either country singlehanded. Should either France or Russia attack Germany without the agreement of the other, Germany would be obliged to mobilize against both. Worse, in a diplomatic situation elsewhere than in Franco-Russian-German relations, which nevertheless threatened a confrontation between Germany and either France or Russia, she was still obliged to mobilize against both. Unlike Austria, which had a 'major' and a 'minor' war plan, the first to deal with a Russian threat, the second with a lesser danger in the Balkans, Germany had only one plan: to mobilize against both her greatest enemies. Mobilization, in the circumstances of the age, would inevitably lead to war.

That had not always necessarily been the case. Nations had mobilized in the past as a means of bringing pressure to bear on a neighbor, yet without the maneuver leading to an actual clash of armies. But developments both in the size of armies and in the speed with which they might be moved to a potential war front had recently invested mobilization with great

Below: Count von Schlieffen, who had completed his war plan in 1906. It was to be executed as it had been laid down.

Left: President Raymond Poincaré of France (white beard) at an airdrome near Paris just prior to the war.

Right: Kaiser Wilhelm II of Germany and his army Chief of Staff von Moltke on maneuvers prior to war.

Far right: A heroic view of the Kaiser.

Below right: Kaiser Wilhelm II in full regalia.

Below: Theobald von Bethmann-Hollweg, German Chancellor in 1914, who gave Austria-Hungary a 'blank check' to invade Serbia at will.

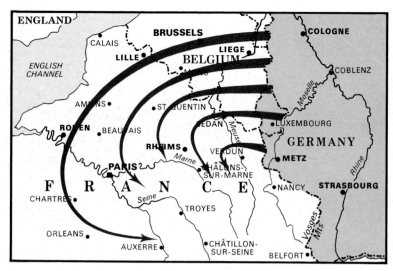

Above: The Schlieffen Plan called for a quick encirclement of Paris within six weeks of the outbreak of war, forcing a French capitulation.

Above: Provincial townspeople are called to the German colors in July 1914.

risk; where a power was threatened, as Germany was, by a war on two fronts simultaneously the danger became all the more intense.

All the powers in 1914 maintained large standing armies in peace, fed by conscription, which in turn fed very large reserves. France maintained a standing army of 500,000, Germany of 750,000, Russia of 1,200,000, and Austria of nearly 500,000. The officers and senior noncommissioned officers of these armies were long-service soldiers. The privates and corporals were conscripts serving from two to three years and then returned to civilian life, but remained on the books of the armies as reservists. With these reservists, France could increase the size of her field army to 3,500,000, Germany hers to 5,000,000. There were still more reservists to be drawn from men up to the age of 50, capable of forming second-line units — called *Territorials* in France, *Landwehr* and *Landsturm* in Germany — who, though not fit to take their place in the line of battle, were able to do tasks on the lines of communication, thus releasing younger men for the front.

These large numbers of active troops, first-line reserves and second-line Landwehr and Landsturm, allowed Germany, in the summer of 1914, to contemplate putting eight separate armies into the field. One, the Eighth, was earmarked to defend East Prussia against the Russians should they manage to mount an invasion. The other seven were to be transported from their mobilization centers to the Belgian and French frontiers, in accordance with the Schlieffen Plan.

It was expected that these armies would encounter the French about 18 days after mobilization, if war should follow. However, the principal ingredient of the Schlieffen plan was concealment. Where Germany would deploy its main force was to remain hidden — and in such a context the word 'if' could not be used. But as the Kaiser was to discover to his anguish, the sequence was that war would follow a German mobilization. He had to face up to the fearful truth that mobilization inevitably revealed the deployment plan, and that the deployment plan told all.

The Kaiser made this horrifying discovery rather late in the day. On 24 July, the day after the issue of the Austrian ultimatum to Serbia, the crisis had deepened. Certain precautionary military measures had been taken by Russia and an announcement was made on 26 July that

she would pass to the 'Period Preparatory to War.' This unfortunately-phrased term, which in fact only meant that the army would prepare to mobilize rather than actually do so, laid itself wide open to misinterpretation. Straight away it was misconstrued by Austria. She had two mobilization schemes — the first (B) for a small-scale war in the Balkans, the second (R) for general war. She had implemented B on issuing her ultimatum to Serbia, anticipating a Serbian mobilization to resist it. Sergei D Sazonov, the Russian foreign minister, expected the Austrians to accept the 'Period Preparatory to War' as a purely precautionary measure, even though it involved bringing the 13 Russian corps on the Russo-Austrian border to a state of readiness. The head of the Russian mobilization office pointed out to Sazonov that he might be expecting too much: that Austria would probably feel itself forced in consequence to order full mobilization, and in that case Germany, as Austria's ally and protector, would also feel herself obliged to mobilize. Presented with this likely outcome, Sazonov, far from deciding to defer the 'Period Preparatory to War' made plans for its implementation. Not

Below: Herbert Asquith, British Prime Minister in 1914, who used the violation of Belgian neutrality by Germany as a pretext to join the war.

Below: Sergei Sazonov, the Russian Foreign Minister, warned the Czar that entry in the war might prove fatal to the monarchy.

Below: Sir Edward Grey, British Foreign Minister, who warned the world that 'the lamps were going out all over Europe.'

Above: Austrian soldiers receive their first pay after the mobilization in July 1914.

Above right: French crowds cheer after the declaration of war was announced.

only that, he also gave orders to prepare the full mobilization procedure, intending to lay both before the Czar for signature. Later, when he saw how the crisis was developing, he would judge which should be put into effect.

The next fatal twist to the development of the crisis was transmitted by France who, as Russia's ally, was naturally concerned by news of her preparatory measures. On 26 July the French government cancelled all military leave and the next day ordered the embarkation of the North African garrison, 100,000 strong. At the same time, the French Ambassador at St Petersburg, Maurice Paléologue began to press the Czar's government about its intentions. French anxiety about the Russian mobilization in the Caucasus differed from the Austrian in that in the event of a war with Germany French national security rested on the supposition of a major Russian offensive in East Prussia — the present Russian precautions thus represented a weakening, not strengthening of France's strategic position. During the next few days, therefore, Paléologue made it his business to move the Russians toward full mobilization. But in his hurry to maintain France's strength, he failed to see that such measures threatened to destroy, rather than preserve, peace. The flood gates of war were already being prized open.

As late as 29 July, however, Sazonov was uncertain about whether to proceed to full mobilization. On that day he received a telegram from Bethmann-Hollweg, the German Chancellor, which he took to be a patronizing and menacing ultimatum. The German ambassador, who was the intermediary, covered the note with the words that it was 'not a threat but a friendly warning,' sentiments which Sazonov chose to disregard. It implied that 'further progress of Russian mobilization measures would compel (Germany) to mobilize and then European war could scarcely be prevented.' Sazonov interpreted this to mean that Germany demanded a humiliating reversal of Russia's self-defensive precautions and accordingly advised the Czar that 'the risk could not be accepted of delaying a general mobilization.' Faced with this uninspiring alternative Nicholas II agreed to allow the whole of his army to be put on a war footing.

On the brink, however, the Czar had second thoughts. A patron of the international peace movement, his concern for peace was genuine. He decided to order not general but partial

Send Out the Army and the Navy

Send out the army and the navy,
Send out the rank and file,
Send out the brave territorials,
They'll face the danger with a smile
(I don't think)
Send out my mother,
Send out my sister and my brother,
But for God's sake don't send me!

Below: British recruits at Chatham Barracks. Some less enthusiastic volunteers sang this song.

БОЖІЕЮ МИЛОСТІЮ,

МЫ, НИКОЛАЙ ВТОРЫЙ,

ИМПЕРАТОРЪ И САМОДЕРЖЕЦЪ

ВСЕРОССІЙСКІЙ,

ЦАРЬ ПОЛЬСКІЙ, ВЕЛИКІЙ КНЯЗЬ ФИНЛЯНДСКІЙ,

и прочая, и прочая, и прочая.

Объявляемъ всѣмъ вѣрнымъ НАШИМЪ подданнымъ:

Слѣдуя историческимъ своимъ завѣтамъ, Россія, единая по вѣрѣ и крови съ славянскими народами, никогда не взирала на ихъ судьбу безучастно. Съ полнымъ единодушіемъ и особою силою пробудились братскія чувства русскаго народа къ славянамъ въ послѣдніе дни, когда Австро-Венгрія предъявила Сербіи завѣдомо непріемлемыя для державнаго государства требованія.

...миролюбивый отвѣтъ Сербскаго Правительства, ...Австрія поспѣшно перешла

У К А З Ъ

В О Е Н Н О М У М И Н И С Т Р У

Признавъ необходимымъ привести на военное положеніе армію согласно данныхъ МНОЮ вамъ указаній, повелѣваемъ вамъ нынѣ же сдѣлать по сему всѣ распоряженія.

Первымъ днемъ мобилизаціи назначить 17ᵒ Іюля.

Николай

Въ Петергофѣ
16 Іюля, 1914 года.
Военный Министръ, Генералъ-Адъютантъ Сухомлиновъ

mobilization. The telegram reached the four military districts bordering Germany and Austria at midnight on 29 July. His soldiers, dismayed at this back-pedalling, then decided to take matters into their own hands. Realizing that international tension had become so acute that a partial mobilization would have the same effect as a general, they prevailed on the Czar to change his mind once again, and order general mobilization for 31 July. Their analysis of the mood of the other Great Powers was correct. Moltke, the Chief of the German General Staff, was acutely alarmed by Russia's partial mobilization in the four western districts and had immediately urged Franz Conrad von Hötzendorf, his Austrian opposite number, to move himself from partial to general mobilization – a departure, he pointed out, which under the terms of their treaty agreement would automatically compel Germany to mobilize also in Austria's support. He had also been working on the Kaiser, explaining that, in his professional judgment, Germany was now in a deteriorating military position in relation both to France and Russia and that she too must proceed to a preparatory phase. On 31 July, therefore, a state of 'imminent danger of war' (*drohende Kriegsgefahrzustand*) was proclaimed throughout the German empire.

Austria had actually been at war with Serbia since 28 July, though neither as yet had taken military action. On the news of the *Kriegsgefahrzustand*, however, Conrad von Hötzendorf declared general mobilization — from state (B) to state (R) — and thus created the situation which guaranteed a full Russian mobilization. The departure taken, pressure was renewed on Moltke and the German general staff. Since the plan hinged on Russia and France going to war simultaneously, thus asking Germany to attack France with seven-eighths of her armed forces, the German General Staff needed to take measures which would delay French mobilization. The German foreign office, acting on the initiative of the Crown Council, accordingly issued ultimata to both countries at the same time. Russia was to cease mobilization within 24 hours, France was to announce her neutrality within 36 hours and, for the duration of the crisis, to hand over two of her greatest frontier fortresses, Toul and Verdun, as a guarantee of goodwill.

As the Germans knew perfectly well, this demanded too much of French goodwill, whose sensitivities had never recovered from the humiliation of defeat by Germany in 1870 and the government rejected Germany's terms without discussion. Since 30 July her covering troops – the portion of her army which was kept permanently on a war footing – had been deployed along the Franco-German frontier, though 10 kilometers short of it in order to avoid further incidents. On 31 July, however, Joffre, Chief of the General Staff, warned the cabinet that:

'any delay in calling up our reservists will have as a result the withdrawal of our concentration points from 10 to 12 kilometers from each day of delay: in other words, the initial abandonment of just so much of our territory.'

A mobilization army order, the equivalent of the *Kriegsgefahrzustand*, had been issued the same day. On the next, 1 August, Joffre advised the

Far left: Czarist announcement of the declaration of war on Germany.

Left: Decree signed by Czar Nicholas II ordering the mobilization on 31 July 1914 (17 July, Russian date).

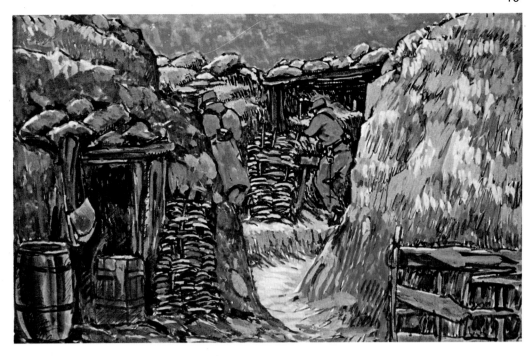

Above: A lull in the fighting in a French trench near the Hultebise farm, painted by Albert Boisfleury. This was a typical scene once the fronts had stabilized following the First Battle of the Marne.

Cabinet that it was unsafe to delay issuing the order for full mobilization any longer, and the posters *Ordre de Mobilisation Générale*, calling all reservists to report to their units, began to be posted up in the streets of Paris at 1555 that afternoon. Five minutes later, Germany ordered her own mobilization.

In the meantime, however, the Kaiser had had his personal moment of anguish. Although long informed of the Schlieffen Plan, he had not faced its full implications. Suddenly, on the evening of M-Day (general mobilization), he could not bring himself to take the responsibility of ordering a major attack on France when the weight of the crisis lay in the East. He summoned Moltke to him at short notice and demanded that the troop trains now loading for departure toward the Rhine, should be redirected and their passengers deployed against the Russians. Moltke, so appalled as to be unable even to remind the Kaiser of France's obligation to attack Germany if she should attack Russia, was reduced to a simple confession of impossibilities. The timetables, he said, perfectly accurately, had been prepared for years. The

mobilization plan was designed to proceed almost literally by clockwork. Any attempt to interfere with it now would only render Germany defenseless, both on the Eastern and Western Front. Their responsibility, therefore, was to push on with the plan, and not to hinder its unrolling; with this reminder of inevitability, the Kaiser acquiesced.

The only major power not yet drawn into the crisis was Britain. She had no alliance which automatically engaged her support to one side or the other. However she was a guarantor of Belgian neutrality under the treaty of 1832. She had been made deeply antagonistic to Germany by the latter's creation of a large battle fleet, whose only visible purpose was to challenge the

Below: French postcard shows the latest models of cars and bikes to be used at the front. Mobilization problems caused a severe strain on the transportation system.

CLÉMENT

PARIS

CYCLES & AUTOMOBILES

Above: German troops are festooned with garlands as they march to the Belgian frontier.

Top: Austrian soldiers say goodbye to their families as they leave for the Serbian Front.

Above right: The 2nd Scots Guards leave the Tower of London for the mobilization center in the New Forest.

Below: French cavalry parade down the Rue de Rivoli on their way to the front.

Royal Navy for supremacy at sea. Also her soldiers had, since 1911, been conducting staff talks with their French opposite numbers to agree on how the British army might act in concert with the French if the British government decided to come to the aid of France in a defensive war against Germany. The outlines of that defensive war now loomed before the Cabinet in London. On the personal responsibility of Winston Churchill, First Lord of the Admiralty, the Grand Fleet had been kept together at Scapa Flow at the end of one of its trial mobilizations on 29 July. The Admiralty had also issued notice of a 'Precautionary Period.' On 1 August, requested by the French government to take incentives to protect the sea lines for troop movement across the Channel, it had ordered full mobilization, which called in the naval reservists and activated older ships of the fleet which did not normally take their place in the squadrons. The Cabinet were not yet ready, however, to order the mobilization of the army, or to give France a firm guarantee that it would come to her aid. Cabinet discussions from 1 to 3 August were sharply divided between those who felt that Britain's vital interests were threatened by the developing crisis on the continent and those who held true to the traditional principles of the Liberal Party — peace and isolation. Sir Edward Grey, the Foreign Secretary, a devoted Liberal and lover of peace, increasingly came to see no way out of the crisis for Britain but a declaration against Germany. 'The lamps are going out all over Europe,' he remarked to a colleague; in that deeply depressed mood he revealed to the House of Commons on 3 August the news both of the existing understanding between Britain and France for military co-operation, and firm news of Germany's violation of Belgian neutral territory. Later that day the Cabinet instructed the War Office to order General Mobilization and, the following morning, after all diplomatic representations had failed to take effect, Britain formally declared war on the German empire.

The Europe of the Great Powers was now at open war. Spain, as politically isolated as she was geographically, economically and culturally, would take no part, neither would Portugal. Italy, newest of the Great Powers, a club to which she only marginally belonged, was calculating her interests on the principle of

Below: Russian civilians demonstrate their patriotism at the outbreak of war in front of the Czar's Winter Palace in St Petersburg.

sacré égoisme — divine selfishness. She would later decide to join the Allies rather than the Central Powers, to which she had earlier been diplomatically committed. The Scandinavian states, Denmark, Sweden and Norway, the last an independent kingdom of only nine years' standing, were neutralist by popular mood, aspiration and diplomatic custom. Holland, whose territory Schlieffen had considered using for the passage of his armies westward toward Paris, was grateful to have been left alone. The smaller Balkan powers — Rumania, Montenegro, Bulgaria and Greece — had as yet no reason to enter the war for reasons of their own, and the interests of none of the Great Powers yet threatened to engulf them. Turkey, propelled by reaction away from Russia, her age-old enemy, toward Germany, trembled diplomatically on the brink of involvement, but had not yet toppled. Switzerland would remain an island of neutral middle ground, physically almost impregnable. Luxemburg had been engulfed without choice by Germany's military necessities. All other countries were at war: France, Russia, Serbia, Britain and, willy-nilly, Belgium, against Germany and Austria-Hungary.

In the East, Austria was finding Serbia a tougher enemy than she had complacently

Above: Viennese citizens hold up portraits of Wilhelm II and Franz Joseph as they celebrate the outbreak of war.

expected. The Serbs, a compact, proud and warlike nation, had mobilized simply and, when three Austrian armies, the Second, Fifth and Sixth (comprising the 'B Contingent' of Austria's War Plan) advanced into her western provinces across the River Drina they were roughly handled. Between 12 August and 20 August they were heavily counterattacked by the Serbs who, fighting on their own territory and with their national survival at stake, outperformed the invaders and forced them back, eventually compelling them to recross the Drina. The Second Army was, in any case, required under Plan R to move from Serbia to Galicia, to take its place in the line against Russia. Thereupon it suffered the humiliation of defeat and was instantly removed from the field of action without having had a chance to revenge its setback. In a week of fighting the Austrians suffered over 23,000 casualties, against an inferior enemy and

Below: Conrad von Hötzendorf, General of the Austrian armies at the start of the war.

Above: General Pau, French commander of the Army of Alsace in 1914.

for no territorial gain. Indeed soon, there were no Austrian soldiers at all inside the Serbian frontier, which was to remain quiet for the next year of the war.

Elsewhere the action was dramatic and large scale. On the Eastern Front, the Germans found themselves almost instantaneously with a major crisis on their hands. All Schlieffen's calculations had rested on the assumption that Russia would mobilize much less quickly than France and would not move to the offensive until her armies were at full strength. His deliberations showed,

Below: Serbian women hung by the Austrians in Macva, August 1914.

on paper, a delay of six weeks between M-Day and the first Russian offensive, and it was in those six weeks that he planned to defeat France. Alas for the calculations — for which, of course, he could no longer be brought to book — Russia behaved in a fashion quite different from that which he had predicted. Far from waiting for the completion of mobilization, a procedure which Schlieffen had rightly calculated would be far lengthier in underdeveloped Russia than in the modernized West, the Czar's Stavka (Grand Staff) decided to attack with its covering force from the outset of hostilities. This force comprised two large armies, First and Second, deployed against the German Eighth Army in East Prussia, as well as four others, Fourth, Fifth, Third and Eighth, which were to face the Austrians in Galicia. The Austrians found the virtually roadless countryside of Galicia difficult terrain in which to develop an offensive, and were slow to move against the Russians. Equally hampered, the Russians were also slow to deploy but, as they planned no offensive action yet, were at less of a disadvantage. In the north, however, they pressed on against all difficulties — First and Second Armies determined to make the most of the opportunity that the German weakness offered them. Russian strategy, which aimed to win a victory not only to safeguard their own territory but also to materially aid the Western Allies in their struggle with the mass of the German army, was one for which France and Britain had the strongest reasons to be grateful. However for the Czar and for Russia, it would have dire consequences.

The officers commanding First and Second Army, Pavel Rennenkampf and Alexandr Samsonov, were on bad terms, which hardly augured well for smooth co-operation between their two armies. Even worse, their staffs, separated by a hundred miles of almost roadless countryside, required to co-ordinate a complicated enveloping maneuver and obliged to communicate by radio, chose not to encode their messages. Radio was an entirely novel means of signalling and the Russians trusted to the fact that they changed their frequencies and

Above: General Otto von Below, Commander of the German Second Army in 1914.

varied their transmission times to shield their messages from the Germans — who, they hoped, might not be searching the air waves. The Germans, however, were. At first the knowledge they gleaned did not do them much good. Max von Prittwitz, the Eighth Army's commander, had unrealistic orders: to stand on the line of the Eastern frontier and hold it fast, if possible by offensive action in Russian Poland. Outnumbered, his three corps commanders — Otto von Below, August von Mackensen, Hermann von François, all to become famous as the war progressed — were defeated on 20 August in the frontier battle of Gumbinnen and forced to withdraw to the line of lakes (the Masurian Lakes) which bisects East Prussia. He also

Above: General Erich Ludendorff, Chief of Staff of the German Eighth Army.

Above: Field Marshal Paul von Hindenburg, Ludendorff's commander and head of the German Eighth Army at Tannenberg.

decided his next move would be to retreat to the River Vistula, thus abandoning most of East Prussia to the Russians.

The thought of the historic heartland of the German military class falling to the despised Slavs put the German High Command into a controlled panic. Moltke was aghast. 'This was the result,' he raged, 'of leaving that fat idiot in command of the Eighth Army. . . .' Prittwitz, once described as the German version of Falstaff ('impressive in appearance, conscious to the highest degree of his self-importance, ruthless, even coarse and self-indulgent') had long been disliked by Moltke, who considered him unfit for his assignment. Now that he could legitimately be relieved Moltke did not hesitate.

He nominated Erich Ludendorff, victor of the recent *coup de main* at Liège, to succeed Prittwitz's Chief of Staff. Shortly afterward he recalled Paul von Hindenburg from retirement to replace Prittwitz. On 23 August the two reached Marienburg, headquarters of Eighth Army and prepared to tackle the crisis. To their considerable relief they found that the Eighth Army's operations officer, Colonel Max Hoffmann, had already formulated a plan which offered the chance of a solution. This was to leave the 1st Cavalry Division to delay Rennenkampf's First Army on the coast, while the bulk of the infantry was transferred on a wide detour by railroad to attack Samsonov's Second Army, whose movements could be anticipated by radio interception. Hoffmann had, indeed, already set the plan in motion and, so impressive was the confidence with which he expounded it, that

Hindenburg and Ludendorff at once adopted it as their own. After all, it might achieve the 'classic double envelopment' of Schlieffen's dreams.

The detraining place of François' corps was near Tannenberg, site of the great battle in 1414 in which the Slavs had won a rare victory over the crusaders of the Teutonic Order. That defeat was about to be avenged. Radio intercepts now revealed that Rennenkampf, impeded by poor roads and lagging supply columns, had actually halted short of the Masurian Lakes and

Below: An Austrian encampment in northern Serbia near Belgrade.

Above: The Russian attack at Tannenberg. The Czarist armies pushed into swampy ground, preparing their encirclement.

Above: The German counterattack at Tannenberg, which forced the Russians to surrender hundreds of thousands of men.

that Samsonov was accordingly at their mercy. His soldiers, 'exhausted and semistarved troops who had barely managed to stumble to the frontier,' fighting among the birch woods and small lakes which dot the sandy countryside of East Prussia, nevertheless gave François four very difficult days. But on 27 August von Below's corps arrived to attack Samsonov's northern flank, with Mackensen following him. Samsonov now realized that he was enveloped and decided to withdraw. Hindenburg was content to let him go, but the fire-eating von François, descendant of one of those Huguenot families which had found refuge from Louis XIV's persecution in Protestant Prussia, pressed his men forward. On 30 August two of Samsonov's five corps were surprised on the march and 60,000 prisoners taken. The total eventually reached nearly 100,000.

Below: Serbian victims of the reprisals by Austria after the assassination of Franz Ferdinand.

Samsonov, appalled at the fate of his offensive, shot himself on the field of battle. The gesture did as little to help Rennenkampf as the latter's hesitant advance had helped him in the crisis of Tannenberg. Now isolated in every sense, Rennenkampf dug his soldiers in on the line of the Masurian Lakes, hoping to ride out the storm of the German counteroffensive. His luck was in. The Eighth Army and its commanders, all tired from the emotional strain and physical exertion of the previous month, moved very slowly to the attack. The Russians resisted their efforts to envelop their right flank and, although eventually forced to withdraw across the Niemen, did so in good order. The Battle of the Masurian Lakes was a German victory, not of the stature of Tannenberg but enough to complete the liberation of East Prussia, and to establish the German army, even in the inferior numbers by which it was represented on that front, as the dominant force in the war in the East. As for Hindenburg he was, as Barbara Tuchman said, 'transformed into a titan by the victory.' For the Russians it was nothing short of a disaster. The Second Army virtually ceased to exist, its commander was dead, two corps

commanders had been captured and three cashiered for incompetence. The French, however, were well satisfied that German strength on the Western Front had been weakened – the Russians had, indeed, as their Commander in Chief put it, made a sacrifice for their allies.

It remained to be seen whether the German armies in the west would have a Tannenberg of their own to celebrate. Walter Bloem, marching southward with the 12th Brandenburg Grenadiers, looked forward to entering Paris, *la ville lumière,* 'the city of light,' as a conqueror. He had reason to be optimistic. All had gone so well since mobilization and deployment that it was impossible to foresee anything but a conclusion to the campaign as successful as that now unfolding in the East.

The campaign had begun with a dramatic success. Long before the war, the German

Below: The Russian advance guard in Poland which was preparing for the disaster at Tannenberg.

Great General Staff had determined that the Schlieffen Plan could only succeed if the gorge of the Meuse, the great river which passes through northern Belgium, could be crossed by its existing bridges, at Liège and Namur. A plan had accordingly been drawn up to seize the former at the very outset of the war by *coup de main*, with a specially picked task force of 13 infantry regiments and a siege train of 210mm howitzers.

The man chosen to command the attack was Ludendorff, a fanatical devotee of Schlieffen on whom he modelled himself carefully, even down to his forbidding personality. A staff officer of some brilliance he was now to demonstrate that his idol's theories could be put into practice, and also to demonstrate his own considerable powers of leadership. Liège was a 'ring fortress,' a central citadel in the city surrounded at a distance by a circular chain of smaller forts. The spaces between the outer forts was supposed to be filled by 'interval troops,' infantry allotted to the fortress commander. Leman, the Belgian general had, however, only been asked to render four of these forts impregnable. Work had not progressed very far before on 6 August the Germans broke in after some stiff fighting. Ludendorff put himself at the head of the leading column and marched down into the center of the city where, with the pommel of his sword, he battered for admission on the door of the citadel. To his frustration, however, the outer fortresses refused to surrender in sympathy, and he was obliged to bring up his big howitzers and reduce them one by one. The explosions of their giant shells as they were 'walked up' to each while the range was found drove some in the fort garrisons mad. Not Leman however, who, bloody but unbowed, was extracted from the ruins of the last fort to fall, on 13 August. He was allowed by Ludendorff, in an uncharacteristic gesture to keep his sword.

Above right: Some of the first members of the British Expeditionary Force take up positions in a Belgian wood.

Right: Belgian infantrymen pause for chow prior to the German onslaught.

Below: Swarms of German infantry cross the rolling hills at the Belgian frontier in the first days of war.

Above: Marshal Joffre on the cover of a French illustrated magazine.

Above far left: The cover of a German youth magazine depicting Crown Prince Rupprecht of Bavaria.

Above left: General Sir John French, leader of the BEF.

Left: 'The Last Gunner,' the legendary defense of the British retreat at Mons, where one gunner held off the advancing Germans until the British forces were safely out of gunfire.

The week-long resistance of Liège had threatened to set back the departure of the 'great wheel' on Paris. In the nick of time, its fall allowed the preordained schedule to be met. It had also threatened to unveil to the French the true center of the German concentration and the direction in which their armies would deploy. However Joffre, at GQG (Grand Quartier Général, French Headquarters), remained resolutely convinced that the focus of German concentration was not in the north, but in the center of France's eastern frontier at Metz. Therefore he considered that the right strategy to pursue was precisely that offensive one which the Supreme War Council had decreed before the war. Plan XVII divided French forces into five armies. Of these the First was to stand on the defensive on the right in the mountainous Vosges. The Second was to attack into Lorraine, toward Metz. The Third and Fourth were to advance into the Belgian Ardennes. All were trained tactically to prosecute the offensive with great vigor, indifferent to enemy fire, and to attack off the line of march with or without artillery support. Colonel Grandmaison, principal advocate of this tactical doctrine, preached that 'infantry which went forward boldly must conquer.'

General Charles Lanrezac, commanding the Fifth Army, subscribed to the tactical doctrine but not to official strategy. He had long believed that the Germans could not resist making use of

the open avenue into northern France which Belgium offered and, positioned as he was nearest the Belgian border, prevailed on Joffre to allow him to extend his flank in that direction. It was toward that flank that the British Expeditionary Force of six divisions of infantry and one of cavalry was making its way. Lanrezac privately arranged with the BEF to bar the approach of the German armies, which he suspected to be descending on the currently unprotected northern plains. While he stealthily sidled northward, however, the experience of other armies tended to reinforce his diagnosis. Between 6 and 11 August the First Army's probing operations in the Vosges encountered strong German opposition. The Second Army, which had begun an advance into Lorraine toward Metz, was resisted by German covering forces and had to fight hard to progress. Though its commander did not know it, the Germans

Above: The French General de Castelnau, who commanded the Second Army which guarded the Ardennes.

were deliberately drawing the Second Army on and on 20 August, overextended in difficult country under a fierce counterattack, it was thrown into full retreat after a two-day battle. On that same day, the French Third and Fourth Armies, pushing through the forests of the Ardennes, came up against major German forces — in fact the Fifth and Fourth Armies, which were wheeling southwestward in conformity with the Schlieffen plan.

The French had not expected to meet the Germans; the Germans, however were more than ready for such an encounter. As a result,

Below: Belgian troops camouflaged their hats with straw at the start of the war.

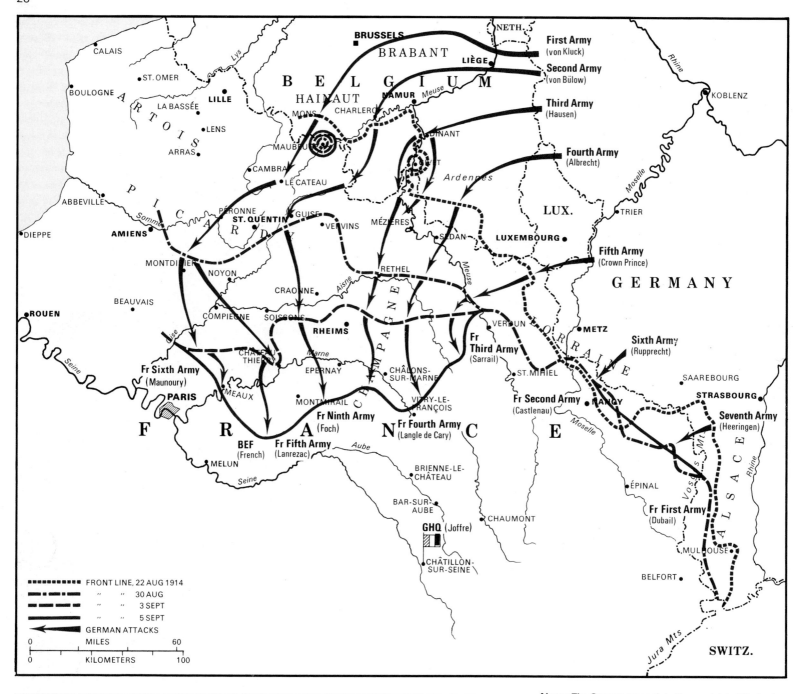

FRONT LINE, 22 AUG 1914
" " 30 AUG
" " 3 SEPT
" " 5 SEPT
GERMAN ATTACKS

	MILES	60
0		
0	KILOMETERS	100

Above: The German sweep into France violated the basic tenet of the Schlieffen Plan. Instead of encircling Paris the Germans hoped to drive toward it and, almost inevitably, failed.

Left: Belgians defend the Willebroeck Canal near Antwerp.

the battle went disastrously for the French who were forced into a hasty retreat. General Sordet's Cavalry Corps, which had been reconnoitering to the north in an empty tract of countryside, also fell back frustrated, announcing that it had seen no major German forces.

In fact, it had simply been in the right place at the wrong time. As it withdrew, the major weight of the German wheeling armies, supplied by Third, Second and First, came hurrying forward. All that now stood in their way was the British Expeditionary Force and Lanrezac's Fifth Army. By constant entreaty, Lanrezac had prevailed on Joffre to allow him to move his army further and further northward, but now it and the BEF were deployed to defend the most important water line guarding the northern approaches — the Sambre-Meuse line between Dinant-Namur-Charleroi and the Mons Canal. On 23 August both were heavily attacked in their positions, the French at Charleroi, the British at Mons. In both places the Germans suffered heavily. They, like the French, em-

Above: Belgians watch as the 2nd Scots Guards advance.

Right: A Belgian armored car and infantry wait for the Germans to arrive.

Below right: Victorious Germans cross the Place Charles Rogier in Brussels, 26 August 1914.

ployed their infantry in direct frontal attacks against the Allies' hasty entrenchments, which were reinforced both by machine guns and plentiful field artillery. The British were expert marksmen and the young German conscripts paid the price. So, too, did they against the French at Charleroi. But their numbers were overwhelming and eventually the weight of their supporting artillery told.

Even so, they might have held the position but for the withdrawal of the French Fourth and Third Armies from the Ardennes. Threatened by that development on their right flank with a German envelopment, both Sir John French, commanding the BEF and Lanrezac came to the conclusion that they must abandon the Sambre-Meuse line and accordingly gave orders for a retreat to begin the following day, 24 August. A similar retreat was taking place all down the French line, as far south as Nancy, where the Germans had relaxed their pressure. The retreat was not, however, a rout. Joffre continued to retain control of his subordinate armies' movements and they stood and fought whenever and wherever they could: on 26 August the BEF fought a successful delaying action at Le Cateau; on 29 August Lanrezac held the Germans for a day at Guise — and there were other, small, successes. But the trend was inexorably southward. Joffre first hoped to hold the line along the Somme, 60 miles north, but his forces were pushed off that river without the chance to make a stand. By 1 September, after 10 days of ferocious marching, the Germans were approaching Paris. There was only one defensible obstacle which lay between them — the line of the Marne. Moltke, who was secure in the German High Command, firmly believed that it would offer no more serious impediment than any of the others his victorious armies had overcome so successfully in the course of their onslaught. True, his armies were tiring and his lines of supply were drawing thin, but that had been foreseen. There now seemed no reason why the culminating act of the Schlieffen Plan, a battle of annihilation before the walls of Paris, should not be triumphantly concluded.

The French Model 1875 artillery gun in action.

2 The Clash of Arms

The walls of Paris was not merely a literary phrase. Alone among the historic capitals of Europe, Paris retained in 1914 its girdle of fortification. London had overgrown its walls in the sixteenth century; Vienna's had been razed to the ground in the 1850s in order that revolutionaries should never again hold the city against the Emperor; Berlin's had been buried in the enormous building boom which followed its elevation to imperial status in 1871; Rome's had never been restored since their breaching by Victor Emmanuel's soldiers in 1870. Paris, besieged in 1870 by the invading Prussians, had been judged by successive French governments to be too tempting and too vulnerable a target and the walls had been allowed to remain. For Paris, strategically as much as politically and culturally, was France. All roads, all railroads, led to it. He who held the capital held the country.

Schlieffen had been aware of the central significance of Paris throughout the years of work on his plan. He accepted from the first that his decisive battle would have to be fought near it, but he could not decide what to do about the obstacle that it presented. He knew that in a crisis its garrisons would come out to fight beside the French field army, unless there was some way of confining it within the walls. His first idea, therefore, was to allot extra troops to the marching mass of his 'great wheel,' whose task would be to invest the city. Try as he might, however, he could not find a surplus of troops to undertake it. The imperial parliament was reluctant to vote funds to raise yet more men but, even if they could have been persuaded to do so, Schlieffen found that however hard he stared at a map of France there was simply no way of accommodating the extra troops in the 'wheel.' There were just not enough roads. The whole road network of Belgium and northern France was required solely to move the armies of the 'great wheel.' For the moment Paris would have to be left uninvested.

This had, however, raised another difficulty which Schlieffen had tinkered with, failed to solve, and finally bequeathed to his successors without disclosing the threat it offered to the great plan's success. It was General Alexander von Kluck, commanding the German First Army at the beginning of September, who had to grapple with the consequences. Paris was dead ahead of his line of advance. The Second Army, commanded by Bülow, was keeping static to his right. On 31 August they crossed the River Aisne and were now approaching the Marne, the last major water obstacle on the route to Paris. Kluck was following the retreat of the British Expeditionary Force but found as he

Above; General, later Marshal Galliéni, military governor of Paris.

Above: General Franchet d'Esperey, commander of the French Fifth Army.

Above: French *cuirassiers* in Paris on their way to the Marne.

Below: Cars and taxis are requisitioned in Paris to bring troops to the Marne.

Above: French troops advance through a village near Paris during the Battle of the Marne.

Right: The rush from Paris by Galliéni's men enabled the BEF to drive between the German First and Second Armies and force a retreat at the Marne.

came inward that the line of march drew him away from Bülow in a direction which threatened to take him west of Paris. At once he saw that if he persisted he would find himself cut off from the rest of the German army by the intervening obstacle of the Paris fortress – with the strong possibility of being attacked by its garrison. On 3 September pilots of the Royal Flying Corps, who the day before had observed Kluck's columns heading southwestward, now reported that they had turned southeast, and that some had turned east to regain contact with the outer flank of Bülow's army. Kluck's army would now pass Paris to the east.

This news quickly filtered to GQG, where Joffre had been busy forming a new army near Paris (to be called the Sixth, under General Joseph Maunoury). General Joseph Galliéni, the Military Governor of Paris, and once Joffre's superior in Madagascar, at once pointed out to the Commander in Chief that Kluck's change of direction offered a magnificent opportunity to launch an attack into his flank with Maunoury's new reserve. Joffre, who had been sitting all day under a tree in a village schoolyard at Châtillon, rose to the occasion. Enormous in bulk, ponderous in speech, (and apparently in thought) his massive calm had served France better in the terrible days of August than, perhaps, the qualities of a more obvious leader would have done. He now demonstrated that he was able to profit from, as well as survive, a crisis. Orders were given that on the following day the French armies should turn about and counterattack along the whole length of the front from Verdun to Paris. The Battle of the Marne was about to begin.

In retrospect the Marne was not a spectacular battle. Fought along a front 100 miles long, few of those taking part were conscious that they were actors in a dramatic turning point of European history. Few of the army commanders in action had grasped any full picture of events. There was little, if any, maneuver during the four days the battle lasted. The Germans simply went on with their frontal offensive, but now they found that the French, instead of turning their backs, showed their faces to the front and attacked. At the eastern end of the battleline the reaction achieved little effect. At the western end, however, the BEF launched a determined counteroffensive spearheaded by the newly-formed Ninth Army under the dynamic Foch ('My center is giving way, my right is falling

back. Situation excellent. I attack.') It was, though, the outflanking move of Maunoury's Sixth Army from Paris which did most to unhinge the German position. Kluck and Bülow, at OHL's orders, first halted and then found front to the west, so as to meet this new threat, a change of activity which spelled doom to the Schlieffen plan.

During the ensuing battles, both against Foch and Maunoury (some of whose troops had been brought to the battlefront in taxi cabs, thus giving birth to a potent legend), the Germans actually established a supremacy. However the appearance of the BEF in the gap which had opened between Kluck's and Bülow's armies, and the paucity of information filtering to OHL over the crackling field telephone, threw Moltke into a panic. 'Where,' he kept asking, 'are the prisoners? Where are the captured guns?' He was convinced that the battle was lost, and on 8 September dispatched a junior staff officer, Colonel Richard Hentsch, from his headquarters at Spa in Belgium to the battlefront, with authority to take the decision to retreat should he judge it to be necessary. Hentsch motoring along the battlefront from headquarters to headquarters soon became persuaded that the situation near Paris was, indeed, critical and accordingly ordered a retreat to the Aisne, to begin the following day. The intention was that it should be only temporary and that, from firmer positions, the Germans should resume their offensive. But, though they could not foresee it, Hentsch's decision was to consign them to those long years of defensive warfare in the trenches, which within a few days, they would begin to dig.

They reached the Aisne on 14 September, exhausted but in good heart. The retreat had been orderly and their defense of the line on arrival was so successful that hopes were still high at the prospect of resuming the offensive. Just as the French, during the Battle of the Marne, had been able to bring reinforcements from either end of the front – Paris and Alsace – along their shortened line of communications, so now the Germans could find extra troops to thicken their line. In September the BEF, the Sixth Army (Maunoury) and the Fifth, now commanded by Franchet d'Esperey, Lanrezac having paid the penalty for having been right too soon, attacked across the Aisne to the heights on the north bank, only to find the German First and Second Armies reinforced and the gap between them now solidly filled. Nothing was achieved in the ensuing three days of fighting except for heavy casualties.

Joffre and Foch, (now promoted to be his

deputy after the magnificent display of moral courage he had shown at the Marne) accordingly decided to dislodge the Germans by an attack upon their open flank. More troops had been brought from the eastern end of the front, where the old frontier fortress towns of Nancy, Toul and Verdun stood as bastions against a German advance, and with these reinforcements the French applied pressure first at Roye, then Arras, then Lens, then La Bassée. Though they did not realize it, they were fighting a hopeless battle. The railroad system was against them. For the Marne, it had worked in their favor, when the Reine–Verdun line had been used to shift troops east–west along the battlefront. Now, however, they were fighting an enemy who could use, as the French put it, another *ligne de rocade*, from Metz to Lille, running north–south at about 50 miles from the successive points of encounter. The superior speed of reinforcement which this facility conferred on German strategy (now directed by Erich von Falkenhayn, who had succeeded the disgraced Moltke on 14 September) nullified any French offensive effort. Fortunately for the Allies, their hold on the coast was secure. British reinforcements landed at Ostend in late September, and the Belgian army, which had fallen back from Antwerp to join them, held the little river Yser which runs through the wet coastal plain of Flanders to the sea at Nicupat. In between, however, lay the small city of Ypres – offering, as it seemed, a last chance to break through into the German rear area. The BEF, transferred from the Aisne to La Bassée by rail on 10 October, and having seen little action on the Marne, was still in fine fighting fettle. They at once began to push forward and, quite by accident, encountered an equal and opposite reaction.

For the Germans had, in the nick of time, managed to form those new divisions for which Schlieffen had searched in vain during the days when he was designing his master plan. Raised from students of all ages who had volunteered at the outbreak of war, they comprised six new corps (XXII–XXVII) to add to the 37 (I–XXI, Guard, I–III Bavaria, and 12 reserve corps)

Right: General Falkenhayn was brought in as German Chief of Staff to replace the disgraced General von Moltke.

Far right: German soldiers take up machine-gun positions near the Aisne, to which they withdrew after the Marne maneuver.

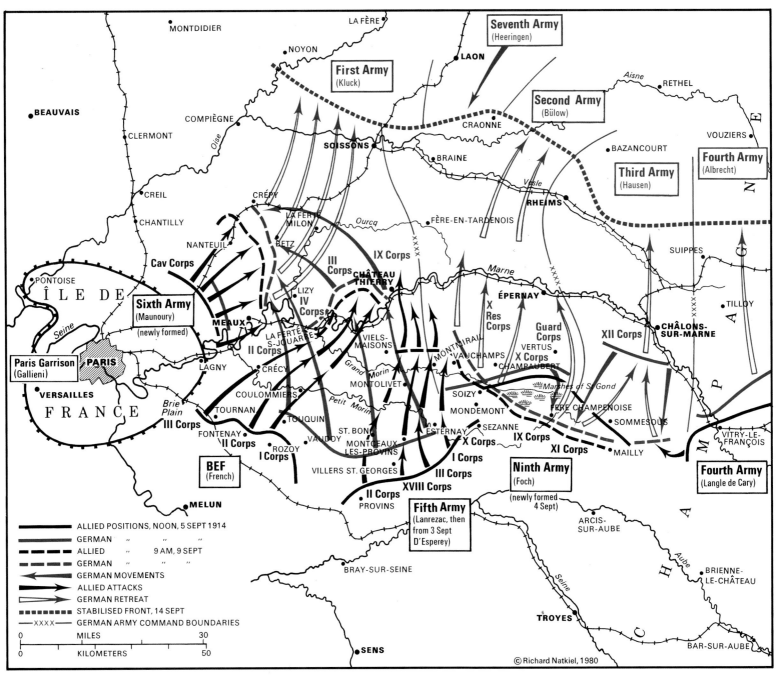

MONTDIDIER · LA FÈRE · NOYON · LAON

Seventh Army (Heeringen)

First Army (Kluck)

BEAUVAIS · CLERMONT · COMPIÈGNE · CRAONNE · Aisne · RETHEL · VOUZIERS

Second Army (Bülow)

CREIL · CHANTILLY · SOISSONS · BRAINE · BAZANCOURT

Third Army (Hausen)

Fourth Army (Albrecht)

CRÉPY · LA FERTÉ MILON · Ourcq · FÈRE-EN-TARDENOIS · Vesle · RHEIMS

NANTEUIL · BETZ · III Corps · IX Corps XXXX · SUIPPES

Cav Corps · LIZY · CHÂTEAU THIERRY · Marne · ÉPERNAY

PONTOISE · ÎLE DE · IV Corps · TILLOY

Sixth Army (Maunoury) (newly formed)

MEAUX · LA FERTÉ S-JOUARRE · II Corps · VIELS-MAISONS · X Res Corps · Guard Corps · XII Corps · CHÂLONS-SUR-MARNE

Paris Garrison (Gallieni) · **PARIS** · Seine · LAGNY · CRÉCY · Grand Morin · MONTMIRAIL · VAUCHAMPS · Vertus · X Corps

VERSAILLES · Brie Plain · COULOMMIERS · Petit Morin · MONTOLIVET · SOIZY · CHAMPAUBERT · Marshes of St Gond · FÈRE CHAMPENOISE · SOMMESOUS

FRANCE · TOURNAN · MONDEMONT

III Corps · FONTENAY · VAUDOY · ST. BON · ESTERNAY · SEZANNE · IX Corps · XI Corps · MAILLY · VITRY-LE-FRANÇOIS

II Corps · ROZOY · TOUQUIN · MONTCEAUX LES-PROVINS · X Corps · I Corps

I Corps · VILLERS ST. GEORGES · III Corps

BEF (French) · XVIII Corps · **Ninth Army** (Foch) (newly formed 4 Sept) · **Fourth Army** (Langle de Cary)

MELUN · II Corps · PROVINS · ARCIS-SUR-AUBE

Fifth Army (Lanrezac, then from 3 Sept D'Esperey) · BRIENNE-LE-CHÂTEAU

BRAY-SUR-SEINE · Aube · Seine

TROYES · BAR-SUR-AUBE

SENS

Legend:
- ———— ALLIED POSITIONS, NOON, 5 SEPT 1914
- ———— GERMAN " " "
- – – – ALLIED " 9 AM, 9 SEPT
- – – – GERMAN " " "
- ← GERMAN MOVEMENTS
- → ALLIED ATTACKS
- ⇒ GERMAN RETREAT
- ▪▪▪▪ STABILISED FRONT, 14 SEPT
- —XXXX— GERMAN ARMY COMMAND BOUNDARIES

MILES 0 — 30
KILOMETERS 0 — 50

© Richard Natkiel, 1980

Far left: A Tommy and a *poilu,* multiplied by millions, made the Entente Cordiale a reality.

Center left: Artillery fire in the hills near Paris, painted by François Flameng.

Left: 'Papa' Joffre, whose masterly patience saved Paris and France at the Marne.

Right: General von Kluck, whose German First Army failed to sweep around Paris as Schlieffen had planned.

Below left: The trenches near Notre Dame de Lorette after a thunderstorm, painted by Francois Flameng.

Below: Messine Ridge in early 1915.

Above: Lewis gunners of the BEF in position near the Marne. Their crash helmets and guns were brought up quickly by the rail line behind them.

Below: Men of the 1st Middlesex struck by shrapnel at the Marne, 8 September 1914.

Far left: Belgian troops land at Ostend.

Left: British reinforcements near Ostend.

Right: French troops in the trenches in Belgium in 1915. By this time their colorful uniforms had been replaced by the horizon blue uniforms which made a less obvious target.

already in existence. Inspired by the ideals of youth and patriotism, these young men came up against the British at Ypres on 20 October. It was indeed a dreadful baptism of fire. Advancing in massed columns, they were repelled with heartrending ease by the rapid shooting — 'the mad minute' of 15 aimed shots per rifle — of the trained British marksmen. Their sheer numbers, however, determined that the British could not break out through the Ypres gap and the BEF dug itself in to resist a fresh onslaught. It came on 31 October with the same result. In those two battles, and a third final assault by the Prussian Guard at Nun's wood directly outside Ypres on 11 November, the Germans lost, killed and wounded 135,000 men, including 41,000 from the volunteer corps. Little wonder that the Germans call this First Battle of Ypres the *Kindermord* (Slaughter of the Innocents).

Meanwhile, the French army had, on a limited scale, gone over to the offensive. From 14 December to Christmas Eve, it attacked in front of Arras and on 20 December it opened a siege offensive in the Champagne, east of Reims, its prewar training area and destined to be the scene of continuous trench warfare throughout the war. There were limited offensives at other points, all also destined to become familiar names in the communiques: The Argonne, a wet, wooded sector north of Verdun; Les Eparges, east of the city; St Mihiel, further south, where a German salient interrupted a vital military line; and the mountains of the Vosges, where French *chasseurs alpins* and German *Jäger* battled it out for possession of crests and peaks (like the Hartmannweilerkopf — *le vieil Armand*) of jealously loved significance.

Little effect was made on the increasingly dense structure of the French line, now continuous from Nieuwpoort on the North Sea to Switzerland. Both sides had exhausted their prewar reserves of ammunition, neither had really large reserves of artillery with which to batter an entrance into the entrenchments. All

Above: French troops pass through the ruined village of Soisy-aux-Bois near the front in early 1915.

armies had suffered appalling casualties — the BEF 80,000 on a strength of 160,000, the Germans and French each nearly a million. In the British and German armies, Christmas 1914 brought on a mood of war weariness and reconciliation. Neither side had yet any real reason to inflict hurt on the other, and at dawn on Christmas day British soldiers in the lines around Ypres were roused by the sound of carols sung across no man's land and the sight of candle-decked Christmas trees rising over the parapets. Behind them appeared the figures of German soldiers, who, in a steady stream, made their way to the halfway line, calling out Christmas greetings and offering schnapps and cigars. They were shortly joined by friendly partners from the British side and, by noon, the whole of the British front had given itself over to fraternization.

In some places the Christmas truce lasted for nearly a week, and it took the intervention of British headquarters to bring it to an end, to the regret of ordinary soldiers in both armies. No such truce, however, had broken out on the French front. Even if the Germans had wished to offer it, the French army was in no mood to respond. Besides their own losses, there were other reasons for which they could not forgive the invaders: the destruction of much that was beautiful and historic in their country, the occupation of an eighth of the national territory, including the most heavily industrialized regions, the imposition of military government on the population of the occupied areas and, above all, the obvious threat of a renewed offensive against Paris which the German presence held out.

Far from wishing to fraternize, therefore, the French army sought to repay in kind what it had suffered. But, as yet, it had not the means to do so. Asked to decide his strategy by the politicians in meetings of the war cabinet, Joffre, impenetrable and incommunicative as ever, replied *Je les grignote* ('I am nibbling the Germans to death'). With his reserves of men and munitions exhausted, he could do no more. But, with the approach of spring, prospects of renewing the offensive brightened. The colonial garrisons yielded an important increment of

Above: Digging of trenches finally began after the race to the sea. Here Germans dig near the Argonne Forest.

Above right: No man's land between Neuve-Chapelle and Armentières.

Above far right: A British field hospital.

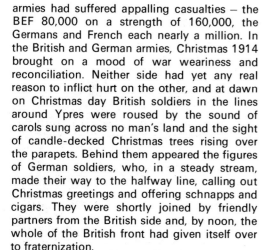

men, augmented by the tightened screw of the conscription machine. The universities and the *grandes écoles* offered a source of replacement for the casualties among regular officers. The cadets of St Cyr, commissioned on the steps of Madame de Maintenon's academy for young ladies on 1 August 1914, swore on oath to meet the enemy in the white gloves and egret feathers of their ceremonial uniforms. All had done so, and most had paid the price. Their places would be taken by students of Science-Po and the Ecole Normale who, in peace, made a cult of their nonmilitary attitude to life. Most important of all, the factories of America, fuelled by the gold reserves which patriotic loan subscriptions had coaxed from the safe deposits of the French bourgeoisie, had begun to tool up for war production and were beginning to make good the vast expenditure of artillery ammunition which the Battle of the Frontiers, the Marne and the Aisne had imposed on the French army.

In May, therefore, Joffre was able to issue detailed orders for a great offensive, whose objects were nothing less than the recovery of the national territory. The map provided a suggestion as to how that might be achieved. On it, the German line described a horizontal S about 450 miles long, one end in the sea, the other touching Switzerland near Basle. At its southern end, high broken country made the line unsuitable for offensive operations. At the other, where the Belgians had let the North Sea into the flood plains of the Yser, an offensive

Right: A British 18-pounder near Armentières, 7 December 1914.

Far right above: Wounded from the Marne arrive at Charing Cross Hospital, London. Medical facilities on the front were virtually nonexistent in 1914.

Far right below: British start to dig trenches near the Ghent-Antwerp road, 9 October 1914.

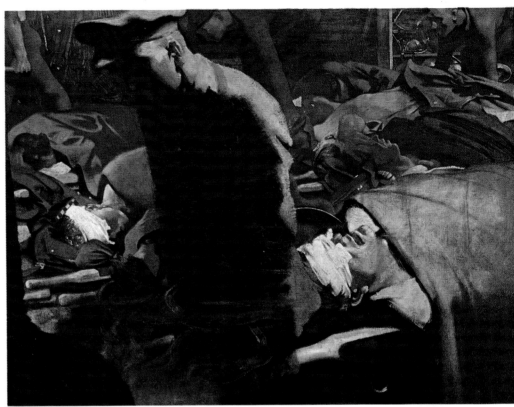

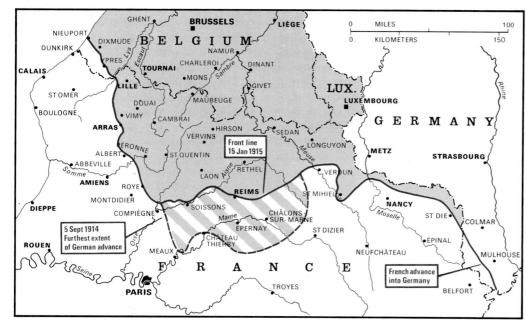

Above: The Western Front at the end of 1914.

would have had to be amphibious to succeed. In between, the countryside offered several routes eastward particularly favorable for an offensive, and Joffre had, as early as December 1915, mentally selected two of them as decisive. They were Arras and the Champagne, on each of which he had already made interim assaults. For May 1915 he planned a large-scale attack at Arras, designed to capture the key feature of Vimy Ridge, from which he could look down into the German positions in the plain of Douai. He had assembled a new army, the Tenth, a great stock of ammunition, and much heavy artillery. That army, despised before the war by French gunners since it could not accompany the infantry in the field on the lightning attacks with which they planned to win the war, was now seen to be the key ingredient of successful strategy. Arsenals and forts had been stripped of every heavy gun, new or old, that could be found. The collection, often more suited to a museum than for action at the front, was fitted with wheels and carriages, in order that it would be able to add its weight to the shoals of 75mm field guns which, against trenches and barbed wire, were proving of little use.

Below: An Austrian hospital, obviously far better than most. Conditions were usually abysmal.

On 9 May the Tenth Army attacked. Among its formations was XXXIII Corps, commanded by General Henri Philippe Pétain, and composed largely of white regulars of the colonial army, hardy and experienced soldiers. Their target was the church which crowned the summit of the Ridge, Notre Dame de Lorette and, within two hours of attacking, they had penetrated two and a half miles into the German lines and seized the crest. Five days of preliminary bombardment, however, had so cut up the ground that Tenth Army's reserves (positioned in any case too far from the front) could not reach the first assailants before they were counterattacked. Once they were under attack, the prospect of deepening the break-in disappeared.

The divisions on either side of XXXIII Corps had done less well, reporting slow progress in what came to be called the *Labyrinthe*. All up and down the Western Front, however, the pattern was the same. The trench system was being transformed, of necessity, into a labyrinth. Official policy on both sides was for a simple layout of entrenchments. A front line, 'traversed' (dug in right-angled zigzag paths, to prevent an enemy who entered at one point firing down the length of the trench); a 'support' line, two or three hundred yards behind; perhaps a 'reserve' line, further back still; and the whole connected transversely by 'communication' trenches, also traversed, which led from the rear into the front

trench. Trenches were dug at least six feet deep – the Germans (whose strategy was defensive in the West) furnishing theirs with deep dugouts excavated under the parapet which went down to a depth of, perhaps, 20 or 30 feet. On the Allied side the dugouts were shallower, due to the fact that both the British and French armies made it their official policy to declare trench positions temporary, Allied strategy being offensive. In practice these official pronouncements of dogma were often ignored. Tactically both sides were offensive at many places up and down the front. Local attacks to capture a piece of high ground, or to iron out an awkward angle, meant that small sections of trench constantly changed hands, and others were hastily dug to protect sections threatened by change of ownership. The result was the growth of a maze of trenches old and new, which to an attacker who inadvertently found himself trapped behind enemy lines presented a puzzle almost impossible to solve and made his task of finding his way out into open country an increasingly difficult one.

Never was this more clearly demonstrated than at Ypres where, sometime before Joffre's attack at Vimy Ridge, the Germans had employed a new weapon to attempt the capture of the cornerstone of the Flanders position from the British. On 22 April both they and the French, whose line abutted on the right, noticed about 1700 hours a curious blue-white mist rising from the parapet of the German trenches and drifting toward them. When it reached their wire the sentries began to cough and choke. As it passed the parapet, it sank into the trench and soon, almost everywhere, French and British soldiers were streaming to the rear, tearing at their collars and gasping for breath. The mist was xylyl bromide, a tear gas, borne by a light evening breeze, behind which the Germans advanced to capture their prize. It was not, however, the first time that gas had been used. That occasion was at Bolimow in January 1915, when the Germans had experimented against the Russians. However the Ypres attack was certainly far more spectacular and threatened devastating results. For on a four-mile front, directly in front of the city, on the evening of 22 April there were no Allied defenses at all.

Just before the Germans reached it, however, and after the gas had dispersed, Plumer, the British commander, was able to scrape together some reserves and race them out to the threatened sector. Due to the fact that it had been fought over in the autumn of 1914, they found old, abandoned trenches everywhere. They hastily improved and connected stretches with their entrenching tools and, when the German assaulting columns appeared, drove them off with rapid rifle fire.

The essential terms of the equation of trench warfare had by now been determined. Wire and trenches required the attacker to use heavy artillery to forge a way for his infantry. Heavy artillery, always in short supply, had to be brought from a distance and its arrival was difficult to disguise. Even when emplaced, its use imposed a dilemma. If employed at the last moment, simply to break gaps in the wire, it might not do enough damage to get the infantry into the enemy's positions. If employed well beforehand, to lay down a long, destructive, preliminary bombardment, or 'artillery preparation,' it would certainly attract enemy reserves to the threatened front and so determine that, whatever success the assaulting infantry had in crossing the front line, they would be counterattacked as soon as they were well inside enemy territory. Neither in a short nor in a long

Carry me back to dear old Blighty,
Put me on the train to London town.
Take me over there,
Drop me anywhere,
Liverpool, Leeds or Manchester.

Above: **Men of the 2nd Battalion, Royal Scots Fusiliers in the trenches at La Boutillerie, winter of 1914–15.**

bombardment could the artillery ensure the neutralization of the most powerful killing-agent on the defending front — the medium machine gun. In the first accurate hits on the machine-gun nests could not be guaranteed, in the second the machine guns were simply taken by their crews into the dugouts, safe from shelling, until the moment came to race up the steps when the bombardment lifted, to let the attacking infantry through.

For the next two and a half years, therefore, all trench-to-trench offensives were to lurch uneasily between hoped-for surprise and assured destruction, until new technical means were at last found to make surprise once again a feasible stratagem. In the meantime the troops at the front began to invent or resurrect a whole array of devices adapted particularly to low-level trench fighting. The Germans, impressed by Russian and Japanese experience in the war of 1904–1905, already had a number of useful devices, like flare pistols, grenades and trench mortars. There were no such things for the British and French, but they soon improvised. Grenades were made from jam tins, mortars from steel piping. There was a short-lived fashion for grenade-throwing catapults, which resembled Roman siege-engines, and a great deal of ingenuity given to the design of peri-scopes, wire-grappling and cutting devices and even body armor. The steel helmet, to be universal (except in the Russian army) by 1916, was still under development, and attracted the opposition of many traditionally minded officers.

Neutral-colored clothing had been adopted everywhere by early 1915. The Germans and the British were already in a camouflage color. The Belgians in black and the French in blue coats and scarlet trousers made conspicuous targets, even against the background of the trenches and both quickly changed — the former to khaki, the latter to a bright 'horizon blue' which muddied itself to an indeterminate gray in the front line.

Equipped and clothed like this, the two sides visited a good deal of small-scale beastliness on each other during the long, inactive summer of 1915. Even though the Germans were on the defensive in the West, while attempting to destroy the Russians in the East, they were ready and able to mount raids, demonstrations and local offensives, and the same ingredients formed the staple diet of the Allied armies. There were French attacks at Metzeral in Alsace, in Lorraine and at Bois-le-Prêtre in the Woevre, near Verdun. On the British front around Ypres, casualties during the summer ran at about 300 a day, in an army of 300,000 infantry, and rose higher whenever there was a flare-up of activity, as at Hooge on 2 June. This château, head-quarters of the BEF in the First Battle of Ypres, had a sentimental value to the British. It was recaptured on 16 June but lost again on 20 July, when the Germans attacked with flame-throwers, a new addition to the armory of trench warfare.

The summer's pause did not, however, imply any acquiescence by the Allies to the German occupation of France's 10 most productive *départements*. On 4 June Joffre sent Sir John French the draft of his plan for an autumn offensive. Like those of December, it proposed a dual attack in Artois and Champagne, intended to break the German line and converge on the headwaters of the Somme east of St Quentin. The German line in between, which formed a large salient, would thus be bitten out, its defenders encircled and forced to surrender and a large enough gap created for a victorious

Below: **A gas school at Barleux in August 1915. Gas warfare was equally devastating for both sides.**

Above: German cavalry near Arras in 1915. Trench warfare made cavalry charges obsolete and usually fatal.

Joffre's plan, though set back by difficulties in the assembly of men, guns and munitions (the British pleaded they would not have sufficient ordnance or artillery available for a large offensive until the spring of 1916), therefore went forward. Scheduled originally for 8 September, it had to be postponed on 31 August, because General Pétain, in the light of his experience at Vimy in the spring, demanded more time to train his artillery more thoroughly. The need to extend the road network in the prewar French training area in Champagne also required more time than had originally been anticipated.

So extended were the Allied preparations that they inevitably came to the attention of the Germans, who, using conscripted French labor as well as the older soldiers of their Landwehr and Landsturm regiments, began in August to construct secondary positions in the rear of the two threatened sections, at distances of two to four miles from the front. They also summoned from Russia an extra four divisions to act as a counterattack reserve. It was against this reinforced line that the Allies began, on 21 September, the first large and prolonged artillery preparation yet unleashed on the Western Front. In Champagne the French had 47 heavy guns to the mile, in Artois 35, the British only 19. Day after day their crews toiled round them, winging shells of 100 to 200 pounds onto the German communications trenches and battery positions deep in their rear, while the 75mm and 18-pounders of the field artillery poured shrapnel and high explosives into the wire and trenches of the front line in order to open the door for the infantry. The German artillery replied as best it could, until beaten into silence or deliberately ceasing to answer, so as to survive until the infantry attack developed.

The attack in Champagne — called by the French the Second Battle — began at 0915 on 25 September. Two armies, Second (Pétain) and Fourth (de Langle de Cary), 20 divisions against six, attacked side by side. They did not

advance to the German frontier. On this occasion, however, while the French army made the major effort on Champagne, that in Artois was to be heavily British. The Tenth Army, which had tried and failed to capture Vimy Ridge in May, would be supported on its left by further British divisions.

Joffre's proposal formed the basis of discussion at the First Inter-Allied Conference, held at Chantilly, seat of GQG, on 7 July and attended by representatives of France, Britain, Belgium, Russia, Serbia and Italy (which had entered the war on 23 May). The French dominated the proceedings, since they maintained the largest army in the West which, though smaller than the Russian, was the only one capable of offensive action against the Germans on a large scale. Joffre had opposed the landings at Gallipoli, which had led to the Mediterranean campaign currently in progress, but his failure to cancel it did not shake his power to dictate when and where the Western Offensive in 1915 should take place. The Russians were grateful for any effort which relieved the pressure on their front. The Italians were occupied with their own offensives, which amounted to the liberation of territory they believed to be theirs by divine right. The Belgians and British, both inferior in military power to the French, were prepared to accept French leadership for practical purposes.

attack in what had become conventional trench fashion, silently and surreptitiously. The two Armies had convinced their soldiers that 25 September was the beginning of the end of the war. The regiments had brought their bands onto the front line to sound the men off to *Ca ira! Sambre-et-Meuse* and the *Chant du Départ*. Many had also brought their colors, those gold bedecked and fringed tricolors, painted with the battle honors of a hundred years of victories, which enshrine the heart of a French regiment. One colonel seized the color from the young officer whose duty it was to carry it, and himself bore it forward over the parapet.

He fell dead within a few feet. The bands, the shouting and cheering, as well as the cessation of the bombardment as it lifted to play on targets beyond the German front line, had given the German defenders all the warning they needed for the 'race to the parapet.' The Germans' starting point was their dugouts, that of the French the other side of no man's land. When the Germans reached it they found their view obscured by clouds of smoke and gas, into which they were forced to fire blind. The result was that along wide sectors of the front the French were suddenly on top of them before they could organize effective resistance. Along a front of 18 miles, the French quickly broke in to a depth of 1000 yards on the left and 2500 yards on the right, capturing in all 10.5 miles of the front line. Some of the strongpoints taken would become catchwords in French military history – the Butte de Tahure and La Main de Massiges, where five projecting spurs of a ridge resembled the fingers of a hand. Some of the bravery shown on that day would also become legendary – by no one more strikingly

Above: British artillery in action near Chusseau–Flaviens.

Below left; German troops carry their heavy machine guns past a French farmhouse.

Below: French troops storm into the plain of their lost province, Alsace.

than General Marchand, the central figure in the Fashoda incident, which had brought Britain and France to the brink of open hostilities in Africa in 1900. He attacked at the head of his colonial infantrymen, was shot through the body and removed from the field to face, it was thought, certain death. However within 10 days he had returned to duty for the closing stages of the offensive.

The closing stages were reached so soon for the simple reason that the Germans were able to man their support line with reserves hastily brought forward from the rear, and to cover it with the artillery fire the French had been unable to silence. The attack in Artois (Third Battle) was not sustained for even that long. There the French had brought their reserves close to the front, hopeful of early success. It did not come, and the German artillery counterbarrage fell into the crowded trenches of the front line, causing terrible casualties and prompting Joffre through his deputy, Foch, to terminate the attack next day.

On the left of this French attack, the British had also opened an offensive at 0630 on the same morning. It became known as the Battle of Loos, after the little village astride the front. This time the BEF was a different attacking force from the one that had opposed the Germans the previous year. Then it had been an army of regulars. There were still prewar regulars in the BEF, but many fewer than the year before – about three-quarters had become casualties. Their places had been taken partly by newly-enlisted men, but mainly by Territorials and new volunteer divisions. The Territorials (not to be confused with the elderly French reservists who also went by that name), were a peculiarly British breed. They were part-time volunteers, who also gave up their Saturdays in peacetime to train for war. They formed in all 14 divisions of infantry and 14 brigades of cavalry, at the outbreak too deficient in equipment and skill to be sent to the front, but now acclimated to the Western Front. The new volunteer divisions were not yet fully deployed to France. Their time

would come in 1916. One, the 15th Scottish, however was ready for Loos and, together with the 47th London Territorial Division, and the 1st, 2nd, 7th and 9th of the old regular army, set off across no man's land on 25 September.

Haig, commanding the British First Army, placed especial confidence for the operation's success in the discharge of a gas cloud. He had calculated on a 20mph wind to carry it across no man's land, but unfortunately the morning dawned calm. Reluctant to cancel the discharge, he told his aide-de-camp to light a cigarette in the garden of his headquarters and, when he

detected a slight eastward drift of the smoke, decided that conditions justified letting his order stand. At the front the breeze was either non-existent or carried the gas in the wrong direction. At best it drifted slantwise across no man's land. At worst it actually blew back into the British trenches. Where it touched the German line, south of Loos, the 47th Territorial Division was able to cross. Elsewhere it actually hindered the attack, hanging about in pockets, so that where the British infantry took off their masks to get a breath of fresh air, they were overcome.

Haig nevertheless judged the attack to be going so well by the early afternoon that, from his headquarters eight miles behind the line, he ordered the reserves forward. They consisted of another two of the new volunteer divisions, 21st and 24th, which had never before been into action. They did not reach the front line until dark, and prepared themselves to attack the following morning. When they did so, a soldier in the German 15th Reserve Regiment reported seeing '10 columns of infantry between Hulluch and Hill 70, each about a thousand men, all advancing as if carrying out a parade-ground drill.' Unable to believe their eyes, the defenders of the position, who had been driven from the front line by the gas the previous day, stood up on the parapets to open fire with rifles and machine guns. The effect was devastating. The army could be seen falling literally in hundreds, but they continued their march in good order and without interruption. Despite the terrible punishment inflicted on them, they went doggedly on, some even reaching the wire entanglements in front of the reserve line which had scarcely been touched by their artillery. Confronted by 'this impenetrable obstacle, the survivors turned and began to retire.' In their advance the two divisions' infantry, about 24,000 strong, lost 8000 killed and wounded. 'Sickened by the sight of the massacre,' the 16th Reserve Regiment's history reads, 'no more shots were fired . . . so great was the feeling of misery and compassion after such a victory.'

Above: The mine craters at Aubers Ridge were home for these men of the BEF.

Below: The barbed wire of a captured German trench at Loos, 28 September 1915.

Hanging on The Old Barbed Wire

If you want to find the old battalion,
I know where they are, I know where they are,
If you want to find the old battalion,
I know where they are,
They're hanging on the old barbed wire,
I've seen 'em, I've seen 'em,
Hanging on the old barbed wire,
I've seen 'em,
Hanging on the old barbed wire.

Above: **Marshal Galliéni studies a map on the Western Front, in the company of other French officers.**

Above: **The fire and smoke of the Western Front in 1915, as the war took on an increasingly ghastly tone.**

Loos was to be last offensive effort of the Allies on the Western Front in 1915. Not only had the September offensives exhausted their reserves of manpower and munitions, they had also cast an incurable blight both upon reputations and the optimistic forecasts of those who had advanced them. In the first months of the war Joffre had dismissed a third of the generals in the French army, at first posting them, as a sop, to Limoges, the command most distant from the front (the origin of *limogé*) then, when the fiction became transparent, simply sending them direct into retirement. The men whom he had promoted in their stead, notably Foch, but also Pétain, Maunoury, d'Urbal, Gourand, Franchet d'Esperey and Debeney, had proved themselves. They had shown themselves capable of taking decisions and of remaining resilient even in the face of the terrible casualty returns which every attack they organized produced. Joffre's own reputation, however, that of Papa Joffre, unpretentious, imperturbable, had begun to crack — if not with the army and the people, then with the politicians. They found his reticence infuriating and his calm a mark of complacency. On the German side, Moltke's removal had brought a soldier of energy and vision, Erich von Falkenhayn, to the head of OHL and he, too, had replaced the dinosaurs of August 1914 with younger, more efficient men. In the British army, Sir John French, Commander in Chief of the British Expeditionary Force, was about to be deposed. His extreme range of mood, emotional approach to military planning and hidden but powerful despair at the failure of the offensives and their human cost had raised a virtual conspiracy against him among his more immediate subordinates. Foremost was Douglas Haig (commanding the First Army), who, through private correspondence with King George V, transmitted 'the feeling of the army' to the highest government circles. On 16 December 1915 French paid the price of his shortcomings and his brother officers' disloyalty and was removed. Haig took his place.

In Britain the war was having its inevitable effect — the phrase 'on the home front' became current. In May 1915 Herbert Henry Asquith, whose heart had never been in the war, had abandoned the attempt to run the government with only the support of his own Liberal party. Thenceforth he became Prime Minister of a coalition, with eight Conservatives in his Cabinet. The new cabinet's most important member was the Liberal Minister of Munitions, David Lloyd George, who brought to the newly-created post a dynamism noticeably absent from other government offices — from the War Office, where Kitchener's early creativeness had petered out, and even from the Admiralty, whose First Lord, Winston Churchill, was eclipsed by the failure of his ill-conceived campaign on the Gallipoli peninsula.

France also had its man of the hour in the Ministry of Munitions, Albert Thomas. Like Lloyd George, he saw that the war needs would be met not simply by exhorting national industry to meet the production targets set it, but by direct governmental intervention to change its structure. In Britain Lloyd George's Munitions Act concentrated the power to distribute orders to the munitions factories into a single office. This power determined that inefficient factories would not receive orders while new enterprises which promised to deliver would. The result was a burgeoning of new engineering workshops in places where industrial work had never before been made available to the population, particularly in the South of England, nearest to the fighting front. At the same time the Munitions Act restricted the right to strike in factories and created a new force of itinerant workmen who had to go wherever labor was shortest.

The labor force was not exclusively male. The migration of enormous numbers of young men to the front, or to the training camps which were staging posts on the way, meant a sudden dismantling of the barriers to female employment in many traditionally male occupations. In July 1914 only 212,000 British women had been employed in engineering. By July 1915 the number had increased to 256,000. A year later, under the impact of Lloyd George's Act, it had doubled to 520,000. A veteran of the mobilization recalled her experiences 60 years later:

'I was in domestic service and hated every minute of it when war broke out, earning two pounds a month working from six in the morning to nine in the evening. So when the need came for women "war workers" my chance came to "out." I started on hand cutting shell fuses at the converted war works at the ACs Thames Ditton, Surrey. It entailed the finishing off by "hand disc." The machine cut thread on the fuses that held the powder for the big shells, so had to be very accurate so that the cap fitted perfectly. We worked 12 hours a day apart from the journey morning and night at Kingston-upon-Thames. Believe me I was very ready for bed in those days and as for wages I thought I was very well off earning five pounds a week.'

Another branch of munition work, filling shells, was commoner than the skilled task of cutting fuses. By the end of 1915 it was done almost entirely by women, the largest concentration being at the national cordite factory at Gretna, on the Scottish border. There 11,000 women worked and were accommodated in purpose-built hostels. A survey revealed that, out of each hundred, 36 had formerly been in domestic service, 20 had lived at home, 15 had been shop assistants and 12 had been laundry workers, farm hands, dressmakers, school teachers or clerks. Soon they were all 'munitionettes.' Those who worked with TNT, which discolored the skin yellow, became known as 'canaries.' They were a familiar sight in the streets of Southeast London surrounding the great armaments complex at Woolwich and Deptford.

Women had also begun to infiltrate occupations long defended as male preserves — tram driving, bus conducting, postal delivery and so on. Between 1916–18 the number of women employed in transportation rose from 18,000 to 117,000. Similar shifts were apparent in the much more traditional society of France. By October 1915 there were 75,000 women employed in the munitions industry, and they had also begun to appear in uniform on the vehicles of the public transport system. Yet, at the same time, those already disenchanted by the war — and they included many soldiers on leave from the front — were offended by the lack of feeling

Above: British girls make up soldiers' rations. Women were used extensively in European factories as the men were taken off to war.

Top left: A howitzer shop in the Coventry Ordnance Works.

Top: A German girl makes cartridges.

Left: Packing fuse heads at the Coventry Ordnance Works.

Below: A French female welder at work making cartridges.

Above: General Ferdinand Foch surveys the fighting near Arras; his destiny was yet to be realized.

for those undergoing the war's harshness displayed by many in the great cities.

In December 1915 the Ballet Russe gave a five-hour performance at l'Opéra, for which a fashionable Paris couturier had previously advertised jewelled gowns at prices of up to 3500 francs. An American, J G Coolidge, said of the packed audiences 'Never in ante-bedlam days have I seen anything more magnificent. The general feeling is that it was a mistake.' However such mistakes were an integral part of the France behind the lines. Restaurants, hotels, theaters and casinos flourished, not only on the pocket money of soldiers snatching a leave from the front. The war had generated a flood of cash and credit, and the earning classes, old and new, were spending unprecedented amounts on entertainment and adornment. A popular department store in the rue de Rennes reported selling a million more articles in 1915 than in 1914, mainly scent and fancy underwear. The war wounded were fêted, but the more realistic accepted that their acclaim would be short lived. 'This year,' said an officer who lost both legs, 'I am a hero. Next year I shall be a cripple.'

In Germany the mood was different. Resistance there to the employment of women in war work was strong, as befitted the most traditional society in Europe. There was little behind-the-lines enjoyment – indeed there was

little to rejoice about. Cut off from the Allies' ready access to the resources of the world beyond Europe by an efficient naval blockade, Germans had already been subjected to bread rationing in January 1915. Importing 20 percent of their foodstuffs, they quickly found that other staples started to fall into short supply, or even disappear completely. Butter was scarce as was fresh meat. The quality of meals, even in an hotel as good as the Berlin Adlon, was, to an American visitor, noticeably poor by March 1915. The hardships of war in an encircled nation made themselves felt in other ways. Nonferrous ores, copper, zinc and tin, were now in particularly short supply, at a time when military demand for them was insatiable and unprecedented. As a result German families were ordered in October 1915 to supply lists to the local authorities of all articles in their possession made of these materials and households were then stripped of them by official collectors. Melted down, the product went to make driving bands for shells, wire for signal cable and electrical contacts.

Yet rumors of the imminent imposition of rationing of all foodstuffs did nothing to shake German commitment to the war or belief in swift victory. 'The people are still well in hand,' wrote the American ambassador, James Gerard, in November 1915, 'constant rumors of peace keep them in hand.' In France, too, enthusiasm, if not for the war then certainly for the gratification of victory of the hated *Boche*, remained high. '*On les aura*' was the catch phrase not only of commanding officers but also of the civilian population. Next year would bring victory, a victory which would wipe out all the humiliations of the past 50 years. In Britain, where Kitchener's New Armies were reaching the peak of their strength and training, there was unbounded public confidence in the belief that the British Empire, once it put forth its strength, would puncture swiftly and completely the pretensions of Germany to dictate the future of Europe by Christmas 1915. '*A Berlin*' had become as popular a watchword as '*Nach Paris*' had been the year before.

Above right: French troops halt for a rest on a march to the front.

Right: Germans watch as a village burns in northern France.

Above far right: Crown Prince Rupprecht of Bavaria and Lieutenant General von Krafft von Dellmensingen in Alsace in 1914.

Far right: German troops in the newly-built trenches in France late in 1914.

Below: An encampment of Moroccan *spahis,* a colorful addition to French forces on the Western Front.

When this Bloody War is Over

When this bloody war is over,
O, how happy I shall be!
When I get my civvy clothes on,
No more soldiering for me.
I shall sound my own reveille,
I shall make my own tattoo:
No more NCOs to curse me,
No more bleeding army stew.

Transports at Lemnos in April 1915 which took part in the fiasco at Gallipoli.

3 The Widening War

On to Berlin was not the only watchword in the Allied camp during 1915. Constantinople – Istanbul as the Turks call it – seemed an equally glittering prize. It could be reached far more quickly and cheaply than the German capital and offered a strategic reward almost as valuable. Turkey had come into the war late. It had been counted in the German camp for years before the war, if only because it had the same natural enemy, Russia. The Ottoman Empire was crippled by weaknesses so severe that even its ambitious and energetic leaders, the Young Turks (all military men) had hesitated to expose it to the strains of a great military effort. They had signed a treaty with Germany on 2 August, pledging Turkish support to the Austro-German cause. However, the unexpected entry of Britain into the war, the poor Austrian showing against the Russians and, particularly, the Serbs, and the French victory on the Marne had further weakened the Young Turks' resolve. Germany had however found a means of tightening the screw.

On 3 August 1914, while their two flag-showing ships in the Mediterranean, the battle-cruiser *Goeben* and cruiser *Breslau*, were racing for the straits of Gibraltar to rejoin the High Seas Fleet, the German admiralty signalled Admiral Wilhelm Souchon to turn about and seek haven in Constantinople. Evading a British pursuit, he did so. A comic pantomime followed, Souchon and his men formally enrolled in Turkish service, exchanging their naval caps for the fez, and the two ships prepared to join the Turkish Navy's order of battle. However, once transpatriated, their mission was to be one of calculated disobedience. Enver Pasha, the War Minister and most pro-German of the Young Turks, collaborated in a scheme whereby the *Goeben* led the few seaworthy elements of the Turkish Navy into the Black Sea. On 28 October, on a slim pretext, they opened fire on such Russian

vessels as they could find and bombarded the Russian seaports of Odessa and Sebastopol. The Sultan, Mahommed V, a cypher in the hands of his ministers, thus found himself a formal ally of Kaiser Wilhelm II and Emperor Franz Josef in the war against Russia, France and Britain.

The French and even the British, despite their compelling Mediterranean interests, might have been content to treat hostilities as a formality had it not been for the supplications of Russia. The Czar had men in millions, more men than any of the combatant powers, but he lacked the guns and the munitions with which to feed them. Outside his own dominions were industrial powers which could supply the goods he needed. After October his sea lanes were blocked by the enemy, the Baltic ports by Germany, the Black Sea ports by Turkey. The answer to the question of how to get supplies through was of importance not only to Russia but to the Western Allies, who had vested large hopes in a Russian steamroller which was now almost broken down for lack of fuel. When, on 2 January 1915 the British ambassador in Petrograd forwarded a request from the Russian government for some diversion to be made to draw off troops from Turkey's invasion of the Caucasus, it prompted an immediate response. Kitchener at once thought of a landing at Gallipoli, gateway of the Dardanelles which led to Constantinople, and Churchill, First Lord of the Admiralty, was equally enthusiastic. While intentions were pondered and plans prepared, Churchill persuaded the War Cabinet to let his Mediterranean fleet attempt to 'force the Narrows' on its own and between 19 February and 18 March a bombarding force of British and French battleships bludgeoned its way up the channel toward Chanak, where the channel was only a mile wide. The naval effort went well at first and the Turkish batteries the fleet engaged

were first silenced and then destroyed. Some blue jackets found that they were able to land and walk about on enemy territory unchecked. However on 18 March a succession of disasters brought the fleet's action to an end. First the old French battleship *Bouvet*, then the British *Irresistible* and *Ocean*, were shaken by explosions and quickly sank. The *Inflexible*, a brand new battlecruiser, was holed soon afterward, then the French *Gaulois* and the *Suffren* were also hit. The last three ships managed to limp away to safety. The Turks, who had inflicted all this damage with a few mines floated down on the current, had shown that the naval effort was doomed.

London and Paris, the latter reluctantly, therefore agreed to commit to a shore landing the military force which it had been gathering in the eastern Mediterranean. It consisted of a French division, which was to land at Kum Kale on the Asiatic shores and make a diversion, and two British and two Australian/New Zealand (ANZACS) divisions, which were to assault Gallipoli itself. One of the British divisions was the Royal Naval Division, which had landed at Ostend the previous October and, for reasons difficult to explain, numbered many writers and poets among its officers. Of these the best known was Rupert Brooke, whose meditation on his own death – 'some corner of a foreign field which is forever England' – had already become the most famous of the flood of war poems which World War I had stimulated and was to remain the best remembered. Writing home to a friend from the troopship, he claimed that 'all my life (I had) wanted to go on a military expedition to Constantinople.' His letter expressed the unspoken wishes of many of his companions and friends from the privileged world of Cambridge, who saw in the war the means to give point to lives which they felt were too soft and purposeless. Rupert Brooke, at the

Left: Winston Churchill, wearing a French helmet, with General Fayolle at Chamblain l'Abbé in 1915. Churchill, as First Lord of the Admiralty, ordered the Gallipoli invasion and was sacked after the fiasco.

Below: The *Goeben*, which was commandeered into the Turkish Navy at the start of World War I.

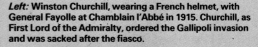

55

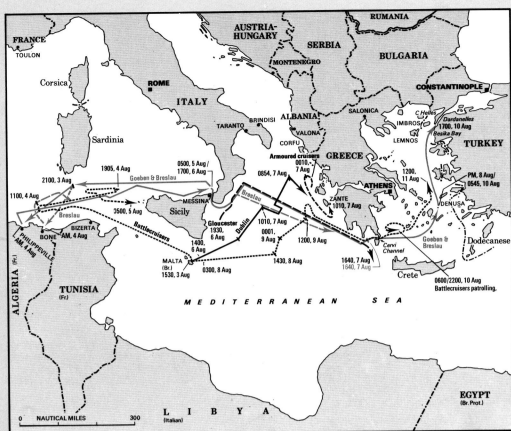

Above: The surrender of the *Goeben,* by Philip Connar. The incident took place at the end of the war.

Top left: Poster celebrating the Turkish defense of Gallipoli.

Above left: Enver Pasha, who led the Turkish defense of the Dardanelles.

Top: The pursuit of the *Goeben* and *Breslau* by the British Mediterranean Fleet.

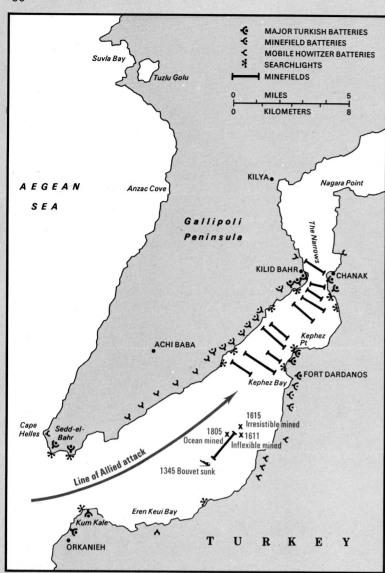

MAJOR TURKISH BATTERIES
MINEFIELD BATTERIES
MOBILE HOWITZER BATTERIES
SEARCHLIGHTS
MINEFIELDS

MILES 0 5
KILOMETERS 0 8

Suvla Bay
Tuzlu Golu

AEGEAN SEA

Anzac Cove

KILYA

Nagara Point

Gallipoli Peninsula

The Narrows

KILID BAHR
CHANAK

ACHI BABA

Kephez Pt

Kephez Bay

FORT DARDANOS

1615 Irresistible mined
1805 Ocean mined
1611 Inflexible mined
1345 Bouvet sunk

Line of Allied attack

Cape Helles
Sedd-el-Bahr

Eren Keui Bay

Kum Kale

ORKANIEH

TURKEY

last moment, was to be cheated, for an insect bite turned septicemic and he died at sea on 23 April, to be buried by torchlight on the island of Skyros among the olives and lemon trees of the Mediterranean world he had loved so passionately in life.

It was a better death than many in the Mediterranean Expeditionary Force were to suffer two days later. A month's pause in the naval bombardment had given the Turkish garrison, now under the command of the German officer Liman von Sanders, the chance it needed to fortify the beaches. When the improvised landings vessels appeared off shore, mainly naval whalers towed by steam pinnaces, but also a collier, the *River Clyde*, converted to discharge troops down ramps, a storm of rifle and machine-gun fire was unleashed on them. At those beaches, lettered S, X and Y, the troops dug trenches at the top of the cliffs they had captured. Had they advanced inland, they would have taken in the rear the Turks who, at the tip of the peninsula, were massacring their comrades at beaches V and W. Alongside the *River Clyde* the sea literally turned red with blood and the expedition commander, General Ian Hamilton, a writer with a sensitive soul, was

Far left: The Allied attack on Gallipoli.

Above left: HMS *New Zealand,* part of the Gallipoli flotilla.

Left: Turkish artillery which bombarded the Allies on the beaches.

Above right: A Turkish shell bursts near the *River Clyde,* a troopship at V Beach at Gallipoli.

Below: HMS *Majestic* sinking off the Gallipoli peninsula. U-Boats were in evidence throughout the assault, harassing Allied shipping.

stricken by horror. He described the sight as 'monstrous; too cold-blooded; like looking at gladiators from the dress-circle.... As men fixed in the grip of a nightmare, we were powerless — unable to do anything but wait. To be safe oneself, except for the offchance of a shell, was like being stretched upon the rack.'

Gradually, the Turkish resistance on the two stricken beaches was beaten down and the landings consolidated. However that did not mean that the tide had turned and the operation had ensured success. Subordinate to von Sanders, whose nerve had been badly shaken, was a young Turkish divisional commander, Mustapha Kemal, later Ataturk. While von

Sanders rode distractedly about the peninsula, Kemal sent for replacements and led them down to seal off the landings made by the ANZACs, most threatening because of their proximity to Constantinople. British inaction in the south then allowed their beaches to be contained also. By 30 April the 'military expedition to Constantinople' had resolved itself into a battle for two tiny footholds on a rocky coast 100 miles from the city.

On 11 May the Turks mounted a mass attack against the beach-heads. So ferocious was the attack, with soldiers dying in their thousands, and so horrifying was the aftermath of suffering among the wounded that the two sides agreed

58

to a truce in order to recover the survivors and bury the dead. The conference was held in a dugout at the beach called ANZAC after its devil-may-care Australasian garrison — one of whom interrupted the conference between Generals Birdwood and Braithwaite and Mustapha Kemal, to enquire, 'Have any of you bastards got my kettle?' Aubrey Herbert, friend and comrade-in-arms of Rupert Brooke, accompanied a Turkish captain to oversee the work of mercy:

'We mounted over a plateau and down through gullies filled with thyme, where there lay about 4000 Turkish dead. . . . There were two wounded lying in that multitude of silence. The Turkish captain said, "At the spectacle even the most gentle must feel savage and the most savage must weep." The dead fill acres of ground. They fill the myrtle grown gullies. It was as if God had breathed in their faces. I talked to some Turks, one of whom pointed to the graves. "That's politics," he said. Then he pointed to the dead bodies and said, "That's diplomacy. God pity all of us poor soldiers."'

The truce did not end the battle, though the initial disaster had ended the current careers of Lord Fisher, who resigned on 15 May, and

Winston Churchill, who was removed from office on 26 May. After a summer of small-scale trench fighting, no different from that on the Western Front except for the heat, flies and unfamiliar diseases, the Allies launched what was to be a final large-scale offensive on 6 August. The troops at the tip of the peninsula were briefed to attack simultaneously with the launch of a new landing at Suvla, 20 miles along it to the north. The landings were successful, but then, as on 25 April, many of the soldiers who had got ashore believed they had achieved all that was expected of them. They sat down, sunbathed, lit fires to make tea and even went swimming. Once again, Mustapha Kemal, now established as the lionheart of the defense, rode about summoning reinforcements until he could be sure that he had sealed off the new landing.

The coming of winter to Gallipoli brought bad weather and despair. On 27 November there was, according to one survivor:

'a terrific thunderstorm, followed by 24 hours of torrential rain, during which the men got soaked to the skin. Then came an icy hurricane; the rain turned into a blinding blizzard; then heavy snow, followed by two

Above: Turkish troops in their trenches near Gallipoli.

Left: British POWs in a Turkish hospital after they had been captured in the Gallipoli campaign.

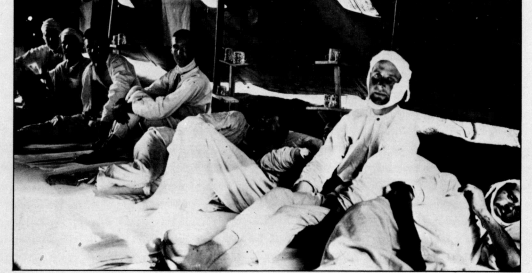

nights of bitter frost. . . . At Suvla, trenches were soon flooded, water-courses became roaring torrents and a wall-like spate of mud and water, several feet high, bore down the corpses of dead Turks and pack ponies into our lines. . . . Streams of exhausted men struggled down to the beaches, many collapsing and freezing to death where they fell. . . . At Suvla alone, during these three dreadful days, there were more than 5000 cases of frostbite. No such storm had been known in these parts for more than forty years.'

Kitchener himself had just left the peninsula after a tour of inspection and, before the climatic catastrophe, had decided that conditions were so bad, and prospects of breaking through to Constantinople so slim, that all the beaches but those at Cape Helles, on the tip of the peninsula,

should be evacuated. By 20 December this had been accomplished. Liman von Sanders attempted an all-out assault on Helles when he found that the rest of the garrison had been evacuated. However, under naval fire and without the overbearing presence of Kemal (who had been transferred) to drive them to battle, the Turks turned and fled. While they remained disorganized, Birdwood, now commanding in place of the sensitive and artistic Hamilton, decided to get the rest of his men off Cape Helles. The last 16,000 were lifted by the navy in a single night on 8 January 1916.

Gallipoli had raised high hopes in those like Churchill, who had planned it as 'a way round,' a 'back door into the fortress of the Central Powers' and in those like Rupert Brooke and Patrick Shaw-Stewart, who had gone there in a spirit of crusade. Their emotions were perfectly captured in Brooke's poem to The Dead:

These hearts were woven of human joys and cares
Washed marvellously with sorrow, swift to mirth
The years had given them kindness. Dawn was theirs
And sunset, and the colours of the earth.
These had seen movement, and heard music; known
Slumber and waking; loved; gone proudly friended;
Felt the quick stir of wonder; sat alone;
Touched flowers and furs and cheeks. All this is
    ended.

These were not the emotions of the common soldiers who had fought and died at Gallipoli. They had learned to hate the place, to feel a grudging respect for the courage and endurance of the Turkish soldier – 'Johnnie Turk' – and to feel there must be a better place to fight a war. The romanticism of the 'Lost Generation' of young officers who felt as Brooke did, and whose feelings were shared by bold spirits in the government like Churchill, had done much to motivate the British to war, just as the wounded patriotism of the French and the frustrated nationalism of the Germans deafened their ears to reason when the pace of crisis began to accelerate. Emotion, as much as self-interest, had generated the war and sustained the warlike urge of the first 18 months.

Above: Turkish prisoners taken in the third battle of Krithia, 4 June 1915.

Top: A British trench captured by the Turks with the remains of corpses and a few rifles.

Below: A village captured by the French shows the *River Clyde,* a British transport, run aground at Sedd-el-Bahr, May 1915.

However by the beginning of 1916 it was realized that emotion could not fuel a war machine any longer. In the West hard decisions were being made about a new sort of battle which would defeat the enemy by allotting him an uneven share of suffering. In the Mediterranean a use had to be found for the army which the Gallipoli defeat had suddenly left unemployed. It came unexpectedly through the intervention of Bulgaria in the war. The Bulgarians were regarded by their Balkan neighbors as little better than the Turks who had so long been their masters — cruel, selfish and scarcely European. There were some reasons for this. In the Second Balkan War of 1912 the Bulgarians had fought their Christian neighbors, who had previously supported them against Turkey in the First Balkan War. They had been defeated, but that had driven them further toward Turkey. Since 1914 the Allies had been busy with flattery and bribes to bring them back

to their side, but the Bulgarians demanded a price higher than the nearest of the Allies, Serbia, would pay. Moreover, Germany had her own urgent reasons for wishing Bulgaria in her camp, notably the need to safeguard her rail connections with Turkey, which ran through Bulgarian territory. On 6 September 1915 she succeeded in binding Bulgaria by a treaty which committed the two countries and Austria to an offensive which would defeat Serbia. Bulgaria at once began to mobilize; news of this prompted the French and British to send troops, partly drawn ·from the force at Gallipoli, to Serbia's assistance. As Serbia had no outlet to the sea, the Allies were obliged to demand passage for this expeditionary force from Greece. The Greek government lacked the power to resist, and the troops were landed at the Greek port of Salonika on 5 October and at once marched against Bulgaria.

The campaign which ensued was to be one of

the most pointless and frustrating of the war. The Central Powers — as the Germans, Austrians and Bulgarians were increasingly known — swiftly disposed of Serbia by a converging attack. The Serbian army, commanded by the aged but indomitable *Voivode* (War Chief), Radomir Putnik, twice avoided encirclement. However, it was forced into an agonizing winter retreat through the mountains of Serbia into Albania, where its survivors, bearing the *Voivode* in a litter on their shoulders, arrived in December. Allied ships evacuated them to Corfu, many so emaciated that they could be carried aboard ship in the arms of the nurses, as if they were sick children. The Austrians were close behind. In January 1916 they compelled the surrender of Serbia's dwarf ally, Montenegro, and then occupied Albania.

Meanwhile the Bulgarians had driven the vanguard of the French Expeditionary Force out of their territory to join the British in their staging area south of Salonika. The two armies constructed a vast entrenched camp as a precaution against a pro-German government coming to power in Greece and sat down to await events. Their inactivity provoked critics of Allied strategy even within the alliance to ribald jests about their function. 'Gardening' it was suggested, and the force became known as the 'Gardeners of Salonika,' with its French commander, Maurice Sarrail, as head gardener. Germans and Austrians were even more cutting. Prisoners of war, their propagandists said, were usually confined in barbed-wire cages. Salonika provided the first example of an army imprisoning itself. Alas, all these jibes were to retain their force almost to the end of the war.

Left: The scene from HMS *Cornwallis* as stores burn ashore after the evacuation of Suvla in late December 1915.

Below: British troops attempt to go over the top to extricate themselves from their beach at Gallipoli. The assault failed.

If in this isolated backwater of the war the tide ran for the Central Powers, in others it was the Allies who enjoyed success. By the end of 1915 all but one of Germany's overseas possessions had fallen. First to go were their Far Eastern possessions. New Zealand troops had occupied Samoa on 29 August 1914, Papua and New Guinea on 17 September and the other Pacific islands — Yap, Nauru, the Peters, Caroline and Marshall Islands — had all been taken by the Royal or Imperial Japanese Navies by the end of November. There had been little or no resistance offered.

The Japanese, who had entered the war on 23 August 1914 precisely because of the pickings it offered, met a different response in September when they undertook the reduction of the most important German naval base in the region, the port of Tsingtao in Shantung Province of China. They found that the German force, which numbered 4000, had entrenched the landward approach to the port and was prepared to fight. Only 10 years before the Japanese had attacked a similar fortification at Port Arthur, Russia's naval base in the Yellow Sea. They tackled the Germans using the same

Above: French General Maurice Sarrail inspects the equipment of a Serbian unit which landed in Greece to join the Allies.

Top left: British troops land at Salonika in November 1915. The assault through Greece was meant to encircle Constantinople.

Top: The pro-Ally Greek Premier Venizelos reviews one of his regiments in Salonika.

Above: A Montenegrin guerrilla force which fought a successful defense of mountain strongholds.

Below: A Sikh unit lands at Tsingtao, China's largest port, after its capture by the Japanese late in 1914.

methods. Like an 18th-century European army, they dug trenches at a safe distance from the German perimeter, brought up heavy guns — the same heavy guns that they had used at Port Arthur — destroyed the enemy's guns and then pushed forward their earthworks. On the night of 6 November the enemy was judged to be weak enough for the delivery of a general assault. The Germans fell in the confusion, and the next morning the Rising Sun flew over Tsingtao.

A token British force, from the Hong Kong garrison, had taken part in the siege. The German possessions in Africa, with one exception, were to fall to colonial forces. Togoland, on the old slave coast, was overrun by columns of black soldiers, West African Rifles and Tirailleurs Sénégalais under white officers by 27 August 1914. German Southwest Africa, which bordered the Union of South Africa and was far larger and better-garrisoned, proved a harder nut to crack. The army, organized to occupy it, was composed exclusively of native white South Africans. Many were Afrikaners, who 10 years before had fought in the three-year war against the British Crown. Now they responded enthusiastically to the summons to march against their enemies, but they had to pause for four months to put down an internal rising led by Lieutenant Colonel Solomon G Maritz, one of the Boer generals of 1899–1902. Then, marching in four converging columns, they invaded the German colony in January 1915 from the landward and seaward approaches and between April and July encircled the enemy garrison at Otavi and forced it to surrender.

Above: The Tirailleurs Sénégalais under French command. Black African troops were used extensively.

Right: A Serbian artillery barrage against the Austrians. Serbia fought hard and well against overwhelming odds.

German resistance in the West Coast Colony of the Cameroons took longer to suppress, the dense jungle impeding the British, French and Belgian drives against the local German defense force, which was not reduced until February 1916. The most stubborn and skillful resistance of all was encountered in German East Africa (Tanganyika). The forces there were no larger, indeed rather smaller, than in Southwest Africa, and the space in which to maneuver no more extensive. However in Tanganyika the German Empire had a commander of genius. Although only a colonel, Paul von Lettow-Vorbeck had the mind of a great general and he understood from the beginning that by a strategy of evasion

and delay he could tie down a far greater number of Allied troops than he had German under command, and so serve the purposes of his Kaiser. He had, in fact, only 3500 whites and 12,000 black Askaris, and his acquaintance with the territory was small, since he had only arrived in the colony in May 1914. He nevertheless succeeded in defeating the first British expedition sent against him from India in November 1914. Its landing was a disaster and, after a confused struggle made more chaotic by the intervention of swarms of vicious wild bees, which seemed to sting only the Kaiser's enemies, the expedition was forced to re-embark on 5 December 1914, only three days after landing.

The British Empire, stung by the rebuff, then gathered its forces in earnest. General Jan Christiaan Smuts, the Boer rebel who had made whole-hearted peace with his enemies, took the campaign against Lettow-Vorbeck in hand, and arrived in the colony in July 1915. Belgian and, later, Portuguese forces made up his strength and in April 1916 a strategy of convoying columns, which had proved so successful in German Southwest Africa, was set in motion. Lettow-Vorbeck eluded all of them, time after time inflicting a local defeat on his pursuers and then slipping away to double back on them in the dense bush and appear on their flank or rear. In January 1917 Smuts, now in demand in Britain as the representative of his country's

contribution to the imperial war effort, left the center of operations. His successors, fellow South Africans, fared no better than he, though the force at their disposal had risen after his departure to 22 battalions of African troops, with several thousand white South Africans still present. Lettow-Vorbeck, reduced to commanding a handful of Askaris, continued to dodge and twist through the interior and was not to surrender until 12 days after the European armistice, on 23 November 1918, when he still had 1500 soldiers under his command. His name belongs to the annals of those great guerrilla soldiers who, true to the logic of their strategy, oblige a larger army to deploy a disproportionate force for an unconscionable time merely to achieve a negative object.

The most famous guerrilla leader produced by the war was T E Lawrence – Lawrence of Arabia. However his operations were a sideshow for the larger forces which tied up the main strength of the Turkish army. As an imperial power Turkey faced two major problems: many of her subjects were non-Turkish and even non-Muslim and her borders were at many points cut off from the center of power in Asia Minor. Also, as the Allies' had control of the sea, they were able to bring their power to bear in remote areas where Turkey was at a disadvantage. Even Gallipoli, because of the lack of rail communications, was difficult for Turkey to defend,

Above: South African Generals Botha and Smuts, who led the Empire's fight against the Germans in Africa.

Below: A column of East African troops under German command which fought a successful rear-guard action under Lettow-Vorbeck to retain a German presence in Tanganyika.

Below: One of Lettow-Vorbeck's German units in Tanganyika.

Below: A British 4.5cm howitzer in action in the Cameroons.

Above: Colonel T E Lawrence, the famous Lawrence of Arabia, who fought for Arab unity and independence despite British intentions to colonize the Middle East.

particularly at a moment when its offensive against the Russians in the Caucasus was going disastrously. The Caucasian border between Turkey and Russia was not served by railroads at all, scarcely surprising as the average elevation on the plateau was 6500 feet. Across it ran a series of mountain ranges with summits between 10–16,000 feet, snow covered even in summer and in winter swept by gales which drove the night temperature to 20 degrees below zero. Twice before the scene of fighting between Russia and Turkey, the Caucasus was known to be difficult campaigning country even in summer. Enver Pasha, the Turkish War Minister, nevertheless decided to attack the Russian Caucasus in winter. In December 1914 he personally led troops up onto the plateau. The Turkish Third Army totalled 190,000 men at the start of the campaign, slightly outnumbering the Russians, but the soldiers lacked winter clothing and were quickly cut off from regular supplies. They had no overcoats, blankets, fuel, tents or decent footwear. They pushed slowly into Russian territory but after a week the Russians counterattacked and defeated three of their former corps, one of which surrendered en masse. Many who escaped capture simply froze to death in the mountain snows. At least 30,000 Turks were buried and by the end of February 1915 the Third Army had been reduced to 12,000 men.

Defeated on the Russian border, the Turks in 1914 were also stretched by the need to defend the southern frontier of their empire in the Persian Gulf. As soon as she entered the war, the staff of the British Army in India conceived a plan to draw away Turkish troops from the Suez Canal region by an attack up the valleys of the Tigris and Euphrates, which it was thought, might also foment rebellion among the Arabs. An offensive strategy in the region would also directly serve to protect the outlets of the Anglo-Iranian pipe lines in the Persian Gulf which, since the abandonment of coal-firing, fuelled the boilers of the Grand Fleet. In November an Indian army expeditionary force landed at the mouth of the Shatt-al-'Arab, the confluence of the Tigris and Euphrates, and marched inland. Weak local forces opposed their advance but were pushed aside and Basra was occupied on 22 January. The Turkish units in these parts, unlike those which had fallen under the reforming influence of Liman von Sanders in Anatolia, had obsolete equipment and were commanded by officers whose ambitions were to lead the easy life of the harem, the divan and the hookah pipe. They made no effort to expel the British force — even though many of its soldiers were Muslim co-religionists, who might have been susceptible to enticement. Their inactivity actually alarmed the Government of India into reinforcing the advance guard,

Below: German machine gunners search for British planes over East Africa. Only a few aircraft were used, as most were needed in France.

Below: British unit, manned largely by Africans, attacks a German strongpoint in Tanganyika.

captured Baghdad. It was then the Central Powers' turn to fail. In September 1917 a joint Turkish-German force, code named *Yilderim* (Lightning), attempted to retake Baghdad but fell to pieces in the roadless wastes of northern Mesopotamia. However Germany and Turkey were determined to take possession of the Russian oilfields at Baku on the Caspian Sea. The Russians had earlier attempted to assist Townshend by launching an offensive from the Caucasus into eastern Turkey and northern Persia. Since Russia's army was falling apart, her two enemies agreed on a plan to take Baku by pincer movements north and south of the Black Sea. To counter them an Anglo-Indian force, named Dunsterforce after its commander General Dunsterville, model for Kipling's schoolboy hero Stalky, set off from Mesopotamia to race them to the objective. In the event, the Turks beat the British to the prize but arrived so fatigued that they were obliged to relinquish it almost as soon as it was taken. Meanwhile on 3 November 1918 the British army in Mesopotamia had captured Mosul, on the headwaters of the Tigris. On the Mediterranean coast of the Turkish Empire another army under General Sir Edmund Allenby was, in September 1918, approaching the capital of Syria, Damascus.

The British campaign in Palestine had begun in February 1915 when an expedition of 20,000 Turks, under German officers, had crossed the Sinai desert and attacked the Suez Canal. This threat to the most precious lifeline of the empire had so alarmed the British government that it thereafter kept 500,000 troops in Egypt. The majority was training for operations elsewhere, but a solid nucleus was earmarked to secure the eastern Mediterranean flank against a renewal of the Turkish menace. This did not recur until

Left: British and Armenian artillerymen use a captured 6-inch Russian howitzer defending the Baku oil fields.

Below right: British artillery dig in to defend the Suez Canal. It was never seriously threatened.

Below: The British march into Kut, during the second attempt to take Baghdad.

which they thought might be in danger of a secret and sudden counteroffensive. The reinforcement, on the contrary, only prompted the local commanders to push further up the rivers into Mesopotamia (modern Iraq). The Turks resisted but were outnumbered and defeated. As the advance progressed the idea seized the British of aiming for Baghdad, from which they could threaten both the Turkish positions in Palestine and Syria and the homeland of Anatolia itself.

In September General Sir Charles Townshend was put in command of a flying column which had the mission of capturing first Kut-al-Amara and then Baghdad. On 28 September he arrived at Kut with a division of infantry and a brigade of cavalry, followed by a long train of boats bringing supplies and munitions up the Tigris, and defeated the Turkish garrison. He at once pressed on, encouraged by a direction from the Viceroy of India that he might 'march on Baghdad if he is satisfied that the force he has available is sufficient for the operation.' He was satisfied, and on 11 November he set off into the desert again with his flotilla of boats following along the river and a column of 1000 mules, 240 donkeys and 600 camels bringing up the rear. On 21 November he encountered strong Turkish positions at Ctesiphon. The pilot of a scouting aircraft who noticed large Turkish reinforcements concentrating in the rear, crashed while on the flight back with the news.

Townshend, therefore, attacked under the misapprehension that his force outnumbered the enemy. He was defeated, forced into an agonizing retreat across the desert and took refuge inside Kut at the beginning of December.

Townshend had directed a siege once before, in the tiny Indian fortress of Chitral in 1895. His triumphant resistance there had made him a hero of the Empire and ensured him the promotion which led him to his Mesopotamian command. However, Kut and Chitral had nothing but Townshend in common. His opponents at Chitral had been ill-armed mountaineers, but at Kut he was penned in by a large, strong, Muslim army commanded by the senior German general, Baron Kolmar von der Goltz. The Turks, legendary diggers, soon surrounded the town with an impenetrable belt of trenches. After a siege lasting five months and the repulse of four attempts by the British outside the lines to relieve the garrison, Townshend was starved into surrender. He, in fact, showed little sign of privation but thousands of his soldiers would soon succumb to malnutrition or disease. However, there was also much disease in the Turkish camp, and von der Goltz himself was carried off by cholera at the moment of victory.

In September a new British effort, directed by the War Office instead of the inefficient Military Department in India, regained Kut. After a year of preparation, General Frederick Stanley Maude, Townshend's replacement, actually

Above: Staffordshire troops at Baladasar after the withdrawal of the Armenians from the fight.

Above: General Townshend who was forced to surrender at Kut in April 1916.

August 1916, when a probe toward the Canal was easily defeated at Rumani. That maneuver decided the British to substitute an active for a passive defense of the Canal, and in March 1917, after months spent pushing forward a railroad and water pipeline along the coast, they began an advance toward Palestine. Gaza, first city of the inhabited Holy Land, was quickly captured, but then evacuated through a misunderstanding.

A new commander, the ferocious Allenby, nicknamed 'the Bull' for his rampaging among inefficient subordinates, arrived in June 1917 with orders to avoid such misunderstandings and win victories. Lloyd George, now British Prime Minister, had given him the order, 'Jerusalem before Christmas,' wanting a seasonal gift for the British people in a year which had

brought them little but sorrow and disappointment. Allenby threw himself into the necessary preparations. A cavalryman of the old school, he was delighted by the presence of large numbers of horsemen, Australian, New Zealand, British and Indian, in his Indian Expeditionary Force. He devised a sound strategy to make use of them. While the infantry and artillery pushed solidly along the coast, he arranged for the cavalry to move on wide outflanking sweeps inland. General von Falkenhayn, displaced from the Western Front by the elevation of Hindenburg and Ludendorff to the supreme command, opposed him with a force of 36,000. However Allenby had nearly 100,000 men and, in terms of quality, the disparity of strength was 'that of a tiger to a tom cat.' On 31 October he swept through Gaza. On 13 November he was under the walls of Jerusalem, and on 9 December the mayor of the city, brought the keys of the gates to the vanguard of the imperial army.

Allenby's next target was Damascus, from which he could stretch out a hand to join forces with the other British army in Mesopotamia. There was a second Turkish army in their rear, based in the far south of the Arabian peninsula, which might threaten their flanks. Fortunately since 1916 that threat had been contained by a home-grown Arab resistance campaign. It was supported and abetted by a British military mission, of which the leading light was a young temporary officer, T E Lawrence. In later life, this strange, introverted man of action was recognized as an intellectual celebrity among his generation. In 1916 he was no more than an apprentice archeologist, temporarily in Khaki. The war had provided an outlet for talents which the excavation of Syrian antiquities had left untapped. Already a fluent Arabic speaker, he had

been a natural choice to join the mission to the Arab rebels in the Hejaz, at the foot of the Turkish pilgrim railroad to Mecca. However mere liaison with the tribes had not satisfied his romantic urge. He had turned himself, in two years, into a full-bloodied guerrilla warrior, satisfying his passion for stealth and subterfuge in a campaign of surprise attacks against the railroad, ambushes of Turkish columns and storm assaults of sleepy desert forts. Under his inspiration, the *Jeish al-Arabi* – 'the army of the Arabs' – had grown into a force of 10,000 by July 1917, when they reached Aqaba, the Palestinian port at the head of the Red Sea. From there he led it along the desert border of Palestine, keeping station with Allenby's advance toward Jerusalem and Damascus.

Politically his greatest triumphs lay ahead of him, but militarily he would never achieve as much as he had in the Hejaz. He described his achievements brilliantly and ensured acclaim for decades. In early 1917 he had fulfilled a long-held ambition to blow up a troop train:

'One entire wheel of the locomotive whirled up suddenly black out of the cloud against the sky and sailed musically over our heads to fall slowly and heavily into the desert behind. . . . The now grey mist of the explosion drifted from the line towards us, and over our ridge until it was lost in the hills. . . . As I watched, our machine guns chattered over my head, and the long rows of Turks on the carriage roofs rolled over and were swept off the top like bales of cotton, which stormed along the roof and splashed clouds of yellow chips from the planking. . . . It made a shambles of the place. The survivors broke out in a panic across the desert, throwing away their rifles and equipment as they ran.'

This ambush ended, like so many Arab operations, in furious and selfish looting:

'The Arabs, gone raving mad, were rushing about at top speed, bare-headed and half-naked, screaming, shooting into the air, clawing one another nail and fist, while they burst open trucks and staggered back and forward with immense bales, which they ripped by the railside and tossed through, smashing what they did not want. . . .'

Sometimes the fighting was more purposeful. In June he had led a camel charge against a Turkish column surprised in the open desert:

'Yells and shots poured up in a sudden torrent from beyond the crest. We kicked our camels furiously to the edge, to see our fifty horsemen coming down the last slope into the main valley like a runaway, at full gallop, shooting from the saddle. As we watched, two or three went down, but the rest thundered forward at marvellous speed, and the Turkish infantry, huddled together under the cliff, ready to cut their desperate

way out towards Maan in the first dusk, began to sway in and out, and finally broke before the rush, adding their flight to Ouda's charge. . . . They were too bound up in the terror against their rear to notice us as we came over the eastward slope; so we also took them by surprise and in the flank; and a charge of ridden camels going nearly thirty miles an hour was irresistible.'

Two years of campaigning in the desert culminated for Lawrence (el Urenz to the Arabs) in the approach to Damascus. Lawrence served as adviser to Faisal, son of the Sharif of Mecca, who desired to make Damascus the capital of a new Arab kingdom. He and Lawrence were acutely anxious to seize it ahead of Allenby's army, which the Arab leadership now saw as the instrument of a policy hostile to their interests. Anglo-Arab antipathy had crystalized in November 1917, when the British government had issued, through its foreign minister, a promise – the Balfour Declaration – to the Zionist movement. This declared that it would assist them in the creation of a national home for the Jewish people in Palestine. Word had also reached Faisal of an earlier understanding, the Sykes-Picot agreement between the British and French, which would retain Palestine and Syria under their control once those territories had been won from the Turks. Therefore, while Allenby's regular armies slogged through the Turkish defenses of populated Palestine during the summer of 1918, Lawrence, Faisal and the Arab army sought a way to Damascus through

the desert. On 19 September 1918 Allenby won a major victory over the Turks, now commanded by the Gallipoli team of Liman von Sanders and Mustapha Kemal, at a place called Megiddo, identified with the biblical battle site of Armageddon. He broke across the mountain barrier into Syria and the Lebanon, but the Arabs were ahead of him. On 2 October, Lawrence and his confederates found them= selves on the outskirts of Damascus. They believed that the Turks and British had already fought through the city:

'But, instead of ruins, the silent gardens stood blurred green with river mist, in whose setting shimmered the city, beautiful as ever like a pearl in the morning sun. . . . We drove down the straight-banked ridge through

Left: British troops pass the Ctesiphon Arch, the site of General Townshend's defeat in November 1915.

Left: General Allenby, who led the successful attack on Palestine and Syria.

Right: King Faisal of the Hejaz (later Saudi Arabia) leads his men who helped the British conquer the Middle East.

Far right: Faisal at Wejh in March 1917.

Below : The British troops, led by General Maude, march Turkish prisoners through the streets of Baghdad after its capture, cheered by Arabs who thought this meant their liberation.

the watered fields in which the peasants were just beginning their day's work. A galloping horseman checked at our headcloths in the car with a merry salutation, holding out a bunch of yellow grapes. "Good news, Damascus salutes you. . . ."'

At their approach to the town hall, they found it:

'packed with a swaying mob, yelling, embracing, dancing, singing. Every man, woman, child in this city of a quarter million souls seemed in the streets, waiting only for the spark of our appearance to ignite their spirits. Damascus went mad with joy. The men tossed up their tarbooshes to cheer, the women tore off their veils. Householders threw flowers, hangings, carpets, into the road before us: their wives leaned, screaming with laughter, through the lattices and splashed us with bath-dippers of scent, poor dervishes made themselves our running footmen in front and behind, howling and cutting themselves with frenzy. And over the loud cries and the shrilling of women came the measured roar of men's voices chanting "Faisal, Nasir, Shukri, Urenz."'

Alas for Faisal and Urenz. Their claim to have beaten Allenby's Australians into Damascus was rejected by the British, who were, in any case, determined and equipped to deny the Arabs any claim to right of conquest. The essential weakness of a guerrilla army was demonstrated as starkly as it could ever be by the steamroller refusal of the British to accept the Arabs as anything but picturesque auxiliaries to their conventional military power. They stuck unapologetically to their plan of dividing Palestine and Syria with the French and admitting Jews

freely to settle in Eretz Israel — 'the land of Israel' as the Zionists call the Holy Land. Lawrence, admitted as spokesman for the Arabs to the peace conference, struggled valiantly to win their case before the court of world opinion, but he was defeated there as decisively as he had been robbed of the fruits of battle on the ground.

There was a sort of justice in his defeat. Every guerrilla leader trafficks as much in propaganda as in deeds. Lawrence must be reckoned one of the great propagandists of the 20th century, a master of both instant personal effect and of lasting literary appeal. In retrospect his achievements appear increasingly transient and insubstantial. He engaged nothing but a small fraction of the Turkish army in Arabia and he inflicted little real damage upon it. Without the prop of Allenby's regulars his 'army of the Arabs' would have been blown like chaff before the wind of the Turks' impatience whenever they had chosen to fill their lungs. He can claim no common standing with Lettow-Vorbeck, whose brilliant campaign of evasion in Tanganyika complemented instead of depended upon the strength of the regular army, and will remain as a classic example of how a guerrilla commander can almost infinitely postpone defeat.

Defeat or victory in these 'outer theaters' ultimately counted for nothing in the scales of World War I. The German colonies, even the territory of the Turkish empire, were peripheral to the forum of the real struggle, which remained where it had begun, on the eastern and western borders of Germany. While Lettow-Vorbeck had been drawing his British and South African pursuers ever deeper into the forests of East Africa and Lawrence had been preparing his spectacular debut on the stage of Arabian politics, the armies of Germany, France and Britain had been gathering their strength for the great battles of 1916 which each believed would bring the conflict to an end. These were to be the battles of Verdun and the Somme.

Above left: Red Cross units carry away the wounded in the fight for Palestine, October 1918.

Left: Indian Bengal Lancers in General Chauvel's march through Damascus after the conquest of Syria, October 1918.

Above right: A British armored car being shelled in Palestine.

Top: The triumphal march into Aqaba.

Above: The triumphal British entry into Baghdad after its capture, 11 March 1917.

Below: Lawrence's forces march into Palestine aboard their camels.

The first British tank unit in action in World War I at Flers, September 1916.

4 Verdun and the Somme

The French High Command, though it had made a token contribution to the Gallipoli expedition, had set its face from the outset of trench warfare against campaigning by the Allies outside France. Its view of the war was simple: that Germany was the strong man of the Central Powers, without whom that alliance would collapse, that the best portion of its army occupied French territory, which was intolerable, and that the right strategy therefore was to attack and keep on attacking until the Germans had been sent packing. As early as 29 December 1915 Joffre had outlined to Haig a plan for a great attack on either side of the River Somme, where the British Expeditionary Force and the French army joined hands. Its objects would be different from those of his earlier offensives, which had been designed to strike at the left and right shoulders of the great bulge which the German line formed in France. The coming battle was to be a straightforward test of strength, in which he who could stand the attrition — *usure*, or 'wearing down' as the

British called it — would emerge the victor. Joffre had chosen the Somme precisely because it was there that the two Allied Armies stood side by side, and could bring their strength fully to bear on the enemy. He suggested that they open the offensive on 1 July 1916 on a front 60 miles wide, and sustain it until the Germans could take no more.

French casualties by the end of 1915 already amounted to 1,900,000, of which a third had been fatal. Joffre nevertheless chose to believe that in the coming offensive he could inflict more casualties than his armies would suffer — a very doubtful belief, since the attacker almost always incurs losses faster than the defender. He buttressed his dubious calculation by his expressed confidence in the superior power of the Allies' artillery which he believed would win ground and kill Germans without proportionate risk to their infantry. Already in French staff circles the idea, later to become an article of dogma, had begun to circulate that 'artillery conquers, infantry merely occupies.'

Above left: The Archduke Friedrich of Austria and General Conrad von Hötzendorf.

Above center: French prisoners captured at Verdun are interrogated.

Above right: General Sir Douglas Haig, who planned the brutal and devastating Somme offensive.

Below: Some of the many thousands of French POWs seized by the Germans at Verdun.

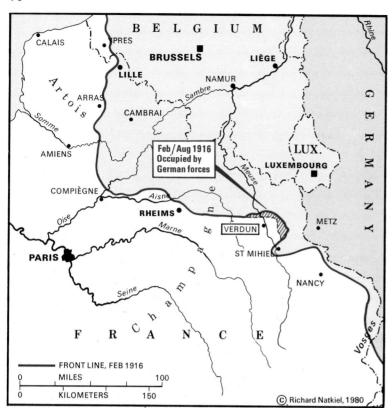

During December 1915 on the other side of the lines a similar idea and a complementary strategic analysis were projecting General von Falkenhayn and his staff toward a decision for an offensive of their own. Over Christmas the German Commander in Chief prepared for the Kaiser an exhaustive survey of the military situation and the options it presented. He now identified the British as 'the arch enemy — the soul of resistance — who must be shown that they had no chance of success.' Since the blockade had begun to bite hard and limited Germany's ability to hold out indefinitely, Britain could only be disheartened by a German offensive, and the only question was where to attack. A landing on British territory was made impossible by her naval strength and the outer theaters, Egypt, Mesopotamia and India, were too remote for German power to be brought to bear. In France, on the other hand, the British were too strong to be attacked directly for though the BEF was smaller than the French army it fought better. It remained therefore to attack one of Britain's allies. Falkenhayn had discussed with Conrad von Hötzendorf, the Commander in Chief of the Austrian Army, which to choose. They agreed that a heightening of the offensive against Russia would be fruitless, for the same reasons which had dissuaded Schlieffen from attacking her in the first place; the distances were too great and the communications a nightmare. Conrad was keen to attack Italy, which had stepped into the war in May 1915 with the unconcealed intention of robbing Austria of her remaining Italian-speaking provinces when she was unfitted to defend them properly. However Falkenhayn did not follow his argument that an Italian campaign would shortly allow the Central Powers' full strength to be turned against France. He thought it would all take too long and it would be better to get at Britain through an attack on the strongest of her allies, France, which was so weakened by the agonies of 1914–15 and likely to collapse under one more heavy blow. Conrad and he therefore agreed to differ. The Austrians decided on a separate attack of their own against Italy in the Trentino. Falkenhayn turned to the map of the French front to choose

Above left: The front line at the start of 1916.

Above: The remains of a French soldier after Verdun.

Above right: Germans dig in at Verdun.

Above far right: A German soldier fights on in a trench abandoned by the French at Fort Vaux, Verdun.

Right: A French soldier who fell at Verdun.

a spot for an executioner's stroke at the neck of Marianne.

The spot he eventually selected was Verdun. Historically one of the great frontier fortresses of eastern France, its fortification had gradually fallen into decay since the last rebuilding in 1885 and since 1914 its strongpoints had been stripped of their heavy artillery to equip the armies in the field. The High Command had judged it safe to take that risk because Verdun seemed to have become a backwater. It stood in a remote angle of the trench line where it crossed the River Meuse south of Rheims, but there had been no heavy fighting there since September 1914. The German garrison on the east bank appeared ready to live and let live and in consequence the French held the area with troops resting from heavier fighting elsewhere. The Germans, nevertheless, enjoyed important advantages in the area. Only a single French railroad ran into the city, and it lay within the range of German artillery. The Germans enjoyed the use of no less than 11 railroads, all of which lay past the heights of the Meuse and so beyond the range of the French guns. In a 'battle of build up,' therefore, the advantage would lie heavily, if indeed not conclusively, with the Germans.

The Germans did not intend to allow the French to build up anything. Overwhelmingly strong in artillery — 221 batteries to 65, theirs included numbers of the 305mm and 420mm heavy howitzers which had devastated Liège and Namur in 1914 — their plan was to challenge the French to commit their unsupported infantry in large numbers to a battle of exhaustion. On 21 February 1916 they opened an enormous surprise bombardment, which included gas and tear-smoke shells. It fell on the positions of the two French divisions which held the eight miles

Above: French troops attack during the Battle of Verdun.

Left: No man's land at Verdun.

Above right: Germans storm across no man's land in the opening stages of the Battle of Verdun.

Far right: Grenades pock-marked the earth at Verdun.

Below: Germans crawl through the barbed wire at Verdun.

of front on the right bank of the Meuse. Nothing like it had been experienced on the Western Front before. Whole trees were uprooted and flung into the air in the woods around Verdun and along mile-long stretches of the front the trenches were completely obliterated. The bombardment was at its heaviest in the Bois des Caures, held by two Chasseur battalions commanded by Lieutenant Colonel Driant. The opening of the battle was doubly bitter for him. Not only did he see his battalions progressively wiped out under his eyes, he himself, who sat in the National Assembly for the Verdun constituency, had been warned of the danger which threatened the sector and had protested against the failure to strengthen its defenses. He was the most famous French imaginative writer about future warfare and had described in graphic detail the particular horrors which a great battle of artillery would inflict on its victims. His understanding of the power of modern armies ensured that his position was the best laid out of any on the Verdun Front, and so paradoxically the agony his Chasseurs suffered in the Bois des Caures was particularly prolonged. It was later circulated that over 100,000 shells fell into his position during the preliminary bombardment, but the concrete shelters and deep dugouts he had had constructed were so strong that most of

his men were still alive when the Germans appeared. They were so heavily outnumbered, however, that although able to hold back the Germans on the first day, on the second their strongpoints fell one by one under sheer weight of numbers. Driant, who had taken absolution from the regimental Chaplain at the opening of the bombardment and behaved throughout the succeeding hours with an almost priestly calm, recognized in the afternoon of 22 February that he would have to abandon his line, which was now being assaulted by flame-thrower teams. Gathering his remaining officers about him he set off for the rear. On the way, he paused to give first aid to a wounded Chasseur, was hit and died with a prayer on his lips. His extraordinary courage and tenacity in the defense of the Bois des Caures impressed not only his own countrymen but also the enemy, one of whom arranged to have Driant's personal effects, which he had found in the command post, sent to his widow via a neutral party in Switzerland.

Thereafter Verdun was to become an increasingly anonymous battle, as the French, responding to the challenge in the style Falkenhayn had hoped they would, began to feed divisions into the stricken fortress, keeping them there until each had suffered the maximum possible level of casualties and then withdrawing it to refit.

Above: Part of the wreckage of Fort Douaumont at Verdun.

Above right: Fort Douaumont before the action.

However, in this opening stage there was to be the opportunity for one more display of individual achievement, this time on the German side. On 24 February the French second line, which had come under pressure as soon as the first had been pierced at the Bois des Caures, suddenly gave way and the Germans were able to rush to the third, formed by the outer line of 19th-century forts – Douaumont and Vaux – and the trenches which had been dug between them. At Douaumont they were only four miles from the city of Verdun itself and, if they could take it, would have only one more line of obstacles to cross in order to achieve victory.

Douaumont was a formidable position. Two fields of barbed wire 30-feet deep were backed by a line of spiked railings eight feet high on the edge of a dry ditch 24 feet deep. Inside stood a low concrete structure 200 yards long and 100 yards wide dominated by armored gun turrets and loopholed for machine guns. Inside was a labyrinth of tunnels and strong chambers with accommodation for 500 men. On the wall of the principal tunnel was inscribed the slogan, 'Rather be buried under the bricks of the fort than surrender.' On 25 August a German sergeant called Kunze appeared on the lip of this forbidding structure. He was in command of a section of pioneers whose task was to remove obstacles for the infantry regiment they were supporting, the 24th Brandenburgs. By some

chance he had lost touch with them and now found himself in the shadow of their principal objective, which seemed uninhabited. Deciding to explore, Kunze found a way through the wire and the spikes, dropped into the moat and crept along the wall of the fort itself. Finding an open loophole, he got his men to form a human pyramid, climbed to the top and entered the fort. No one challenged him and he set off to find the enemy. In fact the fort was held by only 60 elderly gunners, some of whom he quickly collected and made prisoner. After he had been in the fort for about an hour he was joined by an officer with his platoon, and between them they rounded up the rest of the garrison and secured the position. For the loss of none of their men, they had cracked the French position.

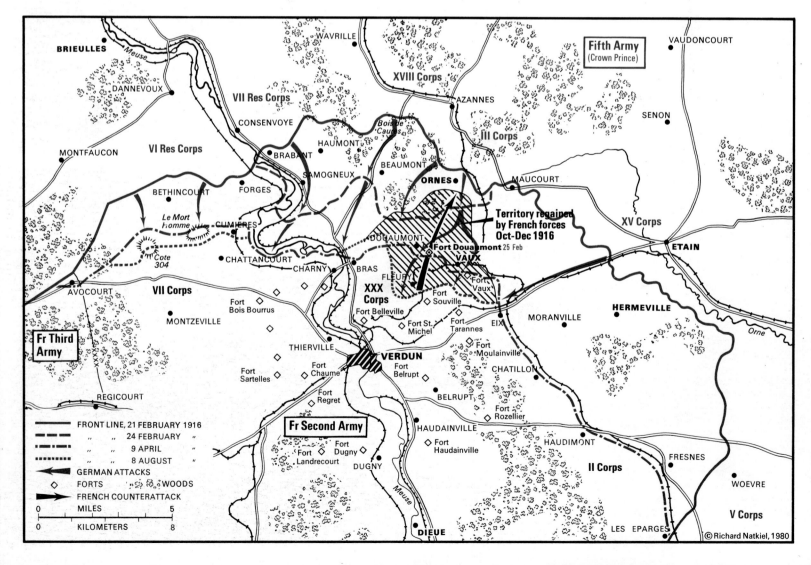

FORT DOUAUMONT
IM VORFRÜHLING
UND
IM SOMMER 1916

138

Above: Fort Douaumont afterward.

Above right: The gunfire at Mort-Homme ridge near Fort Douaumont.

Right: Germans inside the wrecked fort.

Below right: French wounded inside the main corridor of Fort Vaux.

Below left: The action at Verdun.

The Germans were slow to grasp the implications of the advantage which Kunze had won for them (and he was to be cheated of the credit, appropriated by an officer who arrived later), and were even slower to decide how to exploit it. By the time they had done so, a new and decisive factor had entered the situation. Philippe Pétain had been appointed to command on the Verdun sector. Pétain was an odd man out in the French army. Extremely individualistic, and contemptuous of fashionable ideas, he had not had a successful prewar career. He was, indeed, on the point of retiring as a 58-year old Colonel at the outbreak of war, and was kept on only as an emergency measure. However his success in commanding a brigade during the Great Retreat quickly won him a division, then a corps and later an army. By early 1916 he had emerged as the general best attuned to the problems of trench warfare and most understanding of the common soldier's problems. By 25 February it was clear that the local commander, General Herr, had lost his nerve. Joffre had chosen Pétain to replace him.

The effect on French morale in the threatened sector was instantaneous. 'Pétain is in control' were the words which ran round the trenches. 'France has her eyes on you' was the message of his first order of the day, but his intervention depended on more than his personal qualities for its effect. He focused at once on the two outstanding problems of the defense; artillery and supply. The French defenders were not only short of guns, those they had were badly coordinated. He ordered all the artillery put under a single command, appealed urgently to the High Command for more heavy-caliber pieces and made his first enquiry every morning, 'What have your batteries been doing? Leave the other details till later.' The garrison was also critically short of supplies. The only railroad into the fortress was single-line and narrow-gauge. He at once ordered the construction of a new standard gauge spur to lead into the city, but meanwhile concentrated his energies on the maintenance and improvement of the single road which provided the only other means of

supply. Ten thousand military laborers were brought to widen the road to seven yards, just enough for a column of trucks to pass in each direction. Quarries were opened to provide gravel which was constantly thrown on to the surface – 750,000 tons during the course of the battle – and trucks assembled from all over France. There had been only 700 in the district when the offensive opened, enough to provide 1250 tons of supplies daily. The garrison needed 2000 tons and another 100 tons for every extra division committed. Within days Pétain's transport Chief, Major Richard, had found another 2800 trucks, which he set to work in a continuous flow from one end of the *Voie Sacrée* (Sacred Way as the road came to be called) to the other, day and night, week after week without stopping. At maximum density a truck started on to the road every five seconds, but the pace along the 50 miles was so slow that a driver might spend 50 hours at the wheel to complete the journey.

By these desperate improvisations Pétain assumed that the Germans would not take Verdun in the first impulse of their attack. 'They shall not pass' (*Ils ne passeront pas*) became the watchword of his strategy. The formation of the initial assault did not cause the Germans to think again. Falkenhayn had code named the plan *Gericht* – Execution Place – and evidence that the French were willing to prolong the battle, at what he believed would be unbearable loss to themselves, was exactly what he wanted to detect. On 6 March, therefore, he opened a new effort against the tortured fortress. Hitherto he had attacked only on the right (eastern) bank of the Meuse. He now intended to march down the left bank as well, while striking to seize the fort next to Douaumont, Fort Vaux. With that in his hands and the French left-bank positions pushed back, he believed that Verdun could be held only at a progressively intolerable loss in French lives.

The new push won an immediate and spec-tacular success. The French infantry on the left bank were taken by surprise and one division broke under the shock. Most of one of its regiments was taken prisoner – an ominous indication of shaken morale to Pétain, who was himself weakened by an attack of pneumonia which had struck him within days of assuming command. To add to the misery of the battle-field, already beginning to assume that appearance of contiguous and overlapping shell-craters which would leave an unforget-table impression on all who saw it, unseasonable snow had begun to fall. The French fell back in the flurries which blinded their artillery observers from one critical point to another, but on 9 March the triumphant Germans found their attack beginning to falter. It had carried them to the northern slope of le Mort-Homme (Dead Man) ridge and the hill called Côte 304 and here they encountered fresh French troops who refused to budge. During the rest of the month the battle raged on for these two beleaguered

Below: French on Mort-Homme ridge at Verdun turn a German machine gun against their enemy.

Above left: Crown Prince Wilhelm, the Kaiser's son and heir to the German throne.

Above: The wreckage of the Fort Moulainville.

Bottom left: Crown Prince Wilhelm in full regalia.

Bottom right: British postcard satirizes German bayoneters.

features. The Germans won ground in the Bois d'Avocourt, between the Mort-Homme and the Meuse, but the two hills held.

The cost was terrible, to both sides — each had lost over 80,000 casualties so far — but the French suffered particularly. A victim of the battle described men coming out of the line:

'Yesterday . . . I saw some regiments returning from the trenches. . . . When you see those mud statues, steps painfully dragging, those hollow faces, haunted eyes and tortured glances, those moving hulks, those bundles of agony on the march, anger possesses the calmest man. What shame! That's what you can make out of men, machines for suffering. Nothing so abominable has ever been seen before. That isn't heroism. That is degradation.'

There was more to come, and yet more anxiety for the French commanders. On 1 May Pétain, promoted to command the Group of Armies of the Center, had left Verdun to his brilliant subordinate General Georges Nivelle. During May he saw French casualties climb to 185,000 and despite heroic defense both the Mort-Homme and Côte 304 fell to the enemy. At the end of the month the Germans renewed the offensive for the third time in an effort code named May Cup. Its main weight was directed on the right bank in the direction of Vaux, the outermost of the forts. Since the loss of Douaumont the French had taken care to see that the forts were properly garrisoned, and Vaux was held by 300 men under the command of a Major Sylvain-Eugène Raynal. The Germans had also learned that the capture of a fort could not be left to the chance presence of a

Below right: German Crown Prince Wilhelm inspects his troops at Verdun.

Far right: The tunnel at Fort Vaux that became the grave of its defenders.

Below: Relief units pour up *la Voie Sacrée* to assist in the defense of Verdun.

hero like Kunze. They had prepared an enormous bombardment and an assault by a special force of the 50th Division, commanded by Major General Weber Pasha, who had distinguished himself in the defense of the Turkish forts at Gallipoli.

Within minutes of the attack beginning on 1 June they were inside the fort, but their leaders had reckoned without Raynal. This rock of French stubborness and courage was determined that Vaux should not fall and, yard by yard contested every corridor and chamber of the interior with the overwhelming numbers which had invaded it. The Germans used flame throwers, gas and grenades to blast their way forward, called down the fire of the terrible

Above: French troops retreat from Fort Vaux along *la Voie Sacrée,* the vital supply line the French kept open to Verdun.

420mm howitzers and, when the fort was still holding out after three days, began mining under the concrete walls in order to blow them up. Still their losses mounted and French resistance held. Handfuls of reinforcements made their way through the murderous barrage to bring strength to Raynal's dwindling band and the French artillery from miles away put down curtains of fire on the German attackers around and on top of the concrete carapace. On 4 June, however, Raynal lost his means of communicating with the rear when he sent off

his last carrier pigeon, which delivered the message 'relief is imperative' and dropped dead in the hands of its pigeon master. (The pigeon was decorated with the *Légion d'Honneur*.) Shortly afterward he received word from his chief subordinate that the fort could no longer depend on its own resources. The cistern gauge was inaccurate and the garrison had only a quarter of a pint of water per man for a few days more. The heat inside, under a June sun, was intense and the garrison began to suffer agonies of thirst. On 6 June the men's thirst became unbearable and at 0330 hours on 7 June Raynal decided that he must surrender. He sent out a white flag party and shortly afterward he was himself ushered into the presence of the German Crown Prince, commanding on the Verdun sector. Even his enemies were prepared to recognize the extraordinary heroism he had displayed and with a gallantry which Allied propaganda would not admit 'Little Willie' was capable, he presented the weary and smoke-stained hero with a captured French sword to replace his own lost at Vaux.

His magnanimity perhaps derived from the victory he felt to be so close, for his army group was now preparing for the fourth and what was believed to be the final offensive. Large quantities of a new gas, phosgene, which the French gas masks could not filter out, had been issued to the artillery and on 22 June a disabling bombardment was fired into the French front on the right bank south of Douaumont and Vaux. The infantry assaulting behind it, which included the crack Alpenkorps division, found the French gasping for breath and already dying from gas-poisoning. They pushed quickly on to the fort of Thiaumont from the roof of which a small party of reckless attackers actually glimpsed the twin towers of Verdun Cathedral, hitherto hidden from them by the hills of the Meuse valley, gleaming in the afternoon sun. However their elan was not to win them

Above: French General Charles Mangin.

Above right: A French trench near Verdun in the winter of 1916–17.

Right: British soldiers in a dugout on the Somme.

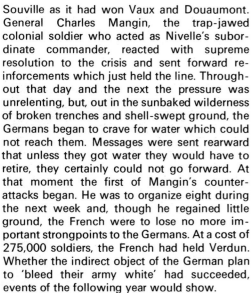

Souville as it had won Vaux and Douaumont. General Charles Mangin, the trap-jawed colonial soldier who acted as Nivelle's subordinate commander, reacted with supreme resolution to the crisis and sent forward reinforcements which just held the line. Throughout that day and the next the pressure was unrelenting, but, out in the sunbaked wilderness of broken trenches and shell-swept ground, the Germans began to crave for water which could not reach them. Messages were sent rearward that unless they got water they would have to retire, they certainly could not go forward. At that moment the first of Mangin's counterattacks began. He was to organize eight during the next week and, though he regained little ground, the French were to lose no more important strongpoints to the Germans. At a cost of 275,000 soldiers, the French had held Verdun. Whether the indirect object of the German plan to 'bleed their army white' had succeeded, events of the following year would show.

Even had the stroke of 22 June succeeded, it would have been impossible for the Germans to continue their offensive, for they themselves became the victims of the enterprise which Joffre and Haig had been planning since the previous December. Their position on the Western Front was essentially defensive and the implications of their numerical inferiority could not be endlessly evaded by spoiling offensives of the Verdun type. The moment of truth now arrived. After two years of war, the British had assembled an army of a size sufficient for them to take over a major stretch of the Allied line and from it to launch with the French a weighty offensive.

This army was both a military phenomenon and a popular social movement, a contingent of a million volunteers who had spontaneously come forward in late 1914 and early 1915 to provide the manpower for 30 new divisions of infantry. The impulse had been provided by Lord Kitchener, hero of the Sudanese and Boer Wars, who had called in September 1914 for '100,000 volunteers' to join the regular army for three years. His appeal had been given a particular point by Lord Derby, political strongman of the industrial and commercial northwest of England, who had appealed in September for the young men of Liverpool to heed Kitchener's call, and for Liverpool to form a battalion of its own for what was already being called the New Armies. Such a battalion was formed at his first recruiting meeting and within days the city had produced three more. Kitchener promised that groups of friends joining together would be allowed to serve together, instead of being scattered throughout the army at large, and so arose the Pals and Chums battalions.

Altogether they were to make up the 9th–42nd Divisions, drawn in groups of six from Scotland, Ireland, the North Country, East Anglia, the West and the Home Counties. Inside each division the battalion titles revealed their particular local origins. The 31st Division was composed of the Leeds Pals, 1st and 2nd Bradford Pals, 1st and 2nd Barnsley Pals, the Halifax Pals, Hull Commercials (local shop assistants), Hull Tradesmen, Hull Sportsmen, Durham Pals, Halifax Pals, Accrington Pals and Sheffield City Battalion. The 34th Division had

two Edinburgh Pals battalions – 15th and 16th Royal Scots – the Grimsby Chums, the Cambridge battalion and eight battalions from Newcastle-on-Tyne and its surroundings called Tyneside Scottish or Tyneside Irish. Scattered through other divisions were battalions with names like Arts and Crafts, 1st Football, Empire, Glasgow Boys' Brigade and Forest of Dean Pioneers. There had always been a strong tradition of voluntary enlistment among the British, and 28 of the divisions in the British Army of 1916 were drawn from the prewar Territorial Force, a part-time army of weekend soldiers who served in their own time without pay. It was the Territorials who had borne the brunt of the fighting during late 1915, particularly at Loos. The New Armies were different, their enthusiasm was not for soldiering as such but for service to the nation in time of crisis. They had joined to win the war and believed that they could do that where the old army and the French had failed. The coming battle was to be their chance.

The spot Joffre and Haig had jointly chosen for the offensive was the River Somme where the French line joined with the British, which had been progressively extended from Flanders as the size of the British Expeditionary Force had grown. Originally Joffre had intended that the two armies should attack in equal strength, on a front of 60 miles with the object of wearing down the Germans and eventually breaking through into open country. Falkenhayn's success in wearing down the defenders of Verdun had vitiated that intention. All that Joffre could provide for 1 July 1916, the chosen date, was eight divisions, to attack on a front of eight miles south of the river. The British, on a front of 18 miles, were to attack with 14 divisions, with three infantry divisions in reserve and five cavalry divisions positioned behind them to exploit the breakthrough when and if it came.

Below: French *poilus* with gas masks in the mud, fire and horror of Verdun.

the Somme was not one generally of foreboding but of gaiety and confidence, emotions all the more readily felt because of their inexperience. One of the New Army divisions, the 9th, which was to lie in reserve, had fought at Loos. The regular divisions committed for the offensive, the 4th, 8th and 29th, had all seen action before, but the rest of the 14 were virgin formations. Many of their soldiers had only recently arrived in France. The infantrymen had in many cases not fired their rifles at the enemy and the artillery, on which so much depended, had in many cases received its guns only at the moment of embarkation in Britain.

The morning of 1 July 1916 dawned bright and sunny, with the mist of promised heat overlying the German trenches. A pilot of the Royal Flying Corps, observing the front from the sky, saw the explosions of the shells appearing on the surface of the mist bank below like the ripples of a stone thrown into a limpid pool. A young artillery officer, Lieutenant Adrian Stephen, recorded:

'the ear-splitting bark of the 18-pounders, the cough of the howitzers, the boom of the heavy guns, sucked into a jerky roar that was flung from horizon to horizon, as thunder is tossed from mountain to mountain. It was wonderful music — the mightiest I ever heard. It seemed to throb into our very veins beating up and down and yet never quite reaching a climax, but always keeping one's nerves on the thrill. And then at last 10 minutes before zero, the guns opened their lungs. The climax had been reached. One felt inclined to laugh with the sheer exhilaration of it. After all, it was our voice, the voice of a whole empire at war.'

More important than numbers of infantry was weight of bombardment, and for this the British and French had assembled more guns and ammunition than had yet been seen on the Western Front. Too many were light guns — 75mm and 18-pounders — but there was one heavy gun to each 60 yards of front on the British sector and to each 20 yards on the French, and 1,500,000 rounds of ammunition. The bombardment opened on 24 June, a week before zero-hour and every day thereafter 200,000 shells were fired into the German lines. The noise could be heard as a dull rumble as far away as the South of England where the Prime Minister, Herbert Asquith, father of two sons at the front and in his heart an opponent of the war, took refuge in endless rounds of bridge to distract himself from thought of the coming holocaust. That thought afflicted the BEF's posts, who sensed the significance of the approaching July and sought words to catch the mixture of dread and elation which word of the battle aroused. Edmund Blunden describes his Colonel's warning that his battalion is off to the Somme:

'We're going South, man'; as he spoke
The howitzer with huge ping-bang
Rocked the light hut; as thus he broke
The death-news bright the sky larks sang;
He took his riding crop and humming went
Among the apple-trees all bloom and scent.
Now far withdraws the roaring night
Which wrecked our flower after the first
Of those two voices; misty light
Shrouds Thiepval Wood and all its worst;
But still 'there's something in the air' I hear,
And still 'We're going South man', deadly near.

Much of the flower of the New Armies was to be wrecked at Thiepval Wood, which lay opposite the British front line at the point where the 32nd Division was to attack — the division which contained the 1st, 2nd and 3rd Salford Pals, the Newcastle Commercials and the Glasgow Tramways Battalions, the Glasgow Boys' Brigade Battalion and the Lonsdales raised on the Border near Carlisle from estate workers in the employment of the famous Yellow Earl.

The mood of the New Armies going south to

Above: German troops move up to the Somme in an early example of motorized transport. Most came on foot.

Below: A 400mm rail gun prepares to fire near the Somme, June 1916.

Above: 1st Lancashire Fusiliers tend their wounded at Beaumont Hamel on the first day of the Somme battle, 1 July 1916.

Up and down the 18 miles of front line, the infantry had been waiting for this crescendo. When it stopped 120,000 individuals, each hunched under a load of 60 pounds of ammunition, kit and rations, climbed out of their trenches, filed through the gaps in the British barbed wire and formed up to move across no man's land. In most places it was about 300 yards wide, but at some as much as 600 yards. The Germans therefore had about two minutes from hearing the end of the bombardment to man the parapets of their trenches and open fire on the approaching British before they were

upon them. Almost everywhere it was to prove time enough.

The Germans in line opposite the 14 attacking British divisions belonged to five divisions, the 2nd Guard Reserve, 52nd, 26th Reserve, 28th Reserve and 12th. For the previous eight days they had crouched in the bottom of their dugouts in the chalk, shaken by the unrelenting crash of explosions above, living on cold food and chlorined water, ears pricked for the least sign of a break in the bombardment:

'At 0730 the hurricane of shells ceased as suddenly as it had begun. Our men at once clambered up the steep shafts leading from the dugouts to daylight and ran singly or in groups to the nearest shell craters. The machine guns were pulled out of the dugouts and hurriedly placed in position, their crews dragging the ammunition boxes up the steps and out to the guns. A rough line was thus rapidly established. As soon as the men were in position, a series of extended lines of infantry were seen moving forward from the British trenches. The first line appeared to continue without end from right to left. It was quickly followed by a second line, then a third and fourth. They came on at a steady pace, as if expecting to find nothing alive in our trenches.'

The Newcastle Commercials were told, 'You will be able to go over the top with a walking stick, you will not need rifles. When you get to Thiepval you will find the Germans all dead, not even a rat will have survived.' Others were encouraged to think that they could 'slope arms, light up pipes and cigarettes and march all the way' and expect that 'the field kitchens will follow you and give you a good meal.' In fact,

Above: Lieutenant General Sir Henry Rawlinson at his HQ on the first day of the Battle of the Somme.

Below: Men of the 2nd Australian Division near Armentières in 1916.

Above: A trench at the Somme. Britain suffered some 60,000 casualties in the first hours of the battle.

two of the British divisions did have a reasonably easy time getting across, because their commanders had ordered their men out into no man's land to lie down close to the German wire while the bombardment was still going on. The rest, who emerged in the long lines noted by the German observer quoted above, were quickly brought under fire by the defenders and began to suffer horrifying loss before they could get to grips with the Germans. As the leading British line approached the rattle of machine-gun and rifle fire broke out all along the whole line of craters and a hail of lead swept into the advancing lines. Some Germans fired kneeling so as to get a better target over the broken ground, while

Below: Tommies with some wounded German prisoners at the Somme, 3 July 1916.

others stood up in the excitement of the moment, regardless of their own safety, to fire into the crowd of men in front of them. Red rockets sped by into the blue sky as a signal to the artillery and immediately afterward a mass of shells from the German batteries in the rear tore through the air and burst among the advancing lines. Whole sections seemed to fall and the rear formations, moving in closer order, quickly scattered. The advance rapidly crumbled under this hail of shells and bullets. All along the line men could be seen throwing their arms into the air and collapsing, never to move again. So terrible was the loss of life in front of many of the German divisional positions that at noon white flags were shown and the German doctors allowed British stretcher bearers to come forward to evacuate such of the wounded as they could.

Douglas Haig and Henry Rawlinson could not as yet know the results of their offensive. The experienced French, south of the Somme, had taken all their objectives for comparatively

little loss. On the British sector the two divisions next to the French had benefited from their advance and also got well into the German lines. Another success had been won by the 36th Ulster Division, recruited from the Protestant Ulster Volunteer Force which had opposed the Irish Home Rule Bill of 1914. Their fiery militarism — perhaps fed by the only just quelled rebellion in Dublin of Easter Week — had won them a success unmatched by any other formation under Haig's command. In every other case, the divisions had either been checked at the German front line or actually halted in no man's land, and the casualties were appalling. All the divisions engaged had lost at least a quarter of their men. The 8th, at Thiepval, had lost half — 5121 killed or wounded. By comparison the German regiment it attacked, the 180th, had lost a mere 280 casualties. Some battalions had effectively been wiped out. The 1st Newfoundland Regiment, one of those bands of colonial volunteers which had responded to the call of the country in her hour of need, had suffered 684 casualties out of 752 men who had gone over the top. In all, 60,000 British soldiers had been hit on 1 July and 20,000 had been killed. The first day of the Battle of the Somme was a tragic disaster.

When this truth eventually dawned on the British High Command, it did not deter preparation for the next stage — an advance from such ground as had been won to the German second position. As it happened, it came off, largely because it was launched at night and took the Germans genuinely by surprise. It was to be the last success won by conventional artillery/infantry methods during the battle, which still had nearly four months to run. The Germans had hurriedly begun to send in reinforcements of men and guns — so weakening their effort at Verdun, as Joffre had hoped — and their numbers rose toward parity with the attackers as each week passed, thus making the likelihood of a

Right: The 10th Worcesters bring in some German POWs at La Boisselle on 3 July 1916.

Below: British casualties at the Somme.

break out even more remote. Haig seems eventually to have recognized the true situation and to have reconciled himself to Joffre's blood-chilling idea of simply settling for *usure*, wearing-down or attrition.

The battle dragged on during August and into September, with casualties running at about 4000 a day and divisions returning to the battle for the second time, sometimes for a third after the gaps in their ranks had been hastily plastered up with new men, fresh from English training camps. Some, in the autumn of 1916, were conscripts, brought in by the new law of January. The volunteering impetus had already begun to run out. Nothing like the New Armies would ever be seen again.

In September there was a flicker of renewed hope for a breakthrough. The first tanks made a brief but spectacular appearance on the battle-field. These new engines of war were the fruit of

Right: Relief at Dawn. The Somme was Britain's most sobering experience in her long military history.

several like-thinking British minds, who had identified the principal problems of trench warfare as early as Christmas 1914. Perhaps first to do so was Colonel E D Swinton, who thought they would be overcome by an armored version of the caterpillar tractor which he had heard of but not seen. The specification for the design was actually written by Maurice Hankey, the Secretary to the Cabinet, and taken up by Winston Churchill, who instituted a Landships Committee at the Admiralty in February 1915.

An experimental model ('Little Willie') had been constructed by the following September and the prototype of the Mark I Tank (a code name) was ready in December. It had been immediately put into production and the first 25 were shipped to France in August 1916 where they were taken over by the newly-formed Heavy Section, Machine Gun Corps. Haig, initially unenthusiastic, was quickly converted to the new weapon, perhaps because he was prepared to clutch at straws to save his Somme offensive.

He included them in the third renewal of offensive effort, called the Battle of Flers-Courcelette, which began on 15 September. It was an attack on a 10-mile front with 12 divisions against six German; as many as had held the original front, but a fraction of the total they had subsequently concentrated there – 30 in all. As usual, the conventional assault was quickly checked by the Germans with machine guns and artillery. However at Flers, when the 36 operational tanks were deployed, the Germans gave up at the sight of these futuristic monsters and the British infantry of the 41st Division followed the leaders deep into the German lines. The Germans who were taken prisoner, Bavarians who normally displayed remarkable stolidity, were described as blue and shaking with fright. The success proved to be very brief. The tanks were too few in number and too slow – their speed was only 3mph – to create a real break in the line and the little hole they made was quickly filled by sending reinforcements to the danger spot.

Haig renewed the offensive on 25 September, again in October and twice in November, the last episode being called the Battle of the Ancre. By then winter rain had turned the churned-up surface of the battlefield into a quagmire and the infantry struggled toward their objectives caked

in mud and soaked by freezing rain and wet fog. The battle petered out at last on 18 November; about 125 square miles of territory, a strip 20 miles long by six deep, had been wrested from the enemy at a cost of 420,000 British and 194,000 French casualties. German losses were optimistically calculated as equal, but were certainly many fewer.

At Verdun the summer and autumn had also cost the French dear. By 15 December, when the battle was also brought to an end by the onset of winter, they calculated their casualties at 362,000. The Germans, who had been attacking and also undoubtedly suffered as hard and, assaulted by a succession of French counter-attacks in October and December, had been forced to surrender much of the ground won at such terrible cost in the spring. Even Fort Douaumont had gone, recaptured in a push engineered by General Mangin on 24 October.

As the third winter of the war descended on the Western Front, therefore, neither side had reason to feel grateful or even optimistic about what had passed. Certainly not Falkenhayn, once the Kaiser's favored general. He too, like Moltke, had incurred the imperial displeasure. The official reason given for his removal was the entry into the war of Rumania, which had yielded to the Allies' diplomatic pressure to join

Above: Royal Australian Battery use their 9.2-inch Mark VI howitzers near the Somme.

Far left: The Western Front at the end of 1916, virtually unchanged from the previous year despite the millions who died.

Below: British and German wounded trudge toward the field hospital during the Battle for Bazentin Ridge near the Somme, 19 July 1916.

Mademoiselle from Armenteers (Armentières)

Mademoiselle from Armenteers,
Parlez-vous,
Mademoiselle from Armenteers,
Parlez-vous,
Mademoiselle from Armenteers,
She hasn't been kissed for
    forty years,
Hinky-dinky parlez-vous.

them in August. Falkenhayn was sent to organize a riposte to that unwise decision, his place in the West being taken by the titans of the Eastern Front, Generals Hindenburg and Ludendorff. The real reason was a belief that his successors would succeed where he was held to have failed, in miscalculating the possibility of waging a one-sided battle of attrition at Verdun and in exposing the defenders on the Somme to the terrible losses they had suffered there.

The discomfiture of individual generals, who retained their health and whole skins, must be counted for little against the suffering which 1916 had visited on their soldiers. The German army might have emerged from the two great Western battles of the year still fit to fight. The ordeal had marked it dreadfully nonetheless. Ludendorff would later say that the summer offensives marked the end of the old German army so heavy were the inroads it made in the ranks of the regular officers and particularly the noncommissioned officers, the backbone of the military establishment. The French army, which had borne a terrible toll in each one of the three years of the war, had been brought to the verge of breaking point, as the crisis of the coming spring would show. The British Expeditionary Force, so buoyant with optimism only six

Above: Corpse of a German soldier at Beaumont Hamel, the Somme.

Bottom left: Men of the 4th Worcestershires pause for a rest behind the lines at the Somme.

Bottom right: Weary British troops return from the trenches near Bernafay Wood, the Somme, in November 1916.

Below: Canadian troops go over the top at the Somme.

months before had been turned in a single season into a grimly hardened legion of veterans, who expected nothing from the war but the chance to do an increasingly burdensome and dangerous duty. 'Where tongues were sound and hearts were light, I heard the Ancre flow,' wrote Edmund Blunden of days spent on the little tributary of the Somme before the battle. Afterward, recalling the grief he had learned there, his lines ran differently:

The struggling Ancre had no part
In these new hours of mine,
And yet its stream ran through my heart;
I heard it grieve and pine,
As if its rainy tortured blood
Had swirled into my own,
When by its shattered banks I stood
And shared its wounded moan.

A torpedo boat breaks through the German flotilla in the
Grand Fleet's spring maneuvers in 1916.

5 War on the Seas

Three weeks before the guns had begun to speak for the opening of the Battle of the Somme, greater artillery had shouted across the gray wastes of the North Sea in the encounter for which the Royal and Imperial Navies had prepared for two decades. Called Jutland, after the land nearest to the Grand and High Seas Fleets' meeting place, the battle had yielded a result so dubious that as yet neither side could decide who had won and who had lost – though both claimed a victory. Even if each suspected that the result contained an element of defeat, there were no regrets. Jutland was preordained, a battle which had to be fought sometime, somewhere. Its event was as much a relief as an ordeal.

If there was a single reason for Britain's decision of August 1914 to join France against Germany, it lay in the insult and threat to her naval supremacy which Germany's building of the High Seas Fleet presented. Throughout the 19th century, indeed since the evening of 21 October 1805, when Nelson had gasped out his life in the cockpit of HMS *Victory* at Trafalgar, the Royal Navy had been unchallenged ruler of the seas. It had consistently maintained a two-power, sometimes a three-power, standard for most of the century, by which was meant that the Royal Navy was maintained at size equal to the two next biggest navies – usually the French and the Russian. However in 1900 the German government had declared its intention of transforming the Imperial Navy from a small coastal defense force into a first-class fleet. The implication of this announcement, by a power which already outproduced Britain in steel and coal and threatened to overtake her in volume of overseas trade, was that the two-power standard could not be maintained in future. An immediate effect was that Britain reconsidered her policy of 'splendid isolation'; in 1902 she signed an alliance with Japan and in 1904 an agreement with France about spheres of influence in the Mediterranean. She also looked to her naval preparedness. It was an age of technical innovation and by 1904 it was clear that a revolution in battleship design trembled on the brink of realization, a revolution which would at a stroke rob Britain of her superiority both in numbers and quality of first-line ships.

Such a revolution had occurred once before, in 1859, when the launching of the first ironclad, *La Gloire*, by France had instantly outdated the whole of the British wooden-walls navy. This new revolution was that of the 'all big-gun

Above: The British Grand Fleet at the Coronation naval review in 1911

Above left: The last moments of the *Scharnhorst* and *Gneisenau,* which were sunk off the South American coast in the Battle of the Falklands in December 1914.

Left: The German High Seas Fleet on exercises in 1914.

ship,' which would make obsolete all the ill-planned late Victorian models, crammed to capacity with guns of every caliber. The Royal Navy, at the behest of its emphatic First Sea Lord, Admiral 'Jackie' Fisher, boldly decided to pre-empt the Opposition and in 1906 launched the first example of the new type, from which in future it would take its name, HMS *Dreadnought.* Armed with 12 12-inch guns and engined with turbines which drove it at over 20 knots, it did indeed make the rest of the Royal Navy's battle fleet obsolete — but also that of every other navy. Britain, moreover, had cleverly geared herself to follow *Dreadnought* with a family of sister-ships and so was quickly set fair to make the leap from superiority in an old technology to superiority in a new. However Germany was not slow to respond. In 1908

the Reichstag voted the money to build 12 Dreadnoughts over the next four years, and at the same time to widen the Kiel Canal, allowing the new, bigger ships to make the transit from the training waters in the Baltic to the potential battle area in the North Sea without entering foreign territorial waters.

At the outbreak of war, which came while a sustained armaments race was in full spate, Germany had built 13 Dreadnoughts and five of the new battlecruisers, a ship with a battleship's guns and a cruiser's speed (though without, its critics emphasized, a battleship's armor protection). Britain had, however, managed to keep ahead and had eight battlecruisers and 20 Dreadnoughts in service, while far outstripping

Germany in numbers of cruisers (102:41), destroyers (301:144) and even submarines (78:30). Most of the ships in the Imperial German Navy were in home waters forming the High Seas Fleet, based at Cuxhaven, Bremen, Wilhelmshaven and Emden, and ready to strike in the North Sea if the Grand Fleet should be caught at a disadvantage. The British Grand Fleet was stationed at Scapa Flow, in the Orkney Islands to the north of Scotland. The strategic logic behind the choice of base was impeccable. Southward, the exit from the North Sea lay through the Straits of Dover, which could be made impassable by mining. As the danger which the Admiralty most feared was the escape of the High Seas Fleet into the Atlantic merchant shipping lanes, the correct place to position its counterpoise was therefore at the other exit, between Scotland and Norway. In the circumstances Scapa Flow, a large archipelagic anchorage, offered the best home for the Grand Fleet.

The Grand Fleet was to spend most of the war in that land of sheep, seagulls, seals and short winter days, watching its shadow image across the North Sea. However, the Grand Fleet

Below: German battleships in a line on exercises, with the *Bayern* astern.

Above: German sailor cleans the gun of a warship of the High Seas Fleet.

Above right: The engine room of a German warship in 1915.

was not the whole Royal Navy. As the maritime arm of an imperial power, the Navy was deployed around all the world's oceans in four squadrons — East India, China, Australia and New Zealand — and also in smaller formations in the West Indies, in the West Coast of Africa and at the Cape of Good Hope, and a large Mediterranean Fleet, based on Malta and Gibraltar. The latter contained four of Britain's battlecruisers. Elsewhere the distant squadrons were composed of cruisers and smaller vessels, including a few remaining gunboats on which British diplomacy had been held to depend in the non-European world during the 19th century.

Germany also had a colonial fleet, based in the few Asiatic or African possessions she had acquired during the last century, as well as some detached cruisers, whose mission would be to raid British commerce when war broke out. The strongest element of the colonial fleet was the East Asian Cruiser Squadron, based at Tsingtao and consisting of the armored cruisers *Scharnhorst* and *Gneisenau*, and the light cruisers *Leipzig*, *Nürnberg*, *Dresden* and *Emden*, all under command of Admiral Maximilian Graf von

Spee. As soon as Japan entered the war, on 15 August 1914, she forced the surrender of Tsingtao and Spee took his fleet (except the *Emden*) into the vast emptiness of the Pacific to evade the much larger Japanese fleet and begin his campaign against Britain's commerce.

News of their departure, and intercepted radio signals of their location, inaugurated the first and most dramatic episode of the naval war. The British Admiralty ordered Admiral Sir Christopher Cradock's South American Squadron to find and destroy them. It was a miscalculation to think that Cradock's ships could match Spee's. They could not, and when the two squadrons met off Coronel, Chile, on 1 November 1914, Spee sank two of the British cruisers without difficulty. News of this humiliation outraged the British public and the Admiralty, repairing a deficiency of which it should have been aware, at once sent two of the Grand Fleet's battlecruisers, *Invincible* and *Inflexible*, to repair it. Their destination was the South Pacific, but Admiral Doveton Sturdee commanding, called first at the Falkland Islands in the south to coal before proceeding round the Horn. On 8 December Spee appeared there, miscalculated the opposition he faced and moved in to attack. As he got closer he detected the battlecruisers' silhouettes and turned tail. All through a long southern hemisphere

Above: 'Jackie' Fisher, Lord Fisher, who created Britain's Dreadnoughts and masterminded the Grand Fleet in 1914.

Below: The Japanese destroyer *Shirakumo* in 1914. She was built in Britain.

Above: King George V aboard HMS *Queen Elizabeth.*

Left: The British battleship HMS *Barham* at Scapa Flow.

Below: The British Fleet in review, July 1914.

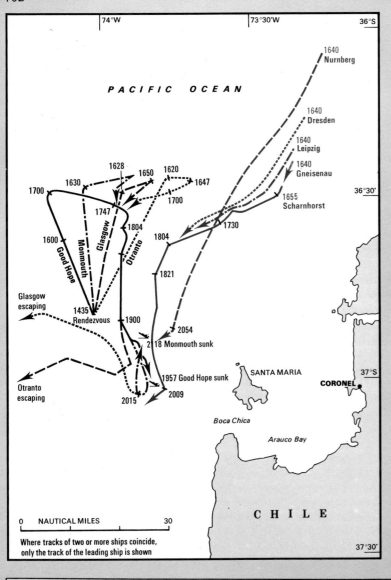

Map 1 — Coronel (Pacific Ocean)

PACIFIC OCEAN

74°W · 73°30'W · 36°S

1640 Nurnberg
1640 Dresden
1640 Leipzig
1640 Gneisenau
1655 Scharnhorst

1628
1650
1620
1647
1630
1700
1700
1747
1804
1804
1730
1821
1600
1435 Rendezvous
1900
2054
2118 Monmouth sunk
Glasgow escaping
Otranto escaping
2015
2009
1957 Good Hope sunk

Good Hope · Monmouth · Glasgow · Otranto

SANTA MARIA
CORONEL
Boca Chica
Arauco Bay
CHILE

36°30'
37°S
37°30'

0 NAUTICAL MILES 30

Where tracks of two or more ships coincide, only the track of the leading ship is shown

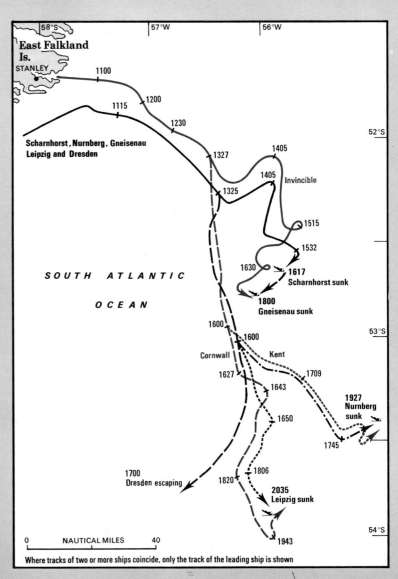

Map 2 — Falklands (South Atlantic Ocean)

East Falkland Is.
STANLEY

58°S · 57°W · 56°S · 52°S

1100
1115
1200
1230
1327
1325
1405
1405 Invincible
1515
1532
1630
1617 Scharnhorst sunk
1800 Gneisenau sunk

Scharnhorst, Nurnberg, Gneisenau Leipzig and Dresden

SOUTH ATLANTIC OCEAN

1600
1600
Cornwall
Kent
1627
1643
1709
1650
1927 Nurnberg sunk
1745
1700 Dresden escaping
1820
1806
2035 Leipzig sunk
1943

53°S
54°S

0 NAUTICAL MILES 40

Where tracks of two or more ships coincide, only the track of the leading ship is shown

Above: HMS *Inflexible,* which helped track down Graf Spee in the Falklands.

Below left: The Grand Fleet patrols the North Sea.

Left: The battles of Coronel and the Falkland Islands tied up part of the British Fleet in the first months of the war.

summer's day the British battlecruisers remorselessly pursued, their greater speed gradually winning back the start the Germans had had. Eventually they closed the range and between 1541 and 1723 hours four of Spee's five cruisers were sunk. Only the *Dresden,* swallowed by approaching darkness, escaped to continue the campaign of commerce destruction.

Her search for prey was to be fruitless, and she was eventually hunted down and sunk at Juan Fernandez – Robinson Crusoe's Island – in March 1915. The disaster at the Falklands still left three German cruisers and four armed merchant ships at sea. The latter, in peacetime high-speed liners, carried only light armament and inflicted little damage before being eliminated. The *Cap Trafalgar* was sunk by the British armed merchant cruiser *Carmania* in the South Atlantic in September 1914, the *Kaiser Wilhelm der Grosse* by the light cruiser *Highflyer* on 26 August off Spanish Morocco, while the *Kronprinz Wilhelm* and *Prinz Eitel Friedrich* were

both interned in American ports in the spring of 1915. The true cruisers were harder to eliminate. *Königsberg,* based in the Indian Ocean, threatened British shipping using the Suez Canal for several months until a converging force of British cruisers drove her up the Rufifi River in German East Africa, where she was scuttled. *Karlsruhe,* operating off the bulge of Brazil, sank 14 British ships before being destroyed by a mysterious internal explosion on 4 November 1914. *Emden,* based in the eastern Indian Ocean, was also sunk in November, but only after she had inflicted serious loss on British shipping and property. In September she shelled and set ablaze the oil storage tanks at Madras, then sank 13 British ships, made use of port facilities at Diego Garcia, a British island so remote that the inhabitants had not yet heard of the war, and sailed out refreshed to sink seven more merchant ships, a Russian light cruiser and a French destroyer. Overconfidence then betrayed Captain von Müller, the *Emden's* remarkable commander. He entered the harbor of Cocos-Keeling Island to destroy its important radio station. However before he did so, the operator summoned the heavier-gunned Australian cruiser *Sydney,* which in a few hours on 9 November 1914, blew the *Emden* to pieces.

Germany was to revive her commerce raiding later in the war and the cruise of her armed

Above: Admiral Graf von Spee (left) commanded the Germans in the South Atlantic.

sailing ship, the *Seeädler,* was to magnetize the interest of the German population at a dark moment. After April 1915 surface – as opposed to submarine – attack on Allied merchant shipping lost almost all its importance.

The German Navy had never invested its real hopes for success in attacks on British shipping. Those were pinned on the High Seas Fleet, smaller admittedly than the Grand Fleet, but in quality, ship for ship, perhaps its superior. The German admirals, Alfred von Tirpitz, Secretary of the Navy, von Ingenohl, commanding the High Seas Fleet, and Franz von Hipper, commanding its battlecruisers, were certainly willing to back their confidence in their ships and men by taking the fleet regularly to sea from the outbreak of the war in the hope of meeting the British on advantageous terms. The first encounter took place on 28 August, in an action which came to be known as the Heligoland Bight. The terms had been miscalculated by the Germans. The Royal Navy's Channel Squadron submarines had been calculating their patrolling pattern and their commander, Commodore Keyes, had decided that it offered an opportunity to strike unexpectedly at the cruisers which escorted the patrolling destroyers. A cruiser

Below: British battle cruisers *Indomitable* and *Inflexible* which led the fight in the Falklands.

ambush, supported by some of Admiral David Beatty's battlecruisers, was accordingly arranged and the trap sprung. Due to mis-understandings, various British Squadrons failed to co-ordinate their actions. However the German ships were well and truly surprised and driven into flight, during which a destroyer, *V-187*, and three cruisers, *Mainz*, *Ariadne* and *Köln*, were sunk by heavier weight of metal.

This setback shocked the German admirals into caution, but the news of the Falkland Islands, which revealed the absence of the battlecruisers *Inflexible* and *Invincible* from home waters, encouraged them to try again — with greater success. In October their aggressive mining policy had caused the sinking of the Dreadnought *Audacious* off the Irish coast, which slightly narrowed the odds. On 16 December, therefore, the High Seas Fleet sallied forth to bombard the British coast, a repeat of a small-scale raid against Yarmouth on 3 November. In fog, the German battlecruisers caused considerable loss of life along the Yorkshire coast and got clean away from the Grand Fleet, which had come out to intercept. Public outrage so stung the Admiralty's pride that it decided it

must retaliate. It began to make reconnaissance in force into the North Sea. The provocation worked, tempting the High Seas Fleet out on 23 January. Next morning, their scouting forces met near the shallows of the Dogger Bank and shortly afterward fire was opened between the leading main units. These were the battle-cruisers performing their function of covering the battleships, and soon a full-scale gun duel flickered along the line of the two squadrons. It was an exchange to which the stouter German ships stood up better than the British. The *Blücher*, not truly a battlecruiser, was hit and eventually sunk but the big German ships absorbed punishment better than the British, among which HMS *Lion*, Beatty's flagship, was so badly damaged that he was forced to transfer his flag to a destroyer. In the resulting confusion of command, the Germans made good their escape.

The loss of the *Blücher* enraged the Kaiser, and he enforced on Tirpitz and Hugo von Pohl, who succeeded the disgraced von Ingenohl, a policy of extreme prudence. They abandoned their policy of raiding toward the British coast, scarcely venturing out of the Heligoland Bight

during the rest of 1915 and exercised the Fleet by taking it through the Kiel Canal to the safe waters of the Baltic, into which the Russian battleships based at Tallinn and Kronstadt did not venture. They also pressed ahead their naval construction program, though they could not outbuild the British. Between 1914 and 1916 they added five Dreadnoughts to the High Seas Fleet, making 18, and two battlecruisers, making seven. The British in the same period built ten and requisitioned three already built for, but not delivered to, other navies, making a total of 33 Dreadnoughts. They also completed another battlecruiser — a type for which only Fisher and Beatty had had enthusiasm — to give them 10.

It was a natural demand of the public in both countries to enquire what all these ships were doing, a question lent edge in Germany by the sharpening pangs of shortage imposed by the British blockade. Under this criticism, the Kaiser relaxed his ban on offensive operations and replaced Pohl with an officer more tempera-mentally inclined to carry action to the enemy, the energetic and aggressive Reinhard Scheer. In Britain too, where the growing affront of German submarine attack was generating

demands for retaliation, there was pressure on Sir John Jellicoe, Commander in Chief of the Grand Fleet, to engage the High Seas Fleet.

These demands were heightened by the reappearance of Scheer's bombardment force off the East Coast in April 1916. Its cruisers and destroyers had had several brushes with light ships of the coastal flotillas in February and March. Now he brought in his battlecruisers to hit the seaside towns of Lowestoft and Yarmouth — the latter for the second time. The Grand Fleet came out, but missed them. Jellicoe set about planning a trap to make certain the next time. Obviously, Scheer too was planning a trap for the Grand Fleet in the same place,

Far left: Admiral Sir David Beatty.

Left: Damage suffered by SMS *Frauenlob* in the Battle of the Heligoland Bight.

Below left: Raiders recalled to the *Emden,* which led a merry chase across the world before she was destroyed.

Below: The battlecruiser action, which opened hostilities in the late afternoon of 31 May.

Above: HMS *Warspite,* active both at Jutland and at Matapan in World War II.

Above right: Admiral von Tirpitz, creator of the German High Seas Fleet.

Right: Admiral Lord Jellicoe, with Beatty the architect of the Jutland victory.

between Jutland and Norway, and news of his departure on 31 May from the German estuaries, detected by British interception of his radio, ensured that these two plans would coincide.

The Grand Fleet steamed southwestward in two large groups. The main force comprised 24 Dreadnoughts and three battlecruisers, with an attendant screen of 20 cruisers and 52 destroyers. Well ahead speeded Beatty's battlecruiser force with six battlecruisers and four Dreadnoughts of the *Queen Elizabeth* Class, almost as fast as the former and as heavily armored and gunned as the most modern battleships — which indeed, was what they were. The High Seas Fleet, also with a battlecruiser force of five deployed ahead (Scouting Group

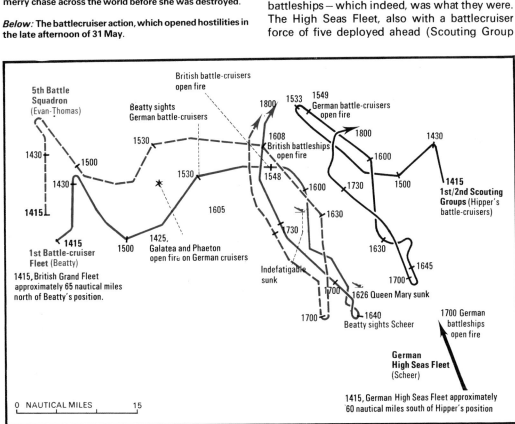

Above: The Grand Fleet moves into line a few moments earlier.

Top: The Grand Fleet moves into action as the first German salvos are fired at Jutland.

Below: Battleships HMS *Royal Oak* and *Hercules* with guns trained to starboard in the afternoon of 31 May 1916, at Jutland.

I), had 16 Dreadnoughts at sea, but had also brought along six older battleships to make weight.

As yet, neither knew for certain that the other was at sea, and their encounter was to be accidental. At about 1415 hours one of the German light cruisers with Scouting Group I spotted a Danish merchant ship and altered course to question her. A British light cruiser of the Battlecruiser Force had also seen the Dane's smoke and gone to investigate. When the cruisers sighted each other they opened fire and radioed news of the encounter. Their supporting battlecruisers turned to back them up and at 1500, to their mutual surprise, came into visual contact. Altering course to shorten the range, Beatty plunged at the Germans, while Hipper turned about to draw the British down onto the heavier guns of the battleships, still 55 miles behind. At 1548 hours the Germans opened fire, and Beatty's ships responded.

A young officer in HMS *Lion* — one of the 'big cats' as she and her sister ship *Tiger* were called — described what he saw:

'My station was in the conning tower and I remember thinking how splendid the enemy battlecruisers looked when they turned to the southward. . . . Both squadrons opened fire almost together, the Germans appearing to fire in ripples down their line starting from their leading ship. The first salvo at us was about 200 yards short, and the next straddled us — one shot short, two hits aft and one over, the two hits temporarily knocking out 'Q' and 'X' turrets.

The German shooting at this time was very good and we were repeatedly straddled but, funnily enough, we were not being hit very often. I remember watching two shells coming at us. They appeared just like big blue-bottles flying straight towards you, each time going to hit you in the eye, then they would fall, and the shell would either burst or else ricochet off the water and lollop away above and beyond you, turning over and over in the air.'

German shooting was indeed very good. Their gun crews were impeccably drilled, their range-finding equipment superior to the British and their shells of better quality. When German shells hit they both penetrated and exploded, which, as the British were later to discover, theirs did not always. The difference was to tell almost immediately. HMS *Indefatigable* was hit

early in the exchange, failed to follow a change of course and then suddenly blew up. The main explosion started with sheets of flame, followed immediately afterward by dense, dark smoke, which obscured the ship from view:

'All sorts of stuff was blown into the air, a 50-foot steam packet boat for example, being blown up about 200 feet, apparently intact though upside down.'

Shortly afterward, another accurate German salvo hit *Queen Mary*. The same observer noticed:

'a small cloud of what looked like coal-dust come out from where she was hit, but nothing more until several moments later when a terrific yellow flame, with a heavy and very dense mass of black smoke showed ahead, and the *Queen Mary* herself was no longer visible. This second disaster was rather stunning, but the only sign from the flagship was a signal, ''Battle-cruisers alter course two points to port,'' — that is towards the enemy.'

Beatty also said to the captain of *Lion*, standing beside him as he issued the signal, 'There seems to be something wrong with our bloody ships today.' *Lion* herself had been saved from destruction by a hair's-breadth when a fire had started in a damaged turret. It is probable that *Queen Mary* and *Indefatigable* had blown up because turret fires had tracked down the ammunition lift into the magazines, a disaster made possible by a design fault. Beatty none-theless had relentlessly gone on, with the bravado which was to make him the most celebrated naval commander of the war, until at 1648 he spotted the enemy, the German battle-ships, and turned northward to lead them toward Jellicoe.

As the gap between the two fleets closed, the screens of lighter ships exchanged fire and suffered losses. However it was the clash of giants which was to count and this occurred at 1815 when Hipper's battlecruisers, now just ahead of Scheer's Dreadnoughts, got within range of Jellicoe's covering squadron of battle-cruisers under Rear Admiral Sir Horace Hood and recommenced their accurate shooting. Within minutes *Invincible*, sister to *Indefati-gable*, had gone her way. She broke in half and the separated pieces ground on the shallow

Top: The British line is broken in the day action at Jutland as the Germans fire with all guns.

Above left: Admiral Hipper, who, with Scheer, led the German High Seas Fleet at Jutland.

Above right: Prince Henry of Prussia (with glasses) and Admiral von Scheer, Commander in Chief at Jutland.

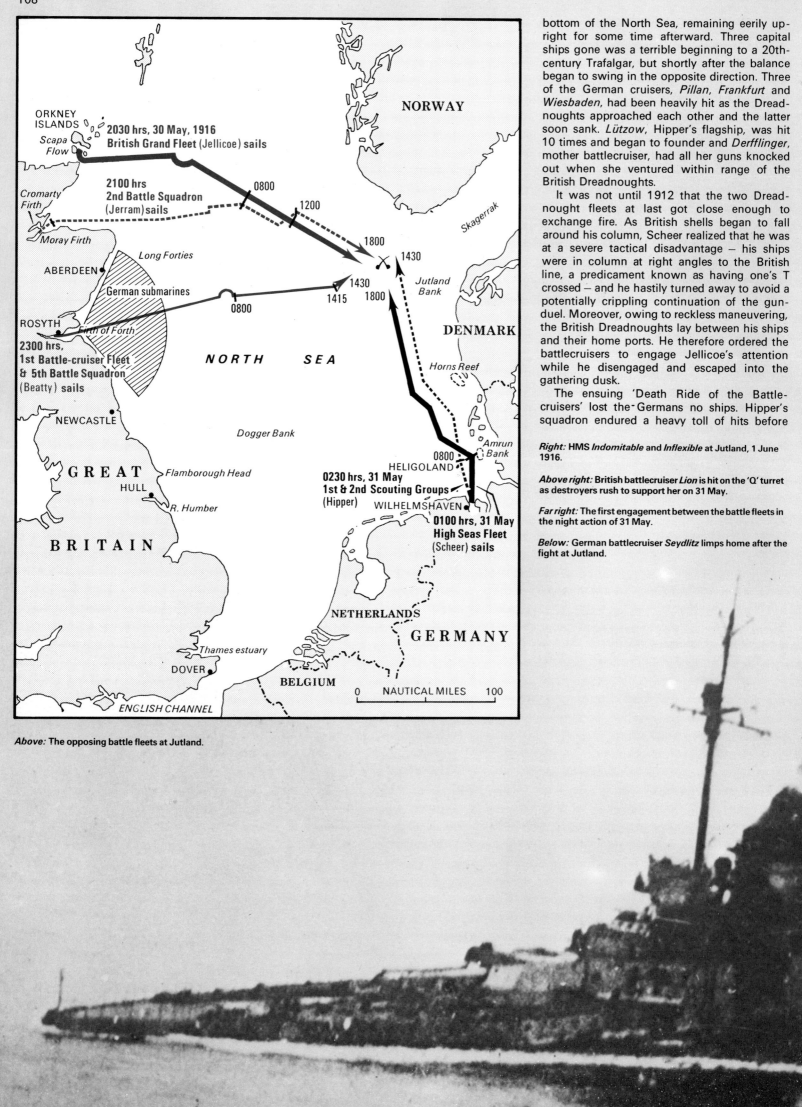

Above: The opposing battle fleets at Jutland.

bottom of the North Sea, remaining eerily up-right for some time afterward. Three capital ships gone was a terrible beginning to a 20th-century Trafalgar, but shortly after the balance began to swing in the opposite direction. Three of the German cruisers, *Pillan*, *Frankfurt* and *Wiesbaden*, had been heavily hit as the Dread-noughts approached each other and the latter soon sank. *Lützow*, Hipper's flagship, was hit 10 times and began to founder and *Derfflinger*, mother battlecruiser, had all her guns knocked out when she ventured within range of the British Dreadnoughts.

It was not until 1912 that the two Dread-nought fleets at last got close enough to exchange fire. As British shells began to fall around his column, Scheer realized that he was at a severe tactical disadvantage — his ships were in column at right angles to the British line, a predicament known as having one's T crossed — and he hastily turned away to avoid a potentially crippling continuation of the gun-duel. Moreover, owing to reckless maneuvering, the British Dreadnoughts lay between his ships and their home ports. He therefore ordered the battlecruisers to engage Jellicoe's attention while he disengaged and escaped into the gathering dusk.

The ensuing 'Death Ride of the Battle-cruisers' lost the Germans no ships. Hipper's squadron endured a heavy toll of hits before

Right: HMS *Indomitable* and *Inflexible* at Jutland, 1 June 1916.

Above right: British battlecruiser *Lion* is hit on the 'Q' turret as destroyers rush to support her on 31 May.

Far right: The first engagement between the battle fleets in the night action of 31 May.

Below: German battlecruiser *Seydlitz* limps home after the fight at Jutland.

being able to disengage and turn to rejoin the Dreadnoughts which, by this sacrificial act, had been able to put a safe distance between them and Jellicoe. As night fell, the two fleets adopted courses which would, in the hours of darkness, bring them once more into gun range. Scheer's heavy ships did indeed encounter Jellicoe's rearguard of destroyers and in the melee British torpedoes found and sank the pre-Dreadnought *Pommern*. Jellicoe remained ignorant of the exchange, and plowed on in the hope of cutting off Scheer before he regained his base. In the darkness he missed contact and turned back to gather his scattered forces for a last search and so allowed the Germans safe home.

In the aftermath the Germans christened the battle the *Skagerraksieg*, the Victory of the Skagerrak. In terms of ships and men lost they had certainly come off better: one old battleship, one battlecruiser, four light cruisers and five destroyers sunk to three battlecruisers, three armored cruisers and eight destroyers; 3039 men killed to 6784. The British consoled themselves with the thought that their ships, built for comparative comfort in long oceanic voyages around their enormous empire, could not offer their crews the same standard of protection as the German ships which were internally subdivided in a much more safety-conscious

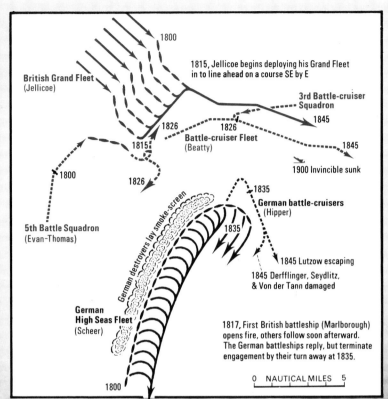

1815, Jellicoe begins deploying his Grand Fleet in to line ahead on a course SE by E

British Grand Fleet (Jellicoe)

3rd Battle-cruiser Squadron
1845

Battle-cruiser Fleet (Beatty)
1845

1900 Invincible sunk

5th Battle Squadron (Evan-Thomas)

German battle-cruisers (Hipper)

1845 Lutzow escaping

1845 Derfflinger, Seydlitz, & Von der Tann damaged

German destroyers lay smoke-screen

German High Seas Fleet (Scheer)

1817, First British battleship (Marlborough) opens fire, others follow soon afterward. The German battleships reply, but terminate engagement by their turn away at 1835.

0   NAUTICAL MILES   5

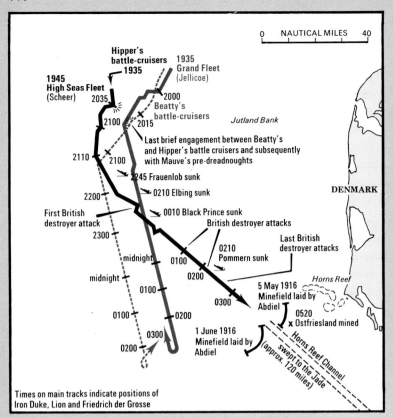

Times on main tracks indicate positions of
Iron Duke, Lion and Friedrich der Grosse

Above: The chase after the High Seas Fleet on 1 June.

Above right: British fleet crosses the German line.

Right: The second engagement of the battle fleets, which forced a German withdrawal.

fashion. However the truth was that German guns, though generally a caliber lighter than the British, were at least as hard hitting, that German range-finding was superior and German shells more penetrating and explosive. British ships also suffered from a serious flaw in the protection of their magazines from plunging fire. But for that, three battlecruisers would not have been blown up.

What comfort the British could take from the Battle of Jutland, as they called it, lay in the knowledge that they had chased the Germans home and retreated at their own leisure — a traditional measure of victory. They could also presume that, if the Germans sought their revenge, the Grand Fleet would again demonstrate its superiority of strength, if not of quality. So Jutland, if not Trafalgar, was a success. Scheer drew the same conclusion. Bethmann-Hollweg, the German Chancellor, insisted that he should take the fleet into the North Sea again in early July and in October to demonstrate that its fighting power remained intact, but both sorties were unsuccessful and against the wishes of Scheer, who was now anxious

The British battle fleet opened fire at 1910, to which the Germans replied. The engagement was broken off when the Germans executed a "battle turn" away at 1918 and the British turned away to avoid torpedo attack at 1923

Below: HMS *Invincible* goes down on 31 May. This picture was taken from HMS *Benbow* as *Badger* comes over to pick up the remaining survivors.

that the navy should concentrate on submarine operations of an unrestricted character.

Germany's U-Boat fleet had grown from 30 U-Boats at the outbreak of war to 111 by January 1917. In February 1915 she declared the waters around the British Isles a war zone and warned that neutral ships which strayed outside a 'safe passage' north of the Shetland Islands would be liable to attack. It was in accordance with this declaration that the great passenger liner *Lusitania* had been sunk off Ireland in May 1915, an attack which outraged the public in the United States since 128 American passengers were among those drowned. As a result, Germany abandoned the policy in August and returned to the practice of sinking ships only after the crews and passengers had been given the chance to escape — a limitation of offensive action which did not, of course, apply to naval vessels. Even within these limitations, the German submarines based in Austrian and Turkish ports in the Mediterranean were able to achieve an impressive level of success. The British were forced to route ships from Australia and the Far East around the Cape of Good Hope, so as to avoid those dangerous waters, and to deploy nearly 500 naval ships in the Mediterranean itself on anti-submarine duties.

This experience worked hard on the imagination of the German admirals. Admiral Henning von Holzendorff, of the German Naval Staff, was able to show in December 1916 that if the U-Boats could sink 500,000 tons of British shipping a month — and sinkings in November had reached half that — then within five months the British would be unable to meet their input requirements and begin to starve. As the German civilian population was going very short of necessities in the winter of 1916 there was little emotional resistance to the idea of visiting some of the same on the enemy among the German authorities. When Holzendorff went on to argue that there were no countermeasures the British could take, and that America could not intervene effectively against the Germans before such a campaign had achieved its object, opposition crumbled. Accordingly, on 9 January 1917 the Kaiser issued orders that German U-Boats should reopen an unrestricted sinking campaign on 1 February. On the day before the German government handed the United States ambassador a warning that, in waters around Great Britain, France, Italy or the Eastern Mediterranean all shipping would be 'stopped with every available weapon and without further notice.'

The effect was incredible. During the last five months of 1917, sinkings of British ships had averaged 37 per month. In February 1918 it jumped suddenly to 105 ships and in April to 127. One out of every four British ships which left port just did not return. The development transformed British attitudes to the outcome of the war overnight. Hitherto they had fought the submarines by positive methods. Antisubmarine vessels had been sent to look for U-Boats, hoping either to catch them on the surface while they were proceeding to patrol stations or to tempt them into surfacing by pretending to be unarmed freighters or fishing vessels — the so-called Q-Ships. Other ships were equipped with nets or explosive paravanes, to be towed beneath the surface in the hope of catching U-Boats under the sea.

The odd U-Boat was caught by one or other of these measures, but once the U-Boats began to attack without surfacing, and to operate far out into the western approaches to the British Isles, these antisubmarine measures rapidly became ineffective. Equally ineffective was a new policy of sailing merchant ships on widely dispersed routes, so as to diffuse the shipping lanes which the Germans patrolled. Though it spared some ships attack in the great waters, they became vulnerable as soon as they approached any of the maritime bottlenecks which led to the British Isles, where the U-Boats naturally congregated. Stationing patrol vessels in the vicinity of the bottlenecks to escort converging merchant ships through merely guided the U-Boats to the best places to find their prey.

There was a strong school of naval thought which argued that merchant ships should be convoyed through dangerous waters, but their opponents pooh-poohed the idea. Their view was that the convoy system had worked in

WHAT A RED RAG IS TO A BULL-

THE RED CROSS IS TO THE HUN.

To the already Long List of Outrages by the HUNS on The RED CROSS both on Land and Sea, there was added on January the 4th This Year, the Sinking without warning in the Bristol Channel of the Hospital Ship "REWA."—Fortunately owing to the Splendid Discipline and the Unselfish and Heroic Conduct of the Officers, Crew, and The Medical Staff, All the wounded, of whom there were over 700 on board were saved,—But three poor Lascar Firemen went down with the ship.

Above: British anti-U-Boat propaganda, based almost wholly on fantasy rather than fact.

Below: The Grand Fleet opens fire at Jutland. Most of the paintings of the battle are somewhat fanciful and melodramatic.

Above: Captain Turner of the *Lusitania,* which, though carrying contraband, was sunk by a U-Boat and helped the British propaganda campaign against Germany.

sailing ship days when raiders were as visible as their victims, but now convoys would merely offer a more tempting choice of targets as the U-Boats could attack from far below the surface. Moreover, the best ships were protected by their speed, a protection which would be nullified if all ships had to travel at the speed of the slowest. Their arguments appeared convincing but, as losses continued to mount, the convoy school became more insistent. Their case was strengthened by the mounting toll of losses which, during the first five months of the new U-Boat campaign, actually exceeded the 500,000 tons a month Holzendorff had predicted would bring Britain to its knees. A strong mine barrier in the Straits of Dover had closed that exit to the shipping lanes but mining of the northern exits from the North Sea was not working. Lloyd George, now Prime Minister, had early been attracted to the convoy argument. Now he threw his weight behind it and in May 1917 this policy was adopted. The

Americans, with a vast army to transport across the Atlantic, were enthusiastic supporters and transferred 34 destroyers to British ports by July. Almost at once an encouraging decline in sinkings developed. In April there had been 169. By July the figure had sunk to 99 and by November to 65.

The reason, unperceived by the anticonvoy school, lay in the characteristics of the U-Boat. Although fairly fast on the surface — with a speed of about 18 knots — it was very slow submerged, capable at best of eight knots for one hour on its electric batteries and, when it remained submerged longer, of proportionately lower speeds. If correctly positioned to intercept a convoy, it could wreak terrible havoc for the short period it was within range. If even a few miles out of position it could not move fast enough to intercept unless it betrayed its position by coming to the surface. Many U-Boat commanders, a brave and aggressive breed, would push their boats' speed to the limit in the vicinity of a convoy. However, in doing so, they revealed their presence to the listening hydrophones of the escort ships and invited heavy and immediate attack by depth charges. This newly developed undersea bomb was responsible for the increasing disappearances of U-Boats throughout 1917. At least six were being sunk each month, a depressing total which the German Admiralty carefully kept to itself.

The Royal Navy was not satisfied, however, by the haphazard results it was achieving at sea, and sought some means to strike at U-Boats where they were most concentrated: in their bases. The chief base for their operations into the North Sea and the Atlantic was at the inland port of Bruges in Belgium, from which they made their way to open waters down two canals, issuing at Ostend and Zeebrugge. Early in 1918 the Admiralty began work on plans to close these two exits and in April a carefully prepared force set out from Dover and Harwich

to tackle this task. The plan was to bring five old light cruisers, filled with cement, into the narrow tidal channels, explode charges in their bottoms and so sink them immoveably in the fairway. Just before midnight on 22 April Admiral Keyes' squadron approached its targets. At Ostend, the Germans had moved the marker buoys at the mouth of the channel and the blockships grounded offshore, but at Zeebrugge they got alongside the long curving mole which protected the harbor from westerly gales and put a landing party ashore. The idea was to distract the Germans' attention, by fighting on the harbor edge, from the arrival of the blockships in the canal. German defenses of the harbor were very strong so HMS *Vindictive*, the amphibious headquarters ship, was studded with guns and crammed with marines and sailors who were to take the German strongpoints by assault.

A naval officer aboard *Vindictive*, Lieutenant Commander Young, was hit as she came alongside, went below to be dressed and came up again to hear 'sudden eruptions of din alternating with dead silence. The wet, jade-green curve of the wall was dimly visible sweeping up out of the dark, and back into it again. The last of the landing parties was going over the brows, and there was an intermittent crackling and flushing of rifle-fire up and down the mole.' Meanwhile the submarine *C-3*, loaded with explosives, slipped up the canal and, after the crew had abandoned ship, was blown up under a viaduct which crossed the harbor. Behind them three blockships entered the canal mouth and, though one was entangled in the protective nets, the other two were sunk as planned. Then, loaded with casualties, but conscious of having boldly completed their missions, *Vindictive* and her escorting destroyers backed off and made for the sea at high speed.

As an antisubmarine measure, the Zeebrugge raid was only a partial success, for the Germans

Above: A British sub is strafed by a German plane whose pilot took this picture.

Top: A British battle fleet zigzags through the water to avoid U-Boat attacks.

Below: A Japanese submarine built in Britain. They were never called into action in World War I.

quickly found a way round the blocks but as an example of derring-do it had a tonic effect on British civilian morale. The German population, though heartened by the military victories of its armies in the spring of 1918, was by contrast deeply affected by the ever-worsening effects of the blockade. In Britain at the height of the unrestricted U-Boat campaign in 1917 there had still been sugar, butter, cheese and meat to buy in the shops, even if the quantities were rationed. The Germans had been rationed for bread since January 1915 and subsequently for other staples as their supply diminished or actually disappeared. The main items of diet were now 'War Bread,' thinned out with inferior grains, swedes and, when available, potatoes. Eggs, obtainable only on doctor's orders, had almost vanished. Citrus fruits were never seen and domestic apples, pears and green vegetables were extremely scarce and costly; a cabbage for instance cost 12 marks. Meat was so scarce that the kangaroos in the *Tiergarten* had been slaughtered for the pot. Little wonder that, as they watched their children grow thin for want of milk and fats, many Germans should wonder to what point the great battles of March or April 1918 had been fought, and ask what was the purpose of the High Seas Fleet.

There had been disorders, fomented by frustration and lack of activity, in the High Seas Fleet in July and August 1917. They were quelled by a mixture of repression and concession; two of the ringleaders were shot but leave and better food were granted to the dissidents. Popular discontent with the failure of the Imperial Navy to break the ring of the

Above: Two Austro–Hungarian seaplanes pick up survivors from the French submarine *Foucault* which they had bombed.

Above right: Fixing a torpedo launcher on a German torpedo boat.

Above far right: A US convoy in camouflage in World War I.

blockade led, in the summer of 1918, to the removal of the navy minister and his replacement by Scheer, who was succeeded in command by Hipper. Together, for the honor of the navy, they planned one last dash into the Channel to engage the British, but it was not to come about. When they gave the necessary orders the stokers drew forces in the stokeholds and declared their unwillingness to leave harbor. The mutiny was suppressed but then flared up again and threatened to spread into a revolt against the Imperial Government itself.

The naval war at sea was essentially, therefore, one of action threatened rather than delivered. The French, Japanese and Russian Navies had taken virtually no part. The Italians and the Austrians had scarcely put to sea — though in the closing stages, Italian swimmers had destroyed the Austrian Dreadnought *Viribus Unitis* by attaching charges to its bottom. The Turkish Navy consisted of scarcely more than the *Goeben* and *Breslau*. In January 1918 they made a last inglorious sortie into the Mediterranean which resulted in the sinking of the *Breslau*. Submarine operations apart, naval action had effectively been confined to the abortive encounters of the Grand and High Seas Fleets, always circumscribed by Churchill's warning to Jellicoe that he was the one man 'who could lose the war in an afternoon.' He had not done so, but equally he had done little positive to win it.

Right: German submarines at Kiel at the end of the war.

Below: British submarine *C-25* under aerial attack.

The last flight of Captain Ball when this air ace's SE5 was hit by a German Albatros.

6 War in the Air

It was only 11 years before 1914 that the first true airplane flight had taken place and only six years before that the pioneers, Wilbur and Orville Wright, had brought their aircraft across the Atlantic to demonstrate to some very inexpert European imitators how the trick could be managed. Yet three years after the great Rheims air meeting of 1908 the Italian army had sufficiently perfected the techniques of the new art to use airplanes against the Turks in its war in Libya. Shortly afterward other aircraft were employed in the Mexican revolution of 1911 to observe enemy troop movements and to take photographs. The Italians had even attempted aerial bombing of the Senussi tribesmen.

These developments had given the major European powers the hint. The French army purchased a Wright biplane in 1909 and established an Air Service in 1910. The Germans founded the Imperial Air Service in 1913. Britain, which had had a balloon battalion since the 1870s, created the Royal Flying Corps, with naval and military wings, in May 1912 and in June 1914 had detached the naval wing to form the Royal Naval Air Service. However the number of aircraft in all these new organizations was small. Britain had 113 military aircraft in August 1914, France 138, Russia 45, Austria 36 and Germany 384, with 30 Zeppelins. Pilots were also scarce, not surprisingly in an age when the armies found it difficult to recruit enough men who knew how to drive motor vehicles. The role of an aircraft was strictly limited to that of serving the military head-quarters to which they were attached. The generals wanted their pilots to bring them

information of the enemy's movements, and saw them as a useful extension of the traditional cavalry scout rather than as pioneers of a new arm in their own right. From the very beginning they were able to fulfill this role. On 22 August 1914 a British pilot operating forward of the British Expeditionary Force observed the approach of Kluck's First Army toward Mons and was able to give advance warning of the impending attack.

Shortly afterward the first recorded instance of aerial combat occurred. On 26 August three British pilots led by Lieutenant H D Harvey-Kelley observed a German aircraft beneath them. They dived on him, surrounded his aircraft and forced it slowly to the ground. Once the trench lines had been established, observation would lose its strategic importance and combat, for control of tactical observation, would become more important. The fixed trench lines made effective artillery bombardment much more practicable than in the weeks of open, mobile warfare, but required observation from the air to check its accuracy and correct the laying of the guns. Pilots began therefore to chase enemy intruders over the lines and in March 1915 a Frenchman, Roland Garros, hit on a new method of attacking. A prewar stunt pilot, and the first to fly the Mediterranean, he had been in Germany giving a flying exhibition when war broke out, and only just made his escape in time. By early 1915 he was an established French military pilot. Aware that in late 1914 two other airmen, Stribick and David, had shot down a German photographic intruder with a hand-held machine gun, he decided to make such a

weapon an integral part of his machine. The obvious place to mount it was above the engine, so that he could fire it along his line of sight, but to do so would destroy the propeller when the gun fired. By experiment he found that steel plates fitted to the propeller would deflect the bullets which did not pass clear through the arc, and thus equipped he took to the air and shot down five German airplanes in two weeks in March 1915.

In April however an engine fault forced him to land behind German lines and his aircraft was captured before he could burn it. A Dutchman, Anthony Fokker, who was assisting the German Air Service with aeronautical design, was called to inspect it, and at once detected the innovation. He also recognized its principal defect, which was that prolonged use would shorten the propeller, and set himself to design a better mechanism. He quickly produced a mechanical interrupter gear which checked the gun's firing when the blades were in front of the muzzle, and so provided the first weapon specifically adapted to aerial use. At least three earlier systems had been invented, but none was as successful as his, which he at once incorporated in one of his remarkable Fokker aircraft. These, superior to any models which the Allies were yet using, were regarded as so valuable that they were not allowed to cross no man's land, but waited behind their own front to attack Allied airplanes which ventured into their air space.

The second year of the war saw the development of aircraft types specifically designed for combat in all the existing air services. France

Below: An Albatros D.V biplane in 1917.

Above: Roland Garros after crossing the Mediterranean.

Above left: A German machine gunner in a Fokker E.1.

Top: Members of the Lafayette Escadrille before a Nieuport.

Top left: The wreckage of two Nieuports in France, 1916.

Above: This is the way bombs were dropped in 1914.

Above: A British airman drops a bomb with a message for the enemy.

had entered the war with Farman pusher aircraft and Blériots, little different from the model in which the inventor had flown the English Channel in 1909. Production was soon to be dominated by two other makes, the Morane-Saulnier and the Nieuport, both fast and maneuverable, with a rotary engine attached to the propeller and rotating around the shaft. This arrangement produced strong torque and so a spectacular ability to make sharp turns in the same direction as the engine was rotating — a great advantage in the dogfighting which was increasingly common.

The Nieuport was so outstanding an aircraft that it was eagerly bought by the Royal Flying Corps when a surplus of production made them available. Meanwhile the British were producing workmanlike aircraft of their own, both from the Royal Aircraft Factory and private firms like Vickers, de Havilland and Sopwith. Most successful of the early designs was the Vickers FBJ known as the 'Gun Bus.' A two seater with a pusher propeller at the rear of the fuselage, it was equipped with a machine gun in the front cockpit which the observer could fire through a wide arc. To score a hit required fine marksmanship, but the early pilots were good shots. It took remarkable skill to achieve, as Captain L G Hawker did in July 1915, three successful attacks in one flight from an airplane fitted with a single-shot carbine fixed at an oblique angle to the fuselage.

The Germans also were busy in the race to outbuild the enemy in quality of aircraft. The Hanuschke of 1914 was soon replaced by the Fokker, at first chiefly in a monoplane form, and then the Albatros and Pfalz. The Germans' main aircraft during 1914–15 were two-seat observation models, to which the single seaters were attached entirely for protection purposes. It would be some time before the Imperial Air Service sought directly to win air superiority over the Western Front.

Moreover, the Germans had a strange social attitude toward flying. Piloting an aircraft was likened to driving a car which, before 1914, gentlemen had employed chauffeurs to do. The first pilots of the Imperial Air Service were therefore recruited from the noncommissioned ranks. Officers acted as observers, in the rear cockpit, from which they told the pilot where

they wanted to be flown. The excitement of the chase quickly broke down these social taboos, as frustrated cavalrymen glimpsed the chance to experience in the sky the triumphs in single combat which the trenches denied them on the ground. Curiously, as a result, many of the German pilots who early achieved fame as fighters were ex-cavalrymen. In the French air service, which was much less snobbish, the first heroes were often ex-racing drivers or sporting heroes who translated their skills into flying expertise. They often made their reputations as corporals or sergeants before being made officers as a testimony to their prowess.

The improvement in the offensive capacity of aircraft and the emergence of highly-skilled pilots transformed the character of air warfare. During 1915 the haphazard encounters of individuals gave way to planned, purposeful air campaigns for dominance over those sectors of the front where great ground battles were in progress. This new policy produced a new sort of airman, the 'ace,' deliberately celebrated by national propaganda as his reward for victory over enemy airmen. An ace was often given command of a fighter formation whose other pilots modelled their performance on his.

The first aces were two Germans, Oswald Boelcke and Max Immelmann. The latter was famous for his extraordinary airmanship, and the development of a new diving turn which put an aircraft into an attacking position, called the 'Immelmann turn.' Boelcke was more than an individualist. Given command of one of the first German fighter squadrons in the autumn of 1915, he set about training it so that in an attack all pilots would co-operate to support the most promising opening in the enemy's formations. He had the good luck to secure one of the early production model Fokker E.1s and with it led his squadron in a series of victories over their British and French opponents which became known as the 'Fokker Scourge.'

The Germans had become so dominant by the spring of 1916 that the French reacted by imitating them and, during the battle of Verdun, formed their own elite fighter unit, which became known as the *Cigognes* (Storks). Equipped with the Nieuport II and later the very

Below: A Nieuport Type 80 biplane.

Above: The funeral procession for German ace Max Immelmann, 1916.

superior Spad VII, both armed with forward firing machine guns, the *Cigognes* — officially Escadrille 3 — quickly dominated the skies over Verdun. The *Cigogne* pilots now gained reputations to rival those of Boelcke and Immelmann, notably Dorme Deullin, Heurtaux and Guynemer. Georges Guynemer eventually achieved the distinction of 'Ace of Aces,' highest-scoring of all French fighter pilots with 54 victories. His career typified that of the extraordinary band of reckless men to which he belonged. Originally rejected for military service because of his physical frailty, he succeeded in enlisting as a mechanic, qualified as a pilot in March 1915 at the age of 21 and shot down his first enemy

airplane a month after being posted to Escadrille 3 in June 1915. He himself was shot down in September, but escaped from no man's land. He was wounded in the air over Verdun in March 1916, by which time he had eight victories, and was shot down from 10,000 feet in September but survived the crash landing. Between November 1916 and January 1917 his score went from 18 victories to 30 and on 25 May 1917, he destroyed four enemy aircraft in one day, two of them within a minute of each other. The strain of his flying had now combined with his poor health to make him obviously unfit for further service. The High Command begged him to give up, so nervous were they of the repercussions of the death of someone who was by now a national hero, but he refused. On 11 September 1917, five days after achieving his

54th victory, he was shot down over Podcappelle, near Ypres. His body was never found. His death, the circumstances of which have never been explained, was indeed a national tragedy, but it was also a personal one. Guynemer had shocked his family on his last visit to them as he had become physically emaciated and nervously drawn. His father, himself a former army officer, begged him to take a rest. He countered with the argument that people would say that 'I have ceased to fight because I have won all the awards.' There was a limit, his father said, to physical strength and he had

Top: Max Immelmann was popularly known as the 'Eagle of Lille.'

Below: Pilots of Escadrille No 3 *Cigognes*. Guynemer is third from the left.

Above: Guynemer with his mechanic on the day of his first victory.

Above: Heurtaux and his biplane of the Cigognes squadron.

reached it. 'Indeed there is a limit,' was his son's answer, 'but it is only there to be excelled. If one has not given everything, one has given nothing.'

Guynemer had the charisma of the mystic. His opposite number on the German side also had charisma but it was rather that of the fire-breathing man of action. Manfred von Richthofen, a regular *Uhlan* officer, and a passionate huntsman, summed up his attitude to the air war in the words, 'I am a hunter. My brother, Lothar, is a butcher. When I have shot down an Englishman, my hunting passion is satisfied for a quarter of an hour.' Eventually Richthofen was to shoot down 80 of the enemy, most in his scarlet Fokker triplane which became his emblem and was the origin of his nickname,

Below: The Richthofen Squadron after it was taken over by air ace Hermann Göring (in the center).

'The Red Baron.' He owed his skill in combat partly to his early experiences as an observer with another pilot, Kurt Wissemann, who suffered from tuberculosis and was determined to die in the air instead of in his bed. Wissemann time and again flew his aircraft to within a few feet of the enemy he was chasing and survival of those risks seems to have convinced Richthofen that he was invulnerable. He set the highest standards of courage and discipline in his *Jasta II.* His favorite expression was that 'one must overcome the inner *schweinehund,*' and he did seem to have succeeded in suppressing within himself every trace of fear and doubt. He filled his room with trophies of the aircraft he had shot down and lit it with a chandelier constructed from the rotary engine of a British victim so that even in sleep he was reminded of aerial combat. He was eventually shot down in a fight with a comparatively inexperienced British pilot. Mick Mannock, the leading British ace, remarked on hearing that Richthofen had come down in flames, 'I hope he burned all the way down.' The Royal Flying Corps pilots who

recovered his body saw that he had an honorable burial, probably a better testimonial of his standing with his enemies.

Burning was all too often the fate of pilots defeated in a dogfight. Of Richthofen's 80 victims, 54 burned in the air. The reason for this ghastly disproportion was that the fuel tank was mounted as close to the engine as possible and on most models the magnetos geared to the propeller shaft by direct drive. A hit which struck the engine almost always ruptured a fuel pipe and, even if the engine was stopped, the windmilling of the propeller would keep the magnetos sparking. Fire was the inevitable result. As the British pilots carried no parachute, they were burned to death in their airplanes or killed by the fall when they jumped free. Almost as horrible was the irrecoverable stall or spin into which some aircraft, or inexperienced pilots, would fall if their control surfaces or engine was damaged while dogfighting. Cecil Lewis has

Above: The Fokker D.1 triplane flown by Manfred von Richthofen. His passenger came aboard from the adjacent triplane.

Right: Manfred von Richthofen, the Red Baron.

Bottom right: An Australian honor guard attends the funeral of the Red Baron.

Below: Lothar von Richthofen (left) with his more famous brother Manfred.

described seeing a fellow RFC pilot attempt to bring down his aircraft with a damaged tail,

'Roberts was a crack pilot . . . and by shutting off his engine he almost managed to avert disaster — but not quite. He could not stop the machine spinning: but he could stop it going into a vertical diving spin. He tried every combination of elevator and bank. No good. The machine went on slowly spinning, round and round and round, all the way down from 8000 feet to the ground. It took about five minutes. He and his observer were sitting there, waiting for death, for that time.'

The worst moment for the French *Aviation Militaire* had been during the period of the Fokker dominance in the summer and autumn of 1915, when they were fighting their great offensive in Champagne. The worst for the Royal Flying Corps came in April 1917 when its pilots had to cover the front of advance during the Battle of Arras. The Germans had now formed 37 *Jagdstaffeln* (*Jasta*) of the Richthofen type, equipped and trained for offensive action, and they were flying a new model, the Albatros D.III, which outclassed the RFC's Sopwith $1\frac{1}{2}$ Strutters, BE2s and RE8s. German tactics, moreover, were not to cross the front but remain over the lines, idling at a high altitude, so that when British airplanes crossed they could dive to attack them out of the sun. If hit, and not burned, they could retrieve a landing place by turning and gliding eastward. As a result, British losses during April amounted to a third of the crews, inevitably falling heaviest on the replacement pilots and observers. Some squadrons attempted to extend the novices' lives by distributing them among the experienced, putting a new gunner with an old pilot in a two-seater, or giving an experienced flight-leader a tyro as a wing man. The old hands, whose survival depended on the quick reactions they had developed, naturally resisted this seeding. They particularly objected that new pilots had the greatest difficulty in seeing the enemy, a trick learned only by those who had survived at least one close encounter.

Left: A British squadron of SE5As in France.

Below: A Sopwith Camel F-1 biplane.

Emergency measures had to be taken to restore the RFC's effectiveness. The Sopwith Triplane flown by the Royal Naval Air Service near the Belgian coast was known to be a match for the Albatros and a squadron was summoned hastily for the Arras Front. It impressed the Germans by its climb and maneuverability so much that Fokker at once set about designing a copy, in which Manfred von Richthofen would cap his reputation, but the numbers deployed were too few to turn the balance. That came later in the summer with the appearance of the SE5 and the Bristol Fighter. It was a remarkable feature of aircraft design and production in those early days that a small improvement in structure or in engine power could instantly outclass existing models and be translated into large numbers of machines very quickly. Aircraft were cheaply and speedily built — the SE5 cost only £837 — and, while they preserved their

Above: A Sopwith Pup biplane, mainstay of the Royal Flying Corps.

superiority of perhaps an extra 10mph or half a minute less to 10,000 feet, could make their opponents' machines virtual deathtraps. The SE5, the Bristol Fighter (Brisfit) and the Sopwith Camel, which all appeared in France in mid-1917, were to redress the balance and hold it for the British until the arrival of the Fokker D.VII in 1918 gave technical ascendancy back to the Germans.

The Bristol Fighter was a two-seater, at first distrusted by its crews because all two seaters had got a bad name from the cumbersome qualities of the 1914–15 models. Its speed, agility and fire power quickly disproved that reputation and many pilots came to regard it as

Below: A Sopwith Camel in France doing a loop.

the best aircraft in British service of the whole war. The SE5, difficult to fly until its tricks were learned, was fast – 126mph – and powerful: 10 minutes to 10,000 feet, against the 12 minutes of the Albatros. It had an in-line engine, which robbed it of turning ability but was a very stable gun platform and carried two machine guns and a lot of ammunition. The Camel, with a rotary engine and all its heavy components mounted in the front seven feet of the fuselage, was extremely maneuverable and was to remain un-challengeable for the rest of the war. Pilots flying Camels shot down more aircraft – 1294 – than any other airplane.

Robbed of technical superiority over the Western Front during 1917, the Germans sought to compensate for it by organizational improvements. The French *Cigognes* had been the first fighter unit formed to win aerial battles (it was now receiving the Spad XIII, which also out-classed the Albatros). The Germans had fought back with the *Jasta*. Now they grouped *Jastas* to form *Jagdgeschwader* of 50 or 60 aircraft. The most famous, formed on 26 July 1917, became known as Richthofen's Circus after its first leader. Its aircraft were painted scarlet and flew together in large sweeps to catch inferior formations of British or French intruders over their lines and destroy or disperse them. The

British, whose air units were tied to the military headquarters over whose sectors they operated, could not at first respond, since corps or armies were unwilling to lend their airplanes to others. As a result, the Germans were able at times to dominate their own skies, so making impossible the work of the artillery observer and recon-naissance aircraft.

While the spectacular battles of the fighter individualists were taking place over the Western Front, another form of aerial warfare had been gathering pace far to the rear. Germany, thanks to the engineering and com-mercial genius of the pioneer aeronaut Count Zeppelin, had entered the war with a fleet of 30 airships – always known to the British as Zeppelins. Their own efforts at building them had proved remarkably unsuccessful and it was perhaps for that reason that they underrated the danger which the Zeppelins posed. At first, the German High Command did not venture to use them against the British Isles. In January 1915, however, some British aircraft raided Germany and the Kaiser decided that provided a pretext for an attack on civilian targets in Britain. Previously there had only been a little bombing of the Channel ports, used by the army for movement to France. On 31 May 1915 the first Zeppelin raid on London took place.

Below left: The Sopwith F-1 Camel, with its 130hp Clerget 9-Bc engine.

Right: Searchlights over London in the first Zeppelin raid in 1915.

Below: A Sopwith Camel after a forced landing at Noyelles-sur-l'Escaut, 8 October 1918.

It was not spectacular. Only one Zeppelin was used, but five people were killed and fires started. By September, however, groups of Zeppelins were penetrating the heart of London and in one raid £500,000 worth of damage was done. On 31 January 1916 nine Zeppelins flew to the north Midlands and killed 59 people. A month later two Zeppelins positioned themselves over Hull, on the North Sea coast, and bombed it at their leisure.

Most of these raids took place at night and so, though timed to coincide with the bright phase of the moon, defeated the efforts of home-based British fighters to find or engage the airships. On 4 June 1915 one Zeppelin, *LZ.37*, had been destroyed while returning from a raid, but it was attacked in Belgium when it had lost height to make a landing. Another had been downed on 31 March 1916, by a combination of gunfire and airplane attack, but it fell into the sea. The first true victory over the 'monsters of the purple twilight' came on 2 September 1916 when Lieutenant W Leefe-Robinson singled out one of a group of 14, *SL.11*, and brought her down near Cuffley, in Middlesex. He was awarded the Victoria Cross for the feat. Three weeks later Lieutenant Brandon repeated the performance by downing *L.33*. By this time the defenses of the capital were extensive and the airship was

Above: An early Zeppelin under construction.

Above: Zeppelin I in a trial run over the North Sea.

Below: Imagination was worse than reality, as this sketch of a Zeppelin over Antwerp shows.

Below: Wreckage of a Yarmouth house hit in a Zeppelin raid in 1915.

Above: Airships *L.13* (largest) with *L.12* and *L.10* set out for a raid on the English coast.

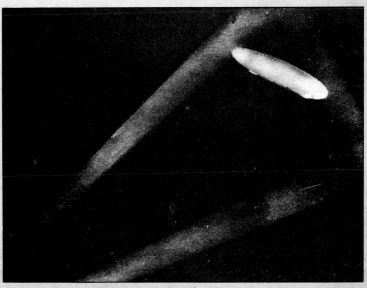

Above: A Zeppelin over London on 13 October 1915 is illuminated by searchlights.

Above: A Zeppelin in 1917, more powerful and dangerous than its predecessors.

Below: King George and Queen Mary came to view the damage of an air raid on Warrington Crescent, London, in March 1918.

Below: Damage caused by a Zeppelin raid on King's Lynn in 1915.

Above: British dirigible over the Dover coast.

constantly caught in the beams of searchlights. Even so, it took Brandon 20 minutes of continuous firing to bring her down. Her end came from lack of power and lift. His bullets had punctured her gas bags and damaged an engine, and she sank lower and lower until her commander decided in desperation to crash land her in Essex.

Given the size and characteristics of the Zeppelins, 5–800 feet long and filled with up to 2,000,000 cubic feet of highly combustible hydrogen, it seems extraordinary that they were not more easily brought down. They owed their invulnerability mainly to the height at which they operated and to the poor quality of ammunition used against them. Warneford, who had destroyed the first Zeppelin in 1914, had managed to catch it at a low altitude and had dropped six 20-pound bombs through its fabric. Miraculously, he had avoided the enormous burst of flame which had resulted. Such feats were difficult to repeat and it was eventually the weather, combined with the improved defenses of London, which drove the Zeppelins away. The increased density of guns and lights around London forced the Germans to fly ever larger formations of airships over the capital and on 19 October 1917 11 Zeppelins which had set out for it were caught in a violent storm. Three were destroyed by the force of the wind, a fourth by anti-aircraft fire when it dropped low for shelter. A fifth was blown out to sea, never to be found again. The other six all lost their way and came down on Allied territory or crashed. After this disaster, the Zeppelin force confined itself to attacking British submarines in the North Sea and to hit-and-run raids. In all, there were 208 Zeppelin flights, during which 5907 bombs were dropped and 522 people were killed.

Concurrently with the later airship raids, the Germans also launched numbers of raids by their large aircraft, generically known to the British as Gothas, after the most successful type.

Airplane bombing began in earnest on 25 May 1917 when the 3rd Bombing Squadron, 16 aircraft strong, left Belgium and made for London. As darkness fell, the pilots lost direction and gave up their effort to reach London, but dropped bombs on Shornecliffe Camp in Essex which caused 100 casualties among Canadian troops there. On 13 June, however, bombing by day, the Squadron killed 104 people near Liverpool Street Station in the middle of London. Public outrage produced an immediate improvement of anti-aircraft defenses, so effective that by September the Gothas were also forced to make their attacks by night. For a time they succeeded in penetrating the defenses of the capital, though they caused little loss of life. The Germans pressed on with forming larger squadrons and on 19 May 1918 sent 40 heavy bombers to London. Thirteen arrived but seven were destroyed, three by fighter attack, three by gunfire and one from engine failure. Thereafter the Germans reckoned the effort too costly. In all their airships and bombers had dropped 8776 bombs and killed 1316 people.

Though the German bombing campaign failed in its attempt to shake the British people's will to sustain their war effort, it remained an impressive military effort. It might have achieved a greater effect had it been more fully co-ordinated. The forces engaged were divided into three, the naval airships, the military airships and the bombers, also under military control. In April 1918 the British took the pioneer step of uniting all their air units — the fighters and sea-planes of the Royal Naval Air Service and the fighters, bombers and reconnaissance aircraft of the Royal Flying Corps — into a Royal Air Force. Its first commander was General Sir Hugh Trenchard ('Boom' to all his subordinates because of his extraordinarily commanding voice).

Trenchard's career had been made by the war. At the outbreak he was an overage major who learned to fly because the new skill seemed to offer the only break in a thoroughly undistinguished career. His seniority in a corps of very young men ensured his rapid promotion as the war progressed and in 1915, rapidly promoted to Major General, he became head of the Royal Flying Corps. On its separation as an independent service this intensely ambitious man determined to find for it a truly independent role. In May 1918 he established a force of 49 heavy night bombers, 75 day bombers and 16 fighters, called the Independent Air Force. He also gave it a precise mission. Rather than simply

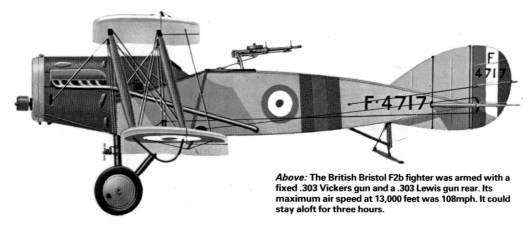

Above: The British Bristol F2b fighter was armed with a fixed .303 Vickers gun and a .303 Lewis gun rear. Its maximum air speed at 13,000 feet was 108mph. It could stay aloft for three hours.

Right: Damage from a Gotha bomber over Paris on 9 March 1918. Bombing raids became more fearsome as the war progressed.

scatter bombs haphazard into large towns, as the German Gothas and Zeppelins had done, he decided to attempt precision attacks on German industrial targets. Naturally he chose the great complex of the Ruhr as his target. In May the IAF attacked Cologne with 33 tons of bombs and between then and the end of the war dropped 540 altogether. Each raid was far heavier and more concentrated than any launched by the Germans against London. However Trenchard, as we can now see with hindsight, overestimated the effect which an offensive on that scale, mighty as it was judged at the time, could have on the economy of a powerful industrial state.

The bombers, though they caused a little public apprehension, never caught the popular imagination in the way the fighters and the pilots did. By 1918 the 'Circuses' squadrons and Escadrilles were working up to their final effort on the Western Front. To the three air forces already engaged, a fourth had now been added, the Air Service of the United States Signal Corps. Its pilots were not the first Americans to have flown against the Germans. That cachet belonged to the dashing volunteers of the Escadrille Lafayette, a squadron of the *Aviation Militaire* formed in April 1916. Despite America's neutrality, numbers of pro-Allied and adventure-hungry Americans were already serving in France, many as infantrymen masquerading as Canadians in the Canadian Imperial Force. A small group had arrived in France in 1914 to form a volunteer ambulance service, a device which kept them on the right side of America's foreign enlistment laws, but the onset of trench warfare had robbed medical rescue of its excitement. One of the ambulance volunteers, Norman Prince, was already a pilot and he conceived the idea of recruiting other American volunteers to fly for the French as an escape from their current frustration. The French authorities at first refused their application but then, recognizing the propaganda value of enlisting volunteers from America, whose neutrality Germany was trying to preserve as hard as the Allies were trying to end it, succumbed. The first seven recruits to the Escadrille Américaine were Prince himself, William Thaw, who had learned to fly at Yale, Kiffin Rockwall, a medical student from North Carolina, Victor Chapman, a Harvard man who had joined the French Foreign Legion in 1914, James McConnell and Elliott Cowdin, from the ambulance unit, and a Texas stunt flier, Bert Hall. After training the pilots were equipped with Nieuport Scouts in May 1916 and sent to Verdun, where they were given the job of attacking the German observation balloons which were directing artillery fire onto the stricken French positions.

'Balloon busting' was not the easy job an attack on a stationary target might seem to be. They were protected by batteries of anti-aircraft guns and by patrols of fighters, which circled at altitude to dive on the 'balloon busters' as they made their attacks. A Belgian, Willy Coppens, was making a speciality of this dangerous occupation and was awarded a Belgian Knighthood for destroying 37 around Ypres. The Americans quickly found how difficult the task was. Both Boelcke and Immelmann were

Right: This biplane became a sitting duck as it straggled behind its squadron.

Above: No 1 Course, Central Flying School. Sir Hugh Trenchard appears on the far right, second row.

Above: A Gotha G.Vd heavy bomber with two 260hp Mercedes engines.

operating Fokker Squadrons over Verdun and on 24 May William Thaw was jumped by three of these German machines and shot down. He was pulled from the wreckage with a cut pectoral artery, but survived. Next day Bert Hall was badly wounded. On 17 June Victor Chapman encountered Boelcke himself, who was shot down and wounded in the head, but in the same week five Fokkers caught Victor Chapman and shot him down. He was the first of the American squadron to die. Rockwell was killed the following day and in the same week Prince, who had been flying long hours, flew into high tension cables on his approach to the airfield in poor evening light. There were replacements — altogether 209 Americans trained as pilots with the French Air Service — but the Escadrille Lafayette was never to be the same again. It was transferred to the American Air Service in France in February 1918 and thereafter operated as a

Below: A Handley-Page bomber at the training depot in Halton Camp, Wendover, England.

normal American fighter squadron. Its glamour and great days were behind it.

It had never included the greatest of the American aces, the extraordinary Eddie Ricken-backer. A poor boy from Columbus, Ohio, between 1910 and 1914 he became America's top racing driver, with an income of $40,000 per annum. In 1914 he broke the world speed record and after America's entry into the war became convinced that a squadron formed of America's other leading racing drivers would prove invincible. His advocacy of this idea achieved nothing and he was eventually persuaded to enlist as personal chauffeur to General John Pershing, the Commander in Chief. Some months of this duty so frustrated him that he insisted on transferring to the Air Service, learned to fly at the end of 1917 and in March 1918 joined the 94th ('Hat in the Ring') Aero Squadron. He shot down his first German plane on 29 April and within a month four more. During July and August he was away from the front with an ear infection, induced by flying at

high altitude. Between the middle of September and the end of October, after his return to duty, he downed another 20 aircraft, making a total of 26 victories, a record achieved in so short a time that it made him one of the most remarkable pilots of the war. His continuing toughness and powers of survival were demonstrated in World War II when the airplane in which he was making a tour of inspection crashed and he spent 21 days on a raft before rescue.

Despite the enormous industrial might of the domestic economy almost all the American squadrons were equipped with French aircraft. Their own aircraft factories were not ready to produce home-designed models until the war was over. Thus the final effort on the Western Front remained a duel between the German and the Franco-British air fleets. In the last months of war it was the Germans who made the most important innovation in aerial tactics. This was

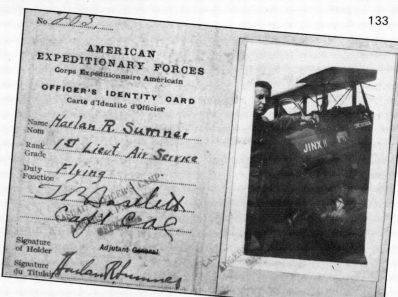

Above: A Gotha G.V is loaded with 110lb and 220lb bombs.

Above right: The ID card of a member of the AEF.

Right: The Handley-Page V-1500 heavy bomber had 350hp Rolls-Royce Eagle VIII engines.

the creation of *Schlachtstaffeln* (Battle Squadrons) which were equipped and trained to support ground troops in an offensive. Special aircraft, designated CL and later J types, were designed and assigned to the *Schlasta*. The J I, when it appeared, was found to be of all-metal construction and highly resistant to ground fire. The *Schlastas* had their first trial during the Battle of Cambrai, where their strafing of the British advanced positions and reporting of the progress of German infantry columns made a major contribution to the success of the counter-attack. The British had also tried 'contact patrolling,' as they called it and were to do so again, but they did not develop the specialized aircraft which the Imperial Air Service had. During Germany's first great offensives of

Above: Germans 'scramble' for their Fokker D-1 triplanes.

Left: Spad two-seater biplanes over France.

Above right: A Spad takes aim at its target.

March–July 1918, the *Schlastas* ranged far ahead of the advancing infantry and were able to indicate to the High Command in which directions it would be most profitable to exert pressure.

The Germans were also able, in the last months of the war, to win back something of the technical advantage in aerial combat which they had lost to the enemy since the appearance of the Camel, SE5, Spad XIII and Nieuport 28. The Fokker D.VII, last of the great Dutchman's designs, did not quite match the speed of the latest models of Allied fighters but it had an extraordinary ability to hang on its propeller at high altitudes while turning and climbing in a dogfight, and so get on an opponent's tail. Lieutenant J M Guder, of the Royal Flying Corps, described an encounter with a D.VII in the summer of 1918:

'There were five of us and we ran into five Fokkers at 15,000 feet. We all started climbing of course — and they outclimbed us. We climbed up to 20,500 feet and couldn't get any higher. We were practically stalled and these Fokkers went right over our heads and got between us and the lines. Gosh, it's unpleasant fighting at that altitude. The slightest movement exhausts you. Your engine has no pep and splutters; its hard to keep a decent formation, and you lose 500 feet on a turn. The Huns came in from above and it didn't take us long to fight down to 12,000 feet. We put up the best fight of our lives but these Huns were just too good for us. . . . I got to circling with one Hun, just he and I, and it didn't take me long to discover I wasn't going to circle above this one. He began to gain on me and then did something I've never heard of before. He'd been circling with me and he'd pull around and point his nose at me and open fire and just hang there on his prop and follow me round with his tracer. All I could do was keep on turning around as best I could. If I'd straightened out he'd have had me cold as he already had his sights on me. If I'd tried to hang on my prop that way, I'd have gone right into a spin. But this fellow hung right there and sprayed me with lead like he had a hose. All I could do was to watch his tracer and kick my rudder from one side to the other to throw his aim off. This war isn't what it used to be.'

Guder got away eventually, but two of his fellow pilots were shot down in this fight, and the renewed 'Fokker Menace' remained the

Left: **Officers of the 103rd Aero Squadron, formerly the Lafayette Escadrille, line up with other Allied officers to receive French decorations.**

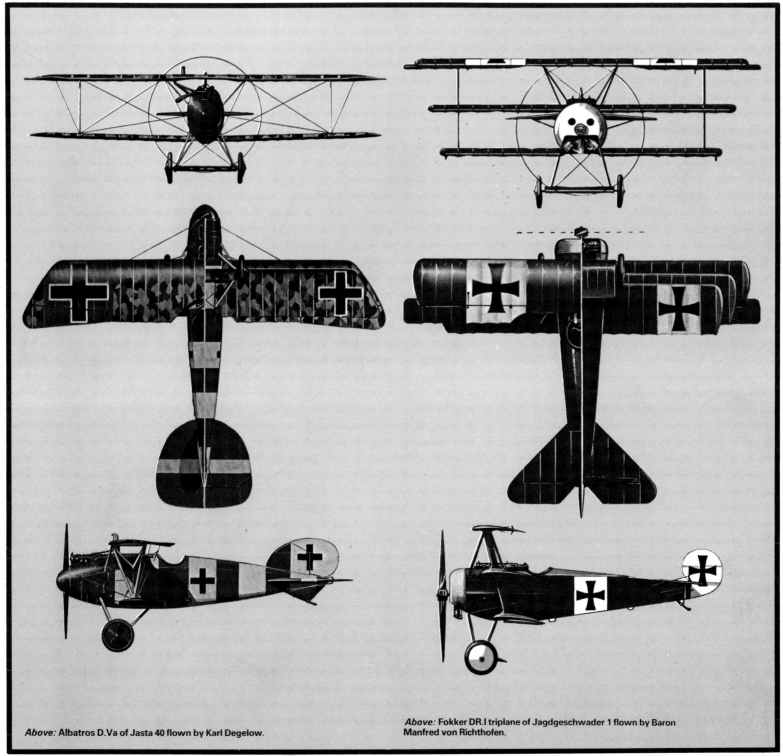

Above: Albatros D.Va of Jasta 40 flown by Karl Degelow.

Above: Fokker DR.I triplane of Jagdgeschwader 1 flown by Baron Manfred von Richthofen.

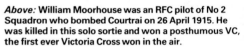

Above: William Moorhouse was an RFC pilot of No 2 Squadron who bombed Courtrai on 26 April 1915. He was killed in this solo sortie and won a posthumous VC, the first ever Victoria Cross won in the air.

Above left: Billy Bishop, with his Nieuport.

Far left: Major McCudden of the RFC, VC.

Left: Major Mick Mannock was a leading British ace, notable for his shyness.

Below: Captain Albert Ball, RFC, VC in his SE5 two-seater. This great ace was killed in combat on 7 May 1917.

Below: Australian-born Major Roderick Dallas in his SE5A of No 40 Squadron. He was credited with at least 51 kills.

dominant factor in aerial warfare until November 1918.

Most of the German strength was concentrated during the last year of the war on the Western Front against the British. In March 1918 there were 1680 German aircraft opposite the British section and only 367 against the French, and an increasing number were Fokker D.VIIs. One of the last epics of the air war was between a formation of these aircraft and one of the heroes of the great individual dogfighting days, the Canadian W G Barker. Like many of the great pilots Barker was a slow starter and had scored only nine victories between October 1917 and January 1918. In the next nine months, however, he raised his score to no less than 49 and on 27 October was flying back to England on a home posting, when he spotted a lone observation plane far below him. Tempted by the chance of one more kill, he followed it down only to encounter no less than 15 Fokker D.VIIs flying an offensive mission. Recognizing attack to be his only hope of escape, he flew head-on into their formation and, in the first shock, shot down two before the others had co-ordinated their maneuvers to encircle him. He had already been wounded in one leg and was soon wounded in the other. He fainted at the controls and his Snipe (an improved Camel) spiralled groundward. The motion revived him but the Fokkers followed him down and he was wounded in the left elbow when he made a suicidal attack, which brought down another Fokker. Intermittently conscious and at ground level, he just managed to hold the machine straight enough to make a landing at 90mph which tore off the undercarriage. The wreckage came to rest close to a British position and the soldiers who dragged him clear raced him to hospital where his life was saved. When examined the remains of his aircraft, which was awash with blood, revealed 300 bullet holes. Barker was unconscious for 10 days but recovered the use of all his limbs and was on his feet to receive the Victoria Cross from King George V on 30 November 1918. His last battle raised his score to 53 and made him the seventh-ranking British ace.

Ace of aces remained Manfred von Richthofen, with 80 victories. Next came the French, Réné Paul Fonck with 75 and the British Major Mick Mannock with 73. Fifteen of the British, four of the French and 11 of the German aces had scores of over 40 aircraft shot down. The victories of the aces of the other air forces — Russian, Italian, Austrian, Belgian or American — were much lower, in the latter's case because of its late entry into the war, in the former because of the altogether lower level of activity in the

Below: Fokker D.VII pilots mount their aircraft in Flanders for a sortie.

skies over their fronts. The sum of these totals is the figure for casualties suffered by the opposing sides. The Germans had lost 5853 men killed, the Royal Air Force 6166.

Was the air war, in retrospect, anything more than a gladiatorial contest? The bombing of the homelands by the 'strategic' air forces clearly achieved very little and certainly inflicted damage which cost far less than the investment in the building of the airships and heavy aircraft which made the raids. It was also ineffective in depressing civilian morale. 'Zeppelins' were quickly a source of English music hall jokes. The tactical air forces achieved a good deal more. During the era of open warfare at the beginning and end of the war, roving pilots had brought nuggets of priceless information to the commanders in headquarters; whether they were used correctly was beyond their power to determine. During the long years of trench warfare, the air forces had wielded the means to make life even more uncomfortable than it already was for the suffering infantry below, by directing the fire of the enemy's artillery into their trenches, or alternatively to spare them the misery by sweeping the skies clean of prying pilots from the other side. It was in those battles for air dominance that the great aces had made their names, and the relief they had brought to

Above: A squadron of Fokker D.VII biplanes in 1918.

humbler warriors earned the adulation that had been heaped upon them. There was another, intangible benefit they had brought. How often did infantrymen testify that, looking up from the mud of their trenches into the blue skies above, their spirits had been uplifted by the sight of airplanes duelling far above their heads; not by the victory of one side over the other, for altitude made the recognition of friend and enemy impossible, but by the reminder that the wheeling and swooping brought that there was still a realm of freedom and movement in the terrible land-locked war that the armies were fighting. Cecil Day Lewis, later Poet Laureate, a pioneer pilot managed to catch the intoxication of fear and excitement that aerial combat brought to warriors and observers in his lines from a pilot's cockpit:

Tempt me no more; for I
Have known the lightning's hour,
The poet's inward pride,
The certainty of power.

Bayonets are closing round.
I shrink; yet I must wring
A living from despair
And out of steel a song.

Russian heavy artillerymen in position in a Polish wood.

7 The Russian Collapse

Hindenburg's great victory at Tannenberg in August 1914, life-saving though it was for Germany, by no means ended Russia's threat to East Prussia and Silesia, or to Germany's feeble ally, Austria-Hungary. Just as at the outbreak it was Russia's generous strategy of a premature offensive which had relieved the pressure on France at the critical time of the Battle of the Marne, so as autumn drew into winter on the Eastern Front French, and later British, activity in the West prevented the Kaiser and his generals from transferring thence any but a few of the divisions originally committed to the march on Paris.

The Central Powers' strategy in the East was defensive. The terrain and the ratio of men to space made defense in the East altogether more difficult than in the West. Measured along its whole length, from the border with Rumania to the Baltic at Memel, Russia's frontier with her two Teutonic enemies was 1200 miles. On 500 miles of front in the West the opposing sides deployed armies far larger than those in the East. They buttressed their lines at several points on major natural obstacles, the flats of the Yser, the heights of the Aisne, the swamps and forest of the Argonne and the mountains of the Vosges. In the East there were a few natural obstacles, like the Masurian Lakes in East Prussia and the Carpathian Mountains on Hungary's border. The Austrian positions stood well to the east of the Carpathians which thus acted as an obstacle to supply and reinforcement of their rear, while, between the northern end of their line and the southern end of the German line in East Prussia,

Below: General Zhilinsky (back to camera) gives out decorations to some Russian officers. Zhilinsky was an incompetent who was sacked in 1914.

the great salient of Russian Poland bulged forward toward the industrial and mining areas of Silesia and the great cities of Breslau and Posen. Russian Poland formed the land bridge between the plains of North Germany and the endless steppe of European Russia, itself as flat as a billiard table for mile after mile. The rivers, the Vistula, the San and the Warthe, ran barely below the level of the flats and, though wide, were easily bridged at almost any point. In the center of the salient stood Warsaw, nodal point of all military comminications in north-central Europe. Geographically, therefore, the advantages stood with the Russians, since they enjoyed the best transport network and were faced by no series of obstacles against which their enemies could buttress a stout defense.

The Russians also had a numerical advantage. They had seven armies in the field against one German and four Austrian. While the Central Powers were divided from each other by nationality, and Austria further divided by language – some scholars counted 15 spoken languages in the Dual Monarchy – the Russians were a single force united by a deep, almost mystical patriotism for Mother Russia. The infantry of the first-line were strong, brave obedient peasants, excellent marchers and busy diggers, who could entrench a strong position overnight without complaint. The cavalry was recruited from countrymen, used to horses and supplemented by light regiments of Cossacks, who made superlative scouts. The Russian artillery had always been good and its materiel was the equal of the German but, as with all classes of Russian equipment, there was not enough of it. Russian industry, though developing faster than that of any other nation's in 1914, faster even than America's, had not yet reached

Above: Russian troops in a Galician trench. The Austrian and German offensives forced the Russians back from their frontiers. After this offensive in early 1915 the German Eighth and Tenth Armies moved forward from the Masurian Lakes and encircled 70,000 Russian troops.

the stage where it could feed a hungry army in full flush of a great campaign. Losses of materiel were therefore serious to Russia in a way which losses of men — whose reserves seemed inexhaustible — were not.

On the other hand, Russian leadership was not impressive. In business life, Russia now offered a career to talented people. In the army, as in the civil service and politics, court influence was dominant, some would have said paramount, and too many of the Russian generals owed their place to patronage. The Commander in Chief was a Grand Duke, Nicholas, uncle to the Czar, and, though a competent administrator, was chiefly distinguished by his enormous height. General Mikhail Alexeiev, the future Chief of Staff, was an adequate military technician but as the rare exception, a man of humble origins who had made his way to the top, lacked the self-confidence and court connections to dictate strategy. The Russian army was also wracked by fierce antipathies between the reformers who were the protégés of the War Minister, General Vladimir Sukhomlinov, and the traditionalists, who looked to the Grand Duke for protection and leadership. The result was that true leadership in the army was hard to find. Sukhomlinov continued the peacetime administration of the army; the Grand Duke, on the outbreak of hostilities, transformed the General Staff into an operational *Stavka* (High Command) which directed strategy. The two retained conflicting powers to appoint commanders and chiefs of staff irrespective of subordinate formations and in consequence often created situations in which the two most important men in a division, a corps or even an army, were not on speaking terms.

None of this augured well for Russian strategy and, as we have seen, its first test in the invasion of East Prussia confirmed the worst of pessimistic fears. However that was against the Germans; against the Austrians the Russians were to do better. The Austrian army, though it had an excellent Chief of Staff in Conrad von Hötzendorf, was beset by internal problems as grave as Russia's. These were complicated by the language problem and constantly threatened by the doubtful political loyalty of the Slavs, particularly the Czechs. Austria-Hungary also had its two-front dilemma, in its case posed by the need to fight the Serbs and the Russians simultaneously. Because of the deployment of 13 divisions against the Serbs it could not match the Russians' strength beyond the Carpathians where they had 1,300,000 men in the field against its 1,100,000. Moreover, weak though the Russian army was in artillery and shell stocks, the Austrian army was even weaker.

This weakness was the salvation of Russia's war effort in the early months of the war. Defeated in East Prussia, she could still achieve victories over the Austrians because Hindenburg's Eighth Army was too small and separated by the Polish salient, too far away to lend help to her ally in front of the Carpathians. Yet the Russians' victories were nevertheless achieved by miscalculation. Both they and the Austrians miscalculated each other's centers of strength and intentions. Conrad von Hötzendorf believed that the Russians did not intend to attack and on 20 August sent his left wing to march round what he had identified as an open flank of the Russian army, south of Ivangorod. On 23 August it met head on a Russian army, under General Alexei Evert, which was pressing forward to make a surprise attack. In a three-day battle at Krasnik the Russians were driven from

Above: Grand Duke Nicholas, the Czar's uncle, was Commander in Chief of the Russian armies from August 1914 until August 1915 after which he was transferred to the Caucasus.

Below: Austrian Chief of Staff Conrad von Hötzendorf surveys the Galician battle front.

142

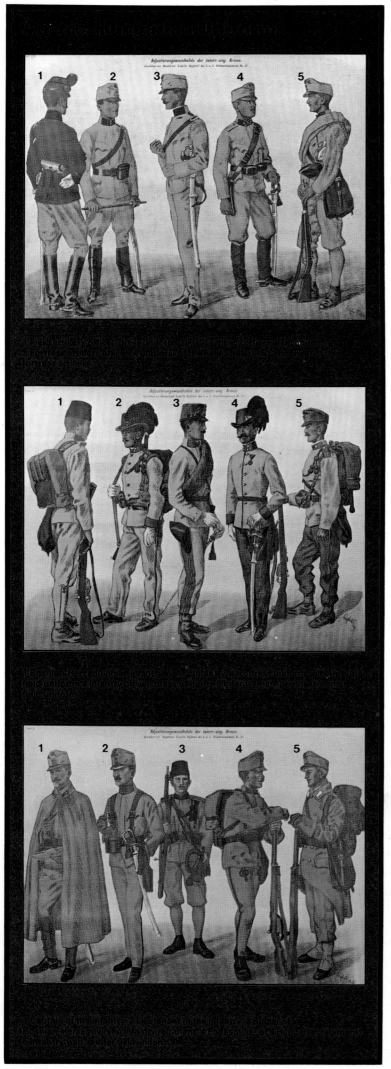

the field and Conrad von Hötzendorf believed he had won a significant victory. This belief was heightened by the fighting at Komarov, from 26 August–1 September, when General Moritz von Auffenberg, commanding the Austrian Fourth Army, almost surrounded his Russian opponent, General Plehve. Then disaster struck. The real Russian strength was further south, along the headwaters of the Dniestr River opposite the great Austrian fortress of Lemberg (Lvov) and on 26 August the advance guards drove into the Austrian lines there and quickly defeated the Austrian Third Army. Following up, the Russians quickly reached positions with three of their armies from which they could easily have enveloped almost the whole of Conrad von Hötzendorf's force in front of the Carpathians.

On 11 September, however, with disaster staring him in the face, Conrad von Hötzendorf was saved by the apparently incurable Russian fault of radioing uncoded messages. A stream of transmissions revealed to him that the Grand Duke Nicholas was planning to send troops on a wide outflanking march around his left, across the Vistula and down the valley of its tributary, the San, which would have cut him off from his escape routes into the Carpathians. He therefore ordered an immediate retreat, first to the San, 50 miles to his rear, and then to the next tributary of the Vistula, the Dunajec, 80 miles

Left: General Mikhail Alexeiev, Russian Chief of Staff in 1915.

Below left: Russian troops in a Galician trench.

Below: A Russian heavy gun position near Przemysl.

beyond that. Lemberg was abandoned, so too was the strong fortress of Przemysl, which guarded the railroad line to it at the San crossing.

The Austrians now standing on the crest line of the Carpathians, which offered the last strong protection before the plains of Hungary were reached, had been forced to retreat 200 miles in two months of fighting, had lost 400,000 men, of whom 100,000 were prisoners, and had disastrously compromised the military reputation of their army.

The Germans felt that their prestige was affected by this reverse almost as much as Austria's. They were also deeply concerned by the threat which the Russians were now able to offer from the positions they had reached to vital German territory. General Nikolai Ivanov, com-

Above: Austrian infantrymen press forward at Lemberg (Lvov).

manding the Russian armies of the southern Front was indeed thinking of advancing into Silesia and simultaneously taking Krakow and perhaps even Budapest, capital of Hungary. Falkenhayn at OHL therefore decided that Hindenburg, now established as the strong man of the Eastern Front, must do something, quickly, to turn the tables. A new German Army, the Ninth, was formed and on 1 October began to move forward into the plains of central Poland, so outflanking the Russians who had driven the Austrians back to the Dunajec. It was now the Russians' turn to anticipate their enemy's movements. Realizing their danger,

Above: German cavalry advance during the Battle of the Masurian Lakes, February 1915.

Below: Russians prepare a counterattack at Lemberg (Lvov).

Ivanov's forces quickly disengaged and fell back, so rapidly that by 12 October the Germans had reached to within eight miles of Warsaw. The Russians did not retreat along their whole front. While Hindenburg was distracted by the thought of capturing the capital of The Grand Duchy and the Austrians by the satisfaction of retaking Przemysl, Ivanov regrouped and struck in between the Germans and Austrians to threaten Breslau. Hindenburg's nerve was gravely shaken by this offensive to which he could find no immediate answer. The Austrians again had to abandon Przemysl and had it not been for an interception of a Russian message announcing Ivanov's intention to pause, Hindenburg might have retreated inside the whole length of the German frontier. As it was in mid-November he scraped together enough troops to make a flank attack into the Russians near Lodz and so check the threat to Breslau. Having robbed the Eighth Army in East Prussia of troops for the Ninth, he could do nothing to help stem a new Russian advance which retook the Masurian Lakes region, nor to help the Austrians, who lost more ground in the Carpathians.

Help, indeed, now had to come from outside Hindenburg's resources and in December, a moment when Falkenhayn was hard pressed in the West, he found eight divisions to send eastward. They were sufficient to form a second new Army, the Tenth, with which after some preparation Hindenburg regained the ground lost in Masuria and even managed to carry the line from East Prussia into Poland. The fighting was

called the 'Winter Battle in Masuria' and lasted from 7–21 February. Conditions were appalling; the attack began in a blinding snowstorm. They were even worse in the Carpathians where the Austrians, spurred on by the Germans who had contributed a small force called the *Sudarmee*, attacked on 23 January. At an elevation of 7–8000 feet, an offensive in mid-winter became what even the Austrian official historian called 'a cruel folly.'

'Mountains had to be scaled, . . . supply lines were either an ice rink or a marsh, depending on freeze or thaw; clouds hung low, and obscured the visibility of artillery targets; shells either bounced off ice or were smothered in mud; whole bivouacs would be found frozen to death in the morning. Rifles had to be held over fires before they could be used; yet even the thick mountain forests were of no great help for fuel, since there was no way of transporting logs out of those primeval forests.'

The Austrians nevertheless made some progress. After a siege of four months, Przemysl fell on 22 March, releasing eight Russian divisions which had been besieging it. This provided the commander of the Southwestern Front, Ivanov, and his chief of staff, Alexeiev, with enough extra strength to be able to recover the ground lost and threaten the Austrians with a renewed offensive across the Carpathians toward Budapest.

This great crisis required a radical solution. The Austrian army seemed threatened with dissolution. Already the Germans were talking of the alliance as being 'chained to a corpse.'

Above: Vladimir Sukhomlinov, who as Russia's Minister of War, administered the army until June 1915.

Austria had mobilized all her reserves in 1914 but had lost 2,000,000 men, many to frostbite and winter sickness by March 1915. Since she had the least efficient conscription system of all the powers, Russia included, she could not properly make good the losses. The young boys of 1915 had to be conscripted because the records of the conscription service were too badly organized to permit calling-up the older men who had been exempted from service before the war. The supply situation was worse. In the Skoda Works in Bohemia and the Steyr Works of Lower Austria, the government had the makings of a considerable war industry. The shell supply office of the War Ministry was perhaps the most inefficient department of that supremely inefficient agency, so managing to achieve even lower deliveries of munitions to the front than on the Russian side. While Germany was producing several million shells a month, Austria managed only 116,000 in December 1914 against a minimum requirement of 240,000. There were 45 different models of gun in the Austrian artillery, a situation which ensured that some models would not receive any shell at all. There was a serious shortage of the supply of other essentials. Hungary, the wheat bowl of the empire, used its political autonomy within the imperial system to supply its own needs first, with the result that workers in the great industrial centers of German Austria began to go short of the food they needed to

sustain a high level of output, and even the men at the front were often hungry. The ever-present temptation to desert, in an army where the Slavs — Czechs, Serbs and Ruthenians — felt a stronger national pull toward their enemies than their rulers, began to manifest itself in actual desertion.

Conrad von Hötzendorf, the Austrian Chief of Staff, quickly abandoned his pride in waging a purely national war against the Russians and by April 1915 was asking the Germans for help — while hinting at the threat of making a separate peace if it was not forthcoming. Falkenhayn had already come to the conclusion that Germany must stretch her resources that little bit further than seemed possible to save her ally and on 13 April asked the Kaiser's permission to send a force to the Carpathians for a counteroffensive. It was to consist of eight divisions, be known as the Eleventh Army and be commanded by the flamboyant cavalryman August von Mackensen, with the steely Hans von Seeckt as his Chief of Staff.

Owing to the inadequacy of railroad communications the German Eleventh Army and Austrian Fourth Army had to assemble by laborious marches along the poor roads. This meant that there was plenty of warning to the Russians that the offensive threatened. Nevertheless, the commander of the Russian Third Army which defended Mackensen's chosen front between Gorlice and Tarnow, just north of the Carpathian chain, refused to believe that he was in danger. This was disastrous, because his entrenchments were weak in the extreme; a single poor trench with a few strands of barbed wire in front of it. The German bombardment which began on 2 May 1915 tore it to pieces in four hours, and the infantry then advanced on a front of 30 miles. In the west, railroads would soon have brought

Above: Field Marshal Paul von Hindenburg, victor of Tannenberg and military hero of Imperial Germany.

reserves to seal off the danger point. In Russia the railroad had neither the capacity nor efficiency to do the job. The roads were so muddy that they prevented an easy withdrawal from the point of danger. The result was that the troops on either side of the break in were trapped in their positions and easily encircled by the attackers whose leading columns meanwhile quickly passed on through the breach. On 10 May Ivanov's Chief of Staff reported to the *Stavka*:

Left: Germans rest in their East Prussian trench during the winter of 1914—15.

Below left: A fanciful view of the Eastern Front.

Below: French propaganda poster urges Slovaks to overthrow their Austrian masters and fight for the Allied cause.

Below: An Austrian army on the march in Galicia.

UŽ SLOVENSKO VSTÁVA,
PUTÁ SI STRHÁVA:

'the strategic position is quite hopeless. Our line is very extended. We cannot shuttle troops around it with the required speed and the very weakness of our armies makes them less mobile; we are losing our capacity to fight.'

He suggested that Przemysl should be abandoned, together with the whole of Galicia (Austrian Poland), that Kiev should be fortified because the Germans would now invade the Ukraine and ended by declaring that Russia must 'renounce serious military activity until we have recovered.' He was at once dismissed but that did not stop a retreat to the River San by Third Army, which had lost 200 guns and 140,000 prisoners in six days.

Bad went to worse. The whole Russian Front in the west was now unhinged and a great backward movement began into White Russia in the north, the Ukraine in the south and toward the Pripyat in the center. By 13 May Przemysl had been surrendered. By 1 July Lodz, in central Poland, had been lost. On 5 August the Germans entered Warsaw. Later in the same month the great chain of Russian fortresses along the Polish rivers fell; Kovno, on the Niemen on 18 August, Novogeorgievisk, on the Vistula on 20 August, Brest-Litovsk, on the Bug on 26 August and Grodno, on the Upper Niemen on 4 September. By that date the Russians had lost at least 300,000 prisoners, some said a million. They had also begun to give up without a fight and, as prisoners, to refuse to run away even when given the chance. The army had also lost 3000 guns in the retreat, as many as it had had at the outbreak of the war.

Dissatisfaction with the High Command be-

came so widespread and severe that the Czar, who resented any criticism of existing arrangements, could no longer ignore it and on 8 September he dismissed the Grand Duke Nicholas by announcing that he was to be appointed Viceroy of the Caucasus — where Russia's war with Turkey was having some success. The Czar alarmed even his intimates by announcing that he would in future command himself. However in practice he left strategy to Alexeiev, whom he brought in as Chief of Staff from the southwestern command. Alexeiev's main quality was a refusal to panic in a crisis, something needed all too often on Russia's Western Front. Contrarily he suffered from an inability to delegate, so that he gave himself chronic migraine by working 18 hours a day. Delegation, however, was difficult in a headquarters where the rest of the staff were, in the view of a visitor, 'either furniture or clerks,' a harsh verdict, even if true, on a group which contained seven generals and 30 colonels.

The change in command did not produce any immediate improvement at the front, even though by the end of 1915 Russia's war industry and bureaucracy had begun to remedy many of the weaknesses which had crippled her armies during the previous spring and summer. With 2,000,000 effective soldiers at the front in January 1916, Alexeiev was able to report to his French allies that they were all now equipped with rifles and the artillery, with 7000 guns, had reserves of 1000 shells per gun, reckoned sufficient for offensive activity even by Western Front standards. The fighting formations had been reorganized into three Fronts, the Northern

Above: Polish refugees and their meager belongings on the road east as the Germans pushed forward in 1915.

Above left: Kaiser Wilhelm II with General von Mackensen (on platform, right) in Campina, Rumania in September 1917.

Below: Russian POWs trudge into captivity during the German advance in Poland.

commanded by General A Kuropatkin, the Western commanded by Evert, and the Southern commanded by General Alexei Brusilov. On each the Russians now had a superiority over their German and Austrian enemies: 300,000 to 180,000, 700,000 to 360,000 and about 500,000 to rather less.

The Western Allies, particularly the French, took advantage of this increase in Russian strength to demand action which would relieve them from the pressure now being exerted by the Germans at Verdun. In March the Russians responded by mounting an attack on either side of Lake Narotch where their Northern and Western Fronts joined, but it was disastrous. Previous experience had revealed that a besetting weakness of Russian offensives was a failure to co-ordinate the effort of their infantry and artillery. The Russian gunners, who regarded themselves as an elite and their weapons as far more valuable than the lives of the infantry they were supposed to support, took no trouble to insure that their shells would disable the German defenders whom the Russians were supposed to overcome. They often fired blind off their maps at positions where they guessed the Germans ought to be, but were not, either because they had prudently evacuated their trenches or had never been there in the first place. The Germans at the end of a week's fighting, 14–21 March, removed 5000 Russian

corpses from their wire. Total Russian losses were 100,000 compared with 20,000 German. It was all terribly reminiscent of the offensive at the southern end of the front against the Austrians the previous December:

'After artillery preparation we went about a mile forward under heavy enemy gunfire. Once we were within 500 yards, we were hit suddenly by devastating machine-gun and rifle fire that had hitherto been silent. There was the enemy in solid trenches with great parapets and dugouts sitting behind 10 or 15 coils of uncut wire, waiting for us. We lay on the frozen ground, for hours, as the snow drifted down. If we were wounded, there was no help because we were so close to the wire. But behind us there were artillery colonels and captains of the General Staff, drinking rum tea and writing their reports — "After brilliant artillery preparation, our glorious forces rushed forward to occupy the enemy trenches, but were held up by counterattack of strong reserves."'

Such strictures on uncaring commanders were altogether too true of much of the Russian army even in 1916. On the Southern Front things were changing. At the root of the changes was Brusilov, the new Front Commander. Formerly in charge of Eighth Army he had been successful in the Carpathian offensives of 1914–15 and he had important connections at court. However his success owed nothing either to patronage or reputation. Unlike almost any other Russian general of the period he had

actually set himself to analyze the nature of the war he was fighting and to find answers to the difficulties which recurred whenever an initial success was gained. As he saw it, the problem in the East was that shortage of supply obviated the possibility of making an attack on a wide front, which was possible only in the more affluent West. Attacks on a narrow front always failed because the enemy could manage to move his reserves to the spot quicker than the attacker could pass his through the breach. The answer was therefore to attack on several narrow but widely separated fronts at the same time, thus confusing the enemy as to which was the main thrust, and trust to psychological factors to widen the gap. Such a strategic surprise required for success, however, radical tactical reorganization. Foreign observers had been startled to discover that on the Russian Front as much as three miles of ground separated the two sides, with still inhabited villages carrying on their business in no man's land. Supporting artillery, as a result, could not reach deep into the enemy's positions while infantry attacks were spotted and broken up long before they reached the enemy's barbed wire. Brusilov changed all that. Along his whole front the first trench was carried forward to within 75 yards of the Austrian trenches and communication trenches and deep dugouts were constructed to shelter the troops moving up to avoid waiting

for the attack. The artillery carefully registered the locations of the enemy's batteries and the concentration points of local reserves.

All promised well, therefore, for Alexeiev's offensive in midsummer. Had his intentions been followed, Evert's much stronger Western Front would have undertaken it. Evert, however, demanded more time for preparation. In the meantime Conrad von Hötzendorf launched his own offensive, the counterpart to the German's at Verdun, in the Trentino against the Italians, an enemy whom the polyglot peoples of the Dual Monarchy were united in detesting. Italy's appeals for relief had to be met, so Alexeiev gave Brusilov permission to attack independently, which he did on 4 June. There were almost no German divisions left opposite his front — only two in the so-called German *Sudarmee* — and in a few hours' bombardment the Austrians, their trenches in ruin, had been reduced to trembling helplessness. When the High Command of the two worst hit armies — Archduke Joseph Ferdinand's Fourth and Pflanzer-Baltin's Seventh — sent up their reserves, they were swept away in a rout and the whole front began to cave in, just as Brusilov had planned. The armies in between, Second and *Sudarmee*, were carried back by the retirement of the flanks and by 20 June all four had lost over 200,000 prisoners to the enemy.

Pflanzer-Baltin's worries were particularly

Above: Artillerymen operate a Russian field gun during their defense of Poland in 1915.

Below: A German transport crosses the Vistula in 1915. Germany conquered Russian Poland throughout that year and invaded Russia proper subsequently.

Above: German cavalrymen enter Warsaw after its occupation in August 1915.

Top: General Brusilov became Commander in Chief of the Russian army in May 1917.

Top left: Austrian troops march into Russia watched by Russian POWs.

Left: Germans pause during their advance in Poland in 1915.

Above: German wounded prisoners are carried into captivity by Russian troops.

Below: Members of the 11th Bavarian infantry cross the Danube in 1915.

alarming because almost all his soldiers were Croats – the most *Kaisertreu* of all the Emperor's subjects – or warlike Hungarians, who were defending their own homeland in any case. Conrad von Hötzendorf appealed for help and the Germans, though scarcely in a position to help, were obliged to scrape together a relief force. It was assembled by 16 June around Kowel on the northern shoulder of the salient Brusilov had created and attacked at once though Falkenhayn did not know it. Brusilov's offensive had now run out of steam itself, after gaining up to 50 miles of territory in places so

that General Alexander von Linsingen, the German commander, did not catch the Russians in disorganized movement but when they had already halted to consolidate. His counter-offensive went slowly.

What saved the situation was an intervention designed to complete the Central Powers' discomfiture, Rumania's declaration of war on 27 August. France and Russia had long been urging her to come in on their side but, surrounded as she was by Bulgarian, Austrian and Austrian-occupied territory her reluctance was understandable. Greedy for Hungarian

lands inhabited by Rumanian speakers she was finally seduced by Brusilov's victory which implied an imminent Austrian collapse. Unfortunately her government and the Allies had miscalculated. Rumania's 23 divisions did not tip the balance in the East. They merely provided the Germans, who continued to display a conjuror's ability to produce reserves and move them rapidly wherever needed, with an easy target. Hindenburg and Ludendorff, who replaced Falkenhayn, disgraced by the failure of Verdun and the surprise of Brusilov's offensive, found no difficulty in assembling an army to

Left: Russian soldiers in gas masks in 1915.

Right: There were no survivors in this action during the Brusilov Offensive.

counter Rumania's invasion of Transylvania, the Rumanian-speaking province which she wanted. In fact they assembled four, the Austrian First, from the southern flank of the Russian Front, the new Ninth, under Falkenhayn in Transylvania, the Danube army under Mackensen, based in Bulgaria where most of its troops came from and a Turkish force which crossed the Black Sea to land at the mouth of the Danube. The Rumanian army which had taken some of Transylvania was thus encircled and quickly began to collapse, an outcome which surprised no Westerner, or Russian who had inspected it at close quarters. One provision of its mobilization orders was to forbid the use of cosmetics to officers under the rank of major. Between 25 September and 26 November the whole of Wallachia, Rumania's main southern province, fell into enemy hands. Bucharest, the capital, fell on 5 December and by 7 January the remnants of the Rumanian army to which the Russians had sent a relief force, had been forced back to the Sereth, a tributary of the Danube. Over half the country, and by far the most productive regions, had thus fallen under occupation and the Rumanians survived only as ancillaries to the Russians to whom they were of doubtful use.

Russia itself was now to undergo a national crisis, ultimately of far greater import to the Allied cause than Rumania's collapse. Despite Brusilov's military victory and the very re-markable adaptation to the demands of war in

Below: Russian soldiers push forward during the Brusilov Offensive in the summer of 1916.

the domestic society and economy, Russia in early 1917 was a deeply troubled country. Although agricultural production had never before been higher, the inflation to which the government had resorted as a means of paying for the war had frightened the peasants into withholding the fruit of their labor. The factory workers of the towns had thus begun to go hungry and to their distress was added the dis-satisfaction of the propertied classes on which war taxation principally fell, who also suffered because inflation eroded their fixed incomes.

On 12 March 1917 self-appointed repre-sentatives of 'workers' and 'soldiers' and some moderate and left-wing members of the Russian parliament (*Duma*) met in the Duma building in Petrograd and formed a council or Soviet. Together with the members of the Duma, it set up a Provisional Government, announcing that the Czar should be deposed. On 15 March the officers of the *Stavka*, convinced by the defec-tion of the Petrograd regiments that the reso-lution was irreversible, conveyed to the Czar their belief that he must abdicate 'to save our country as well as the dynasty, and in order to have the war prosecuted to victory.'

Far left: German soldiers lie dead during the Rumanian campaign of 1916.

Left: Rumanian troops on the march to Bitro in the Carpathians, 1916.

Not a sound broke the oppressive silence. The doors and windows of the imperial train were tightly closed. 'Ah! if only this painful silence could be over,' recounted General Danilov, who acted as the *Stavka*'s spokesman:

'Suddenly with an abrupt movement the Emperor turned toward us and declared in a firm voice. "I have made up my mind. I have decided to abdicate in favor of my son Alexis," whereupon he crossed himself with an ample sign of the cross. We, too, crossed ourselves. "Thank you all," he went on, "thank you for your brave and faithful service. I trust it will be continued under the reign of my son."'

The Czar eventually abdicated in favor of his brother, Grand Duke Michael, rather than his son, but the change was of absolutely no significance because of the ineffectiveness of the Provisional Government which had demanded it. Its authority was daily challenged by the Petrograd Soviet which demanded a republic, and undermined by the unpopularity of the war, which Alexander Kerensky, the Minister of War who had become the leading man of the regime, was determined nevertheless to carry on. He appointed Brusilov Commander in Chief, with orders to repeat his success of the previous year by opening the offensive against the Austro-German front. It began on 1 July 1917, a dual blow by 31 divisions against General Felix von Bothmer's *Sudarmee* and five days later against the Austrians on the Dniestr by another 13. Although the Germans had been warned, the attack had considerable initial success. The Russian soldiers however would not resume the advance after it had been temporarily halted. When out of sight of their officers they began to drift away from the front and after the German counterattack of 19 July the drift became a flood. The Russian front line was quickly driven back to the positions occupied before the so-called Kerensky offensive, where the remaining troops subsided into listless and surly inactivity, accepting orders only from the Soviets which had been elected to represent their views to the Provisional Government:

Left: Bulgarian trenches in 1917 as the war widened in the Balkans.

Below: Rumanian wounded take a bath in a field hospital.

'The trenches are incredibly defiled,' an observer recorded, 'in the narrow communication trenches and those of the second line the air is thick and close. The parapet is crumbling away. No one troubles to repair it; no one feels inclined to do so and there are not enough men in the company. There is a large number of deserters; more than 50 have been allowed to go. Old soldiers have been demobilized, others have gone on leave with the arbitrary permission of the Soviet. Others again have been elected members of numerous committees, or gone away as delegates; a while ago, for example, the Division sent a numerous delegation to 'Comrade' Kerensky, to verify whether he had really given orders to advance. Finally, by threats and violence, the soldiers have so terrorized the regimental surgeons that the latter have been issuing medical certificates even to the "thoroughly fit."'

Despite the failure of 'his' offensive, Kerensky, who in July became head of the Provisional Government, was unwilling to make peace. The Germans, anxious to end their Eastern campaign so that they could transfer strength to the West for a decisive campaign in the coming spring, therefore decided on an offensive to break the Russian army for good. The spot chosen was Riga, on the Baltic coast, from where Major General Max Hoffman, the Chief of Staff on the Eastern Front, believed it might even be possible to reach Petrograd. He nominated the artilleryman Bruchmüller, who had organized the bombardment for the counterattack to Kerensky's offensive, to plan the blow. Its secret ingredient was the use of massed batteries of artillery which opened fire without having previously ranged their guns. Although the gunners thereby sacrificed some accuracy they preserved surprise, which was devastating. The infantry advancing after the five-hour bombardment found almost no Russians present. Nine thousand were taken prisoner; the rest had run away. This behavior spelled doom to the Provisional Government. It was now threatened from within by General Lavr Kornilov, the general who had served notice on the Czar. After Brusilov's failure in the Kerensky offensive, Kornilov had taken his place as Commander in Chief and in September marched on Petrograd with the intention of turning the Provisional Government out. The attempt failed because his troops refused to follow him but it provoked Kerensky into releasing the Bolshevik leaders from jail, as a means of breaking the rising. As a result the Petrograd garrison began to heed the words of the Petrograd Soviet in preference to those of the Provisional Government. Since May the Soviet had increasingly come under the influence of Bolshevik émigrés who had returned home on the news of the Czar's depo-

Above: Alexander Kerensky, who led the Provisional government after the Czar's overthrow.

sition. Leon Trotsky had come from America, Vladimir Illych Lenin from Switzerland at the instigation of the German government, which had provided him with the notorious 'sealed train' as a means of transport.

The Germans had taken that decision because, though deeply hostile to Bolshevism they were prepared to compromise their political principles in the hope of strategic profit; the collapse of the Russian war effort from within. The result was by no means immediate, for Lenin's arrival in April was followed by months of intrigue before he was able to capture unshakeable control of the Petrograd Soviet. However when he did so, he struck decisively on 7 November (28 October Old Style). A Red Guard of workers, soldiers and sailors turned the Provisional Government out of its offices and on 8 November Lenin and his Council of People's Commissars proclaimed a Government of Workers and Peasants. Trotsky was installed as Commissar for Foreign Affairs, Josef Stalin, then a minor figure in the Bolshevik Party, as Commissar for the Nationalities.

Lenin and Trotsky proceeded, as the Germans had hoped, to open peace negotiations at once. Delegates from the two countries met at Brest-Litovsk, just behind the existing front line, and an armistice was arranged between Russia and the Central Powers to begin on 16 December. It proved difficult to move from the armistice to conclusive peace. The Russians, though threatened by imminent civil war at the hands of what were coming to be called the 'Whites' (in contradistinction to the Bolshevik 'Reds') were determined to ignore their own military helplessness and extract from the Germans an acceptance of the territorial status quo. Their terms were 'peace without annexation.' The Germans and Austrians, aware that it was not Allied policy to extract peace terms which would strip their two empires of their non-German speaking lands, signified their agreement, on the understanding that the Allies ratified the 'no annexation' clause and that the Russians excluded from it Poland and the Baltic States. Germany intended to set up an independent

Finland, Lithuania, Latvia, Estonia and a re-constituted Poland as client states of her own. Germany's hand was strengthened by the appearance at Brest-Litovsk of a self-appointed delegate from the Russian province of the Ukraine with a request that the Central Powers recognize his homeland's independence by concluding a separate peace with him.

Trotsky maneuvered with agility around the Germans' uncompromising insistence on their terms. As he had no cards to play, he was eventually compelled to withdraw from the negotiations, declaring his policy to be 'no peace no war.' However the Central Powers had meanwhile signed the so-called 'bread peace' with the Ukraine on 9 February, which gave them the right to station their troops on Ukrainian soil, and automatically transferred its produce from Russia to the hungry peoples of Germany and Austria. Defeated, Trotsky re-turned to Brest-Litovsk and on 3 March signed a treaty even harsher than that originally proposed, whereby Russia was obliged to cede the southern Caucasus region to Turkey. Mean-while the Finns, under the redoubtable ex-Czarist General Carl von Mannerheim, had declared independence and a White army had put down a Red rising sympathetic to the Petrograd Soviet.

The stage was now set for the most tragic passage in Russia's 20th-century history. At least three White armies were preparing to open civil war against the Red Army — created by

Trotsky — of the Workers' and Peasants' Government. With the Ukraine under German occupation, the Allies chose to regard the Bolsheviks as in the enemy's camp and so began to prepare expeditionary forces to intervene in Russia on the side of the Bolsheviks' enemies. This 'imperialist intervention' would lend sub-stance to the Bolsheviks' claim that the Whites were antipatriotic as well as antirevolutionary and allow them to call successfully on all Russian nationalists to join them in the fight for independence. A surprising number of ex-Czarist soldiers — officers as well as men — proved ready to do so. They included Brusilov, who became Inspector General of Trotsky's cavalry, Klembovski, a Czarist Corps Com-mander in 1914, Karbyshev, chief engineer of the Southwestern Front in 1914, and Kirey, artillery commander of the Czar's Ninth Army.

In the prism of history the Russian Revolution now appears as by far the most important out-come of the First World War, its effects dwarfing even those of Germany's ultimate defeat and Austria's dismemberment. At the time, its importance was judged chiefly in terms of the setback it caused to the strategy of the Allies, confronting them as in 1917 with the dread prospect of a one-front war with their chief enemy the German Empire. What is forgotten in the West, and concealed in the East, is how stoutly the Russians had fought, and how near they had brought the Central Powers to disaster in both 1914 and 1916.

Top left: The German and Austrian delegates at the Brest-Litovsk treaty signing, 3 March 1918.

Top right: Crowds scatter to the tattoo of sniper fire in Petrograd's Nevsky Prospekt during the first days of Russia's March Revolution in 1917.

Above: Germans fire at retreating Bolsheviks in early 1918.

Retreating Italian troops during the Austrian offensive in
Venetia, 1917.

8 1917: the Breaking of the Armies

At the beginning of 1917 the Western Allies had reason to believe that the year would go well for them. Russia remained a powerful ally which was retaining most of the Austrian and a third of the German army on the Eastern Front. Italy occupied the rest of the Austrians on the Isonzo, had successfully weathered Conrad von Hötzendorf's offensive in Trentino and seemed set to wear her way gradually through the barrier of the Julian Alps into the plains of Slovenia. There was growing expectation that America would enter the war bringing to the Allies as plentiful a supply of men as she was already contributing of food and munitions. The French and British still felt that their armies were in good fighting shape. The British army was stronger than it had ever been, with nearly 60 divisions, 3,000,000 men, in the field, most of them in France. The French with 100 divisions had survived Verdun, won back much of the ground lost there and made good at least some of their losses with new young conscripts and older men 'combed out' of civilian employment and static military units. Their material power was also on the increase. While the blockade progressively starved Germany of the essential metals and minerals, as well as the food, which her war machine required, the French enjoyed a glut of world production of both raw materials and finished goods, including increasing quantities of shell from American as well as their own factories. There were new weapons to add to their armories, not just improved models of heavy guns and airplanes — during the summer and autumn of 1917 British and French pilots would establish command of the skies over the Western Front — but also the tank, tested experimentally on the Somme and now in mass production in both countries.

Above: Poster for the French second War Loan invoking the slogan Verdun, *On les aura* (we will have them!).

Left: French soldiers prepare another advance over the bodies of their fallen comrades.

Right: General Nivelle, whose long awaited offensive threatened to destroy the remaining morale of the French Army.

So confident were both High Commands of their growing strength that they had planned for 1917 yet another great joint offensive. As in 1915 Joffre had called a conference at GQG at Chantilly in November 1916 to co-ordinate arrangements. Russian, Italian, Serbian, Belgian and Portuguese – whose country had declared war on Germany in March 1916 – had been present as well as British and French representatives. There was agreement to maintain pressure on all fronts, including those of the 'outer theaters' in Mesopotamia, Palestine and Macedonia. In France there was to be a renewal of the offensive on the Somme, excluding only that part of the front worst devastated by the fighting of the previous summer. Later, an offensive in Flanders would 'clear the Belgian coast,' thus unhinging the German line in the West and capturing the U-Boat bases of the North Sea. There was no thought of seeking peace on the strength of the achievements of 1916. Indeed, a peace initiative on the part of the new Emperor of Austria-Hungary, Karl I, who had succeeded the venerable Franz Josef in November 1916, met no response from the French government and a similar proposal by the Marquess of Lansdowne, a former Conservative Foreign Minister, which he circulated to the British Cabinet, was also ignored. The Pope's appeals went unheeded and, more significantly, so did those of President Woodrow Wilson of the United States who on 22 January 1917 appealed for all combatants to accept 'peace without victory.' The rejection of these appeals by the British and French is explained in part by the conditions for which they knew the Germans were still holding out: the cession of the Belgian Congo to Germany; surrender of the Briey-Longwy iron-ore area by France; establishment of German influence in Belgium or, in default, the surrender of Liège; 'improvement' of Austria's frontier with Italy, Rumania, Serbia or Montenegro – the rump of the latter was to be given to Albania; cession of some Serbian territory to Bulgaria and the further limitation of non-Turkish vessels' rights to use the Dardanelles. The seriousness of the German position was emphasized to the Allies by what they knew of the growing influence of Hindenburg and Ludendorff over the German government. As popular dissatisfaction with the hardships caused by the war grew and middle class resentment of socialist defeatism was reinforced by the war inflation's erosion of fixed incomes, the German establishment was demanding not a more conciliatory but a more extreme, triumphalist policy, since it now grasped that only through total victory could it recover all that it had lost through the war.

Joffre therefore pressed forward with his

Above: Some of the first British tanks in action near Amiens, 1917.

Below: A British tank obliterated near Cambrai.

Above: Britain's new Prime Minister David Lloyd George visits the Western Front.

Left: German sharpshooter in the front line in 1917.

plans in the confidence that he was doing the right thing for the alliance, but suddenly his own position of leadership was shaken. The military dictatorship toward which Hindenburg and Ludendorff were moving in Germany had long applied in France, at least within the war zone and the war committees of government. Foolishly, Joffre had sustained the emergency exclusion of members of parliament from the 'zone of the armies' and strictly curtailed the freedom of the press. On 13 December the Prime Minister, Aristide Briand, yielded to parliamentary protests so far as to promote Joffre to the meaningless post of 'technical military adviser' to the government, with a young general, Nivelle, as his executive representative at the front. That failed to quell dissatisfaction and he was compelled to secure Joffre's resignation on 26 December. Foch, his longtime protégé, a ferociously effective fire-eater but a man with many enemies, was simultaneously removed from command of Northern Army Group (though he was soon restored as commander of Eastern Army Group).

Nivelle's was a surprise appointment. A comparatively junior general, he had made his name under Pétain at Verdun, where he had planned the artillery tactics which had first matched and then overwhelmed the German gunnery offensive. As a tactician his star was in the ascendant. As a personality, he was favored by the politicians because his manner was open and explanatory in striking contrast to the sphinxian silence of Joffre. He enjoyed the timely advantage of speaking perfect English, the language of his mother. Moreover, once appointed he began to promise results. Joffre's caution had not allowed him to suggest that 1917 would be anything more than a year of attrition. Nivelle spoke of victory:

'Only the destruction of the principal mass of the enemy's forces,'

Left: British Signal Service operators with gas masks at a forward position in the front line.

he explained to Lloyd George, who was pressing for an attack in Italy,

'can bring about the end of the war. The principal mass of the German forces is on the Western Front. . . . It comprises 130 out of 200 divisions, and includes the best troops. To beat them, it is necessary in the first place to break through the trench system. Is this operation possible? To this question the army of Verdun, in the fighting between 24 October and 15 December (1916) has given an affirmative answer.' (These were the successful local offensives which had recaptured Forts Vaux and Douaumont, so making Nivelle's reputation.) 'We will break through the German front when we wish, on condition that we do not attack it at its strongest point, and that the operation is carried out by a sudden surprise attack and is not extended beyond 24 or 48 hours.'

In private conversation, Nivelle expanded on this optimistic promise. 'I have the secret,' he exulted. After three years of war and a dozen attempts on the inviolability of the German trench system by French and British armies, he believed that he had found a formula which had hitherto escaped the questing minds of all the commanders and staff officers in the two great Allied Headquarters, as well as those of the German army which had also 'found the secret' before Verdun. In essence, his plan was to assemble an enormous mass of artillery in secrecy and open fire without warning along the whole chosen front of attack, and deep into the enemy positions behind. The intended effect was to destroy all opposing German batteries and paralyze the enemy's means of communication and reinforcement. At the same time deep masses of infantry would move forward, following a rolling barrage at a distance of only 70 meters from the curtain of exploding shells. When they had occupied the enemy trenches, a solid block of reserves would pass onward, to be followed by the cavalry which would exploit the breakthrough by debouching into open country.

Skeptics might argue that the formula looked little different from that attempted by Haig on the Somme in July 1916. Pessimists might mutter that he had selected the least promising sector of the front for his attack, since it was to be on the Chemin des Dames, the ridge where the first Allied counteroffensive of the war had miscarried in September 1914. Nivelle's optimism was unshaken — even in the face of

the most remarkable event yet to occur on the Western Front; a secret German withdrawal from the center of the great salient which he planned to pinch out. Part of Nivelle's scheme was for the British to attack a week earlier at Arras, north of the Somme, so as to draw off the German reserves from the Chemin des Dames. On 16 March, however, it was noticed that the enemy's normal artillery fire was dwindling along the whole of the Somme Front and when reconnaissance was made the German lines were found to be weakly held. Bad weather and indecision inhibited any vigorous probing and 29 German divisions were thus allowed to steal back 30 miles to a new but enormously strong position, later to be called by the Allies the Hindenburg Line, which the Germans had

Above: Austrian troops prepare to throw hand grenades in September 1917.

surreptitiously constructed between Arras and the Chemin des Dames.

The British offensive, which opened on 9 April in a raging snowstorm could not therefore strike into the northern flank of the Germans' Somme salient, since it had disappeared, nor could it draw off the whole of the German reserve, since the shortening of their line had increased its size. The British chose to regard the battle of Arras as a success — which it was in terms of ground won on the battlefield — but strategically it was of no significance, and therefore a positive setback to Nivelle's plan. Moreover, he had talked. The eloquence of his

Below: David Lloyd George is greeted by General Haig and Marshal Joffre in September 1916.

Below: Aristide Briand served as a War Minister and Prime Minister of France during World War I.

exposition, which had so impressed Lloyd George, was not a talent he kept for private performances. Anxious to change the command arrangements on the Western Front so that the British Expeditionary Force should become a tool of a single unified command, he had used his charm, and his ideas, on dinner-party audiences all over London in January. Word had inevitably filtered to the Germans of a coming offensive on the French Front and aerial reconnaissance had then pinpointed the spot for them. Toward it they had moved the divisions released by their withdrawal to the Hindenburg Line, so that whereas in January there had been only 18 divisions along the Chemin des Dames, by April there were 42 with 2451 guns, to oppose 46 French divisions with 3810.

Yet, just as Nivelle's optimism remained intact, so did that of this attacking army. Corporal Georges Gandy of the 57th Infantry Regiment describes the mood in the last days of preparation:

'The air was filled with enthusiasm and a heroic mood prevailed in each of us. Officers and soldiers refused to go on leave so as not to miss the great offensive. "Boy, what an attack," the *poilus* (front-line soldiers) were saying to each other, "eighty divisions to go over the top. We've never been that many! This is it, pals! If we don't get them this time, we'll never get them."'

When the French infantry did jump off to 'get them' on 16 April, however, they found that Nivelle's promise of possessing 'a secret' meant no more than any of the other empty words of generals in the three hard years which had gone before. Observing from a distance a French officer of the new tank arm saw:

'Our men's wave, unbroken a moment ago, spread out again and then progressing in zigzag fashion. Here and there the men would crowd together without advanc-ing, having met some obstacle which we couldn't see, most likely one of those accursed, still intact barbed-wire networks.'

Soon afterward the first wounded began to make their way back and their hasty explanations gave the observer a clue as to what was happening:

'A helmetless lieutenant, his clothes torn and a wound in his chest, walked slowly toward our group. "If only you had been with us. We found nothing but barbed wire. If it hadn't been for that, we'd have been far ahead by now, instead of being killed where we stand." "We just couldn't keep moving," shouted an alert corporal, who was using his rifle as a crutch. "Too many blasted machine guns, which we couldn't do anything against."'

In fact 16 April was a disaster comparable to the first day of the Battle of the Somme. The hospital services were overwhelmed even as far away as Paris where the trains took the wounded, and members of parliament, able for the first time to witness the effects of a battle at close quarters, were appalled. Nivelle nevertheless gave orders that the attack was to be renewed the next day, and the subsidiary offensive in Champagne ('The Third Battle of Champagne') maintained. By 20 April the Aisne valley had been regained and 20,000 prisoners taken. Nivelle, cheated of his breakthrough, was outwardly more certain than ever of victory and decided to use his reserves for a final big push on 25 April. Subordinate commanders pleaded for only a modest maintenance of pressure, but he was adamant. The government was now alarmed and insisted Nivelle wait until 5 May, meanwhile appointing Pétain Chief of Staff, a post vacant since Joffre had been made Commander in Chief at the outbreak of the war. On the appointed day, heavy artillery fire preceded the assault. A Sergeant of the 128th Regiment describes what followed:

'In the early morning of 6 May, at the appointed hour, our men were full of dash when they launched their assault. They practically reached their objective, at least in the gap where our artillery had opened a gap in the enemy's defense zone. This was very little, as no

Above: A French attack on German positions near the Aisne, 16 April 1917.

Above right: 5th Australian Infantry Brigade parades through the Grande Place of Bapaume in March 1917 in utter disregard of the ruins around them.

Below: German storm troops train near Sedan in 1917.

Top far left: Camouflaged British armored car and gun near Arras in 1917.

Center far left: The battlefield at Mont des Sapins near the Aisne in April 1917.

Bottom far left: Aerial view of Mont Cornillet, Champagne, in May 1917.

Left: Tommies carry a wounded buddy back to their lines.

Top: French advance first wave hits the Chemin des Dames as the Germans retreat in the background.

Above: Marshal Philippe Pétain, the inspiration of French *poilus* during and after Verdun.

Above: General Sir Herbert CO Plumer, later Lord Plumer, British commander at the Third Battle of Ypres.

less than 16 gaps had been expected but the observations made by the Colonel and the battalion commanders had not been taken into account by the higher staff. The 2nd Battalion ran into an intact barbed-wire network and into the fire of the German machine guns, which our artillery had not been able to neutralize. The regiment was relieved on 15 May and the position it had conquered was lost. Our men were deeply disappointed. They realized that their sacrifices were useless, perhaps even needless.'

The government decided to relieve Nivelle and replace him with Pétain on 15 May. His was a name the troops trusted and the French Government hoped that he, as a man known to value the lives of his soldiers, would be able to restore the shaken morale of the divisions which

had taken part in what had come to be called the 'Nivelle offensive.' Its effects had spread even wider, deeper and faster than had been feared. During the month of April the French army had lost 100,000 men by official record; unofficially the figure was put at 200,000. In the five armies which had taken part in the attack, there began an outbreak of what the High Command called 'acts of collective indiscipline' which have since been generally recognized as mutinies. The 'indiscipline' took the form of infantry units refusing to go up to the front; demonstrations against the war, particularly by men returning from leave; the flying of red flags; throwing stones at transport and rear-area troops; minor sabotage of the railroad and occasional attacks on officers, usually ones already unpopular. The disorders affected 54 divisions altogether, over half the French army, and were eventually quelled by a mixture of bribes and threats. About 55 men identified as ringleaders were shot and 300 men were sent to Devil's Island. Another 20,000 were court-martialled but their sentences were commuted. At the same time, more generous leave was promised, family allowances to soldiers' wives increased and canteens and recreation facilities in the zone of the armies improved. Loyal men held the line while the work of rehabilitation went on and the artillery, which was not affected by the mutinies, continued to keep up its program of fire into the German lines. Pétain travelled ceaselessly about the front, assuring the soldiers that he had their welfare at heart, and gradually the army was weaned from its resentment and inactivity, which in retrospect is perhaps best thought of as a large-scale military strike rather than a mutiny. Curiously, no word of it reached the Germans until it was over. Though the mutineers had, in fact, always assured their officers that they would defend their trenches if forced to do so. What they refused to do was attack.

The onus of the effort on the Western Front Army during the troubled summer of 1917 therefore fell upon the British Army. Still strong despite the losses of the Somme, and in good

Above right: Two men of the Scots Guards in the mud of Ypres (Passchendaele).

Top far right: An expression of public doubt during the Third Battle of Ypres.

Below: Mine crater at Messines Ridge, June 1917.

WHAT A LIFE! LLOYD GEORGE GIVES THE KID
THIRTY BOB TO COME INTO THE WORLD, AND LORD DERBY
GIVES THE FATHER TWO AND NINE TO GET OUT OF IT!

WAR NEWS
ANOTHER
GREAT
BATTLE-
ENORMOUS
CASUALTIES!

Above: German infantrymen return from battle. German morale remained high as French and British morale declined after three years of attritional war.

spirits even though it was now depending upon conscripts instead of volunteers to fill the gaps in its ranks, the BEF was ready for another offensive as soon as Arras was over. Haig, a strategic free agent as long as Pétain was occupied with the mutinies, had his own firm ideas about where that offensive should take place. He had made his name in Flanders, at the First Battle of Ypres in 1914; when all seemed hopeless he had strapped on his sword, mounted his horse and ridden out up the Menin Road to die among his troops. The line had held and his death had not proved necessary, but the epic moment had fixed in him an obsession with Ypres. It was a purely British battlefield, at the furthest point of the line from the French sector. Any success won there would redound solely to the credit of his army. To a fierce patriot like Haig, that prospect was extremely enticing; it

Left: German bodies in a Passchendaele trench, July 1917.

Right: German POWs are paraded through a Belgian town by their Canadian captors.

Below: A horse-drawn water cart breaks down in the mud of Ypres, August 1917.

GIVSEPPE ZVCCA

LA VANGHETTA
DEL FANTE

DISEGNI DI DVILIO CAMBELLOTTI

ANNO XVII   APRILE 1916

LA LETTVRA

was made all the more so by the narrow escape he had recently had from subordination to Nivelle.

Between 4 May and 2 June, therefore, he secured the agreement both of the French High Command — who urged him to take all the pressure he could off its front — and his own government, though the latter was now becoming very suspicious of his costly schemes, to mount an attack 'to clear the Belgian coast.' As a preliminary his Second Army, commanded by Sir Herbert Plumer, undertook to widen the Ypres salient by the capture of the Messines Ridge. This attack, which opened on 7 June had, like all Plumer's operations, been meticulously planned. Two thousand guns covered the advance of nine divisions, which was preceded by the explosion of 19 enormous mines (one failed to explode and the fusing mechanism was lost; activated by a bolt of lightning in 1956, it left a crater as large as a small field). The German defenders were either blown out of existence, stunned by the bombardment, or easily taken prisoner. Limited though it was in scale, Messines was the first wholly successful British battle of the war so far.

It augured well for the coming third battle of Ypres (Passchendaele, as it came to be called).

Haig now decided to transfer planning responsibility from Plumer to his own protégé, Hubert Gough, a cavalry general of 47 who had won notoriety before the war for his part in the so-called 'Curragh Mutiny.' Haig's apologists were later to argue that Passchendaele required a boldness which the painstaking Plumer could not manage. Boldness may well have been in Haig's mind but what the particular circumstances of the Ypres Salient required was exactly that step-by-step method which Plumer had made peculiarly his own. For here the terrain favored the defender very strongly. Beyond the little walled-fortress city the open plain rose in a series of shallow swells toward the distant Passchendaele ridge from which the Germans could observe every movement in the British positions. The ground, moreover, was waterlogged, a potential marshland which a combination of rain and heavy shelling would

Far left: Italian propaganda poster of 1917.

Left: Italian magazine of 1916 depicts an idealized version of their mountain troops' struggle against the Austrians.

Right: Anti-Communist Italian propaganda in 1918.

Below: Stretcher bearers bring back a wounded comrade near Boesinghe, Ypres, August 1917.

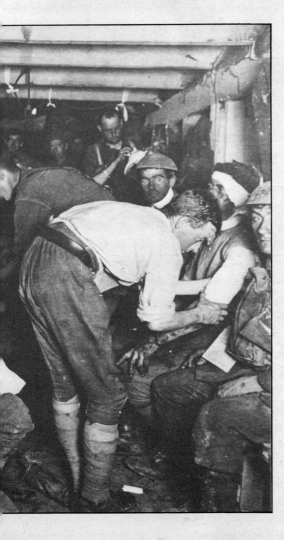

quickly turn into a quagmire. Heavy shelling was a necessity, because the Germans had fortified this part of the front in great depth, studding their trench lines with concrete pillboxes, many of which had been built inside derelict cottages and farm buildings so that their construction was concealed from British observation.

The battle began on 31 July after a week's bombardment and as it opened so too did un-seasonably heavy rain. It continued until 4 August, by which time two miles of ground had been won and 32,000 casualties suffered. Gough, declaring this to be the 'first stage' of the battle, then announced a pause. The attack was renewed on 6 August and persisted for two days, but only a sliver of ground was captured. The German commander opposite professed himself unworried by the offensive, since he had ample reserves, the best of which were now held back and committed only when a British thrust had pushed in deep enough to lose the support of its own artillery.

Doubt in the wisdom of Haig's battle had now spread from the Cabinet to his own officers. Brigadier Baker-Carr, visiting General Head-quarters at Montreuil from the front, expressed his disquiet with 'candor and vigorous language' over lunch, announcing that 'the battle was dead as mutton' and had been so since the second day. After lunch he was summoned to the office of General Davidson, the Director of Operations:

'On entering, I found him seated at his table, his head in his hands.

"I am very much upset by what you said at lunch. . . . A man of your knowledge and experience had no right to speak as you did."

"You asked me how things were and I told you frankly."

"But what you say is impossible."

"It isn't. Nobody has any idea of the conditions."

"But they can't be as bad as you make out."

"Have you been there yourself?"

"No."

"Has anybody in Operations been there?"

"No."

"Well then, if you don't believe me, it would be as well to send somebody up to find out."'

Baker-Carr's description had been of a battle-field reduced to a series of interconnecting ponds, water-filled shell holes, on which all roads and tracks had disappeared and men were sometimes drowned in liquid mud. Even Haig was now shaken by the lack of progress and mounting toll of lives and turned to Plumer again for a solution. That steady old soldier, asked to clear the right-hand side of the salient into which the British were attacking, demanded time so that he could make proper preparations. He was favored by a spell of sunshine and drying winds so that when his meticulous attack began on 25 September all went well for some days. A succession of short advances, each like the Messines success of June, carried the British to the crest of the ridge from which the Germans had hitherto overlooked Ypres. Haig was encouraged and ordered a similar advance on the left-hand side of the salient, to begin on 9 October. The rains of autumn, which could not be explained away as seasonal bad luck, now set in uninterruptedly and turned the last month of the battle into a soldiers' hell.

An Australian officer on 10 October found the slope below Poelcapelle:

Above far left: Men of the 13th Durham Light Infantry on the Menin Road Ridge before their attack on 20 September 1917 near Veldhoek.

Above left: Wounded at an advanced dressing station near Ypres.

Below: British troops pull an 18-pounder out of the mud near Langemarck, 16 October 1917.

Above: Germans cut down trees to block an Allied advance near Havrincourt, 20 November 1917.

Top: Austrian troops advance during the Trentino offensive of 1916.

Below: Canadians bring in their wounded at Passchendaele, 6 October 1917.

Above left: 'Clapham Junction,' looking toward Sanctuary Wood at Passchendaele, 23 September 1917.

Top right: A 5.9-inch naval gun is captured at Cambrai, 29 November 1917.

Above right: German prisoner is captured at Havrincourt near Cambrai, November 1917.

Above: Leicester Regimental machine gunners in a captured second-line trench at Cambrai, 20 November 1917.

'littered with dead, both theirs and ours. . . . I found about 50 men alive, of the Manchesters. Never have I seen men so broken or demoralized. They were huddled up behind a pillbox in the last stages of exhaustion and fear. The Germans had been sniping them off all day and had accounted for 57 – the dead and dying lay in piles. The wounded were numerous – unattended and weak, they groaned and moaned all over the place. Some had been there four days already. Finally the company came up – the men done in after a fearful struggle through the mud and shell-holes, not to speak of the barrage. The position was obscure – a dark night – no line – demoralized Tommies – and no sign of the enemy. I spent the rest of the night in a shell hole, up to my knees in mud and with the rain teeming down.'

Despite these awful scenes, Haig – and whatever his faults of stubbornness and monomania, he did go and look for himself – refused to call off the offensive until the beginning of November, justifying his persistence by the stated need to hold the best line possible for the coming months of winter. When on 10 November 'Passchendaele' was officially closed down it had cost 240,000 British casualties. At its deepest point, the advance had been pushed six miles into enemy territory on a front of 10 miles. Ypres was still in a salient, if a slightly larger one. The Belgian coast remained uncleared. The German line had not been unhinged. Haig was convinced that he had done the right thing.

He was aware that his supporters in the Cabinet had dwindled in number and that Lloyd George was anxious to be rid of him. This sense of insecurity had prompted him earlier in the autumn to take up the proposals of the new Tank Corps for a tank offensive on a part of the front as yet untouched by heavy fighting. It had been carefully prepared during the last bitter stages of Passchendaele and was ready by 20 November. The place chosen was the ground in front of Cambrai, between Ypres and the Somme, high chalk downland, dry and unpitted by shell fire. Four hundred and seventy-six tanks had been assembled and, after a brief dawn bombardment, they lumbered off into the

German positions, the infantry of eight divisions following cautiously behind, with five cavalry divisions – 25,000 horsemen – waiting in the rear for the chance to ride deep into enemy territory.

The Germans whom the massed tanks found in their trenches were, almost without exception, terrorized into instant surrender by the appearance of the monsters. The Hindenburg Line was breached for little loss of life and at the end of the day the front had been advanced three miles. Yet a clear breakthrough had once again eluded the British army. The fault for that lay with the commander of the division attacking in the center of the front, the 51st Highland. Mistrusting the tanks, he had ordered his infantry to keep their distance. As a result, the tanks going forward unsupported had been destroyed by gunfire. When the infantry, who might have driven off the gun crews, came up they were shot down by machine gunners, who would have been silenced by the tanks had they still been in action.

A week after the initial success, the Germans counterattacked, reclaimed most of the ground lost and even captured an unwary British general asleep in his pajamas in his command dugout. Haig did his best to minimize the extent of the humiliation but it gave Lloyd George the excuse for which he had been looking to forbid him any more fresh troops who would, in the Prime Minister's view, only be wasted in pointless or ill-organized attacks. Further force was given to his determination by a sudden and chilling turn of events in Italy whose government had been forced by it to make urgent appeals for men and guns to the French and British.

Italy's war thus far had been an even more depressing essay in fruitless attrition than the Western Allies'. She had declared hostilities against Austria in May 1915 with the declared aim of winning from the Dual Monarchy those pieces of Italian-speaking territory which she claimed as *Italia irredenta* – unredeemed Italy. In particular she wanted the Trentino in the north, and Trieste in the east, toward which her main offensive effort was made throughout 1915 and 1916. Unfortunately, Trieste lay across the high

Above: The Kaiser and Prince Rupprecht inspect a heavy British gun captured at Cambrai.

Above right: Men of the 51st British Division cross a German communications trench near Cambrai in November 1917.

Right: British tanks pass captured German guns on the way to Bourlon Wood, Cambrai, in November 1917.

barrier of the Julian Alps and the Italian armies had spent two years attempting to win footholds in the mountains on the far side of the Isonzo River which crossed its foothills. No less than 11 Battles of the Isonzo had been launched. Very little ground had been won if any, but enormous losses had been suffered; over 600,000 casualties. Despite that the size of the Italian army had been built up to 60 divisions, many men returning from the United States to volunteer for the patriotic war, and in the Eleventh Battle, fought between 18 August and 12 September 1917, the Italians had caused a serious breach in the Austrian line which threatened a breakthrough. General Count Luigi Cadorna, the Italian commander, at once laid plans for a new effort, word of which so alarmed Conrad von Hötzendorf and his chief Staff Officer, General Arthur Arz von Straussenburg, that they appealed to the Germans for help.

During late September and early October, Hindenburg and Ludendorff found six divisions to send to the Italian front, of which four were mountain-trained. They included the Alpenkorps, a division of Bavarian ski troops to which was attached the Württemberg Mountain Battalion. Already notable among its officers was a company commander, the young Erwin Rommel. The coming battle was to offer him the fullest opportunity to demonstrate his dash and fire in attack. Early in the morning of 24 October the German and Australian artillery opened fire on the Italian lines, using shells filled with a gas against which the Italian gas masks gave no protection. When the Fourteenth Army, the Austro-German attack force, moved into the Italian trenches it found them largely deserted. The defenders had fled before the deadly cloud. Particularly important were the footholds obtained by the attackers at Caporetto and

Above: Italian Alpine troops depicted in a Sunday magazine.

Above: General Pietro Badoglio, who made his reputation in both world wars.

Tolmino (Karfreit and Tolmein), because there the Isonzo crossed the front, to run in a loop behind the Italian lines. Advances down its valley from either place thus acted as pincer movements around a huge chunk of the Italian garrison, and would cause their capture. Rommel was quick to see the possibilities. When his regimental commander looked like showing too much caution, Rommel simply took his leave and departed into the mountains, carrying with him his 250 Swabian mountaineers.

In the next 36 hours Rommel and his men captured 9000 Italian prisoners, including a whole regiment of 1500 which he trapped between the fire of his machine guns in a narrow valley. So outstanding were his exploits that he won the *Pour le mérite*, the order founded by Frederick the Great to honor the greatest acts of courage and leadership. The success at Caporetto, as the battle would be called, exceeded individual deeds of derring-do. The

Italian reserves, marching up the roads to the fractured front, began quickly to be outflanked by enemy mountain troops who were moving behind them along the mountain ridges. Reserve positions quickly became the front line and then had to be abandoned because they had been taken by the enemy. On 25 October the situation was already so desperate that Cadorna had to order a retreat to the Tagliamento river, well inside Italian territory, and toward it the Second Army (one of the three on the Isonzo) which had taken the brunt of the Caporetto Strike, began to make its way. In truth no authority could have stopped it. Of its men, 180,000 had already been taken prisoner; the remaining 400,000 were a crowd of stragglers and fugitives. No sooner had they reached the Tagliamento than the speed of the enemy pursuit convinced Cadorna that they could not stop there. So he gave orders to fall back again to the Piave, which runs into the sea only 15 miles North of Venice. The Italian army

had retreated, when it was reached on 10 November, over 60 miles in two weeks and abandoned not only all the territory it had gained in three years of war but a great swathe of the homeland to Austrian occupation.

The personal consequences of the disaster were swift. Cadorna, never a popular general as he was considered to be indifferent to casualties, was dismissed and replaced by General Armando Diaz. In Britain and France which had by mid-November dispatched 11 divisions to help shore up the Piave front, the politicians' patience with their generals, whom they felt should have taken steps to aid the Italians earlier but had selfishly ignored the danger, was growing very thin. Lloyd George would dearly liked to have sent Haig Cadorna's way. However, unable to find a satisfactory substitute, he agreed with the French Prime Minister a plan to set up a Supreme War Council, to which the generals would be subordinate, which would have the power to survey and provide for the strategic needs of all the fronts as a unity.

The French Prime Minister with whom Lloyd

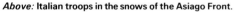

Above: Italian troops in the snows of the Asiago Front.

Above right: A fallen Hussar on the bleak Italian Front.

Right: A fanciful depiction of the skill of Italian Alpine troops.

George dealt was new: Georges Clemenceau, the 'Tiger.' Though new, he was not young, indeed at 78 he was one of the oldest members of the French parliament. His spirit was that of an impatient hothead, and his character was very much to Lloyd George's taste:

Below: Italian General Luigi Cadorna, who was quickly dismissed after the Caporetto disaster.

Below left: Victims of the Central Powers' breakthrough at Caporetto.

Far left: Italian Bersaglieri officers present a dashing appearance.

Left: An Austrian 30.5cm artillery piece in Zompicchia in November 1917.

Right: Austrian storm troopers break out of their foxholes for an assault.

Below: Italian Marines go over the top in 1917.

Right: General Cadorna was replaced by General Diaz as Chief of Staff of the Italian forces.

Above: Clemenceau visits the front line.

Left: Hoisting a '75 gun up an Italian peak.

'He had insulted every prominent politician in France and conciliated none. He had no party or group attached to him. I once said of him that he loved France but hated all Frenchmen. That is a substantially fair account of his personal attitude throughout his career.'

By the end of 1917 there was no French politician who commanded wide respect in parliament. Clemenceau's offensiveness was therefore irrelevant. His fighting temper very much was not. Raymond Poincaré, the President, had decided that the choice of leader lay between Clemenceau and Joseph Caillaux, who was a notorious defeatist and would probably organize a peace party out of like-minded deputies. Therefore, though he cordially disliked the 'Tiger' (he had suffered his insults), he decided to entrust him with the government, a decision he communicated on 15 November.

Five days later the old man stood before the chamber of deputies and delivered a battle cry of a speech which quashed all German hopes of bringing France to a negotiated peace:

'We stand here before you,' he declaimed, 'with but one thought; to pursue the war relentlessly. No more pacifist campaigns, no treachery, no semi-treachery. Only now, nothing but war. Our armies are not going to be caught between two fires. Justice shall be established. The country shall know that it is being defended.'

Left: Italian Alpine soldiers in position atop a rocky crag near the Austrian frontier.

His arrival transformed the atmosphere of French politics and also its personnel. Caillaux was imprisoned for treason in January 1918, and Jean Malvy, the Minister of the Interior, was sentenced to five years in exile. Bolo, a political intriguer believed to be in German pay, was guillotined for treason in April 1918 and scores of other lesser agents of defeatism or espionage were also executed or imprisoned. Most exotic if probably least significant of the victims of the purge was Mata Hari, the dancer and courtesan, who was shot in the moat of the Château of Vincennes. She made a dramatic impression by refusing to be blindfolded and blowing a kiss to her lawyer from the execution stake.

The French army, rested during the summer months, had been weaned back to the offensive in October by Pétain, who had arranged a few carefully prepared small attacks which were calculated to be successful. The appointment of Clemenceau ('Foreign policy? – I make war. Home policy? – I make war. Everywhere, always, I make war.') had a further heartening effect on its morale. The mood of the British army was less certain. Wilfred Owen, writing an epilogue to the year, remembered that:

'last year at this time . . . I lay awake in a windy tent in the middle of a vast terrible encampment. It seemed neither France nor England but a kind of paddock where the beasts are kept a few days before the shambles. I heard the revelling of the Scotch troops, who are now dead, and who knew they would be dead. I thought of the present night (31 December 1917) and whether I should indeed survive . . . but I thought neither long nor deeply, for I am a master of elision. But chiefly I thought of the very strange look on all the faces in that camp; an incomprehensible look, which a man will never see in England; nor can it be seen in any battle. It was not despair, or terror, it was more terrible than terror, for it was a blindfold look, and without expression like a dead rabbit's. It will never be painted and, no actor will ever seize it. And to describe it I think I must go back and be with them. We are sending seven officers straight out tomorrow. I have not said what I am thinking this night, but next December I will surely do so.'

Wilfred Owen would not live to see December 1918. He had already written his own epitaph, and that for the men whose faces he had watched with such clinical pity at base camp:

Above: Digging trenches atop the Dolomites.

Above right: Austrians capture an Italian town in the Alps.

Above far right: The Kaiser visits the former Doge's Palace in Passariano on the Italian Front.

Below: Wilfred Owen, the Welsh war poet.

Right: Italian POWs march into captivity near the Piave.

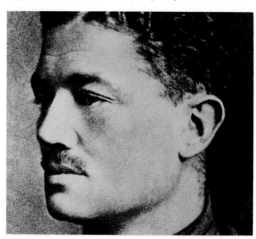

What passing bells for those who die as cattle?
– Only the monstrous anger of the guns.
Only the stuttering rifles' rapid rattle
Can patter out their hasty orisons.
No mockeries now for them; no prayers nor bells;
Nor any voice of mourning save the choirs –
The shrill, demented choirs of wailing shells;
And bugles calling for them from sad shires.
What candles may be held to speed them all?
Not in the hands of boys, but in their eyes
Shall shine the holy glimmer of goodbyes.
The pallor of girls' brows shall be their pall;
Their flowers the tenderness of patient minds.
And each slow dusk a drawing-down of blinds.

The British army had not broken in 1917, but it had been brought to the brink. Too many of its soldiers had now died like cattle for the remainder to hope for anything much more from the war but survival, national or perhaps personal. They were waiting on both for the coming of the Americans. So too was the other great intact army of the World War, the German. It had work to do before the doughboys arrived.

Some of the first American troops sent to France arrive at St Nazaire.

9 The Yanks are Coming

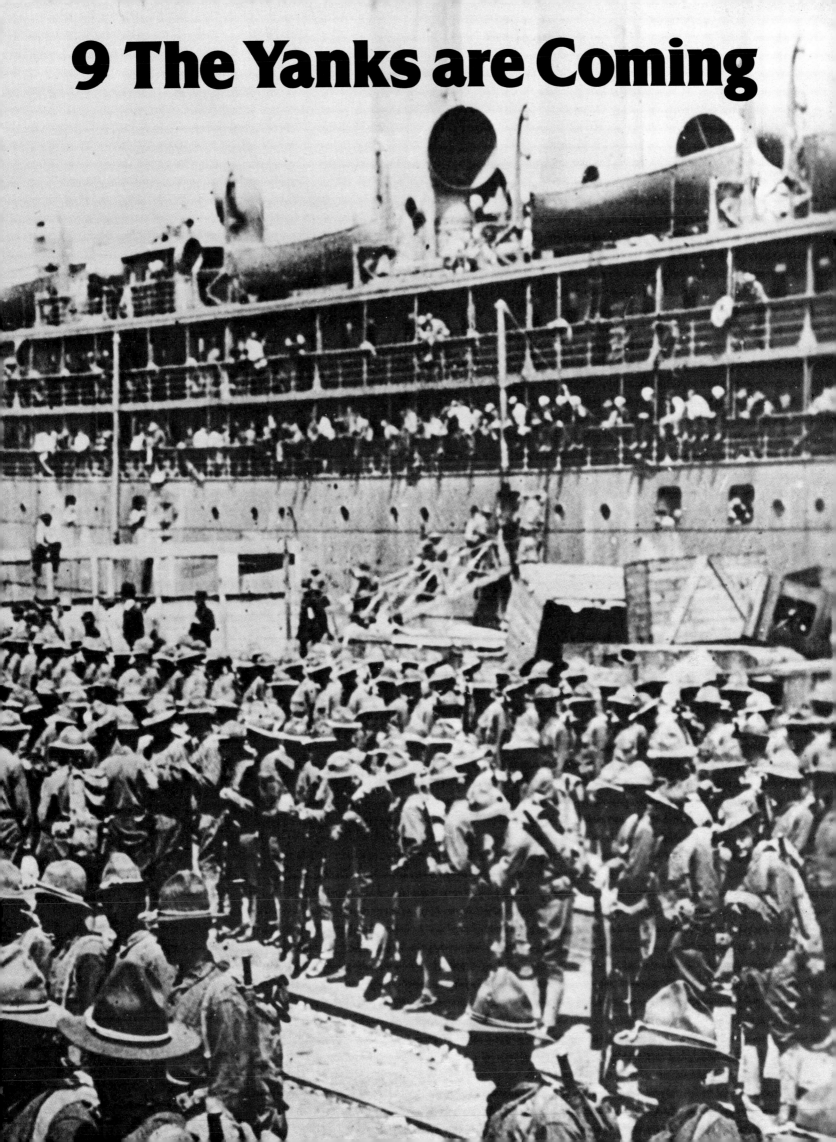

America had struggled against entering the war. It was being fought far from her shores. It threatened neither her territory nor, apparently, her vital interests. The large German minority in the United States, descendants of immigrants who had sought the good life there in the 19th century, were vociferous in opposition to American entry, against which the traditional voice of American isolationism also spoke loud. There were other minority groups, particularly the Irish, who had good reason to oppose any change of policy which would benefit Britain. Had Germany played her diplomatic cards sensitively she might well have ensured the continuance of American neutrality even if that neutrality had favored Britain or France rather than Germany. Germany chose not to do so. Since she could not benefit from the commercial connection with the United States, while the Allies could, she sought to interrupt it by attacking the mechanism of blockade which the Royal Navy had created even though such interruption had inevitably to lead to the sinking of American ships, or the loss of American lives carried in foreign ships sailing to European ports. The first great incident of the sort was the sinking of the *Lusitania* off Southern Ireland on 8 May 1915 which, though a British liner, carried many Americans among its 2000 passengers. The attack, coming only three years after the sensation of the *Titanic* sinking seemed like a deliberate re-enactment of a natural disaster, and outraged American opinion which, for a time, led to the cessation of 'unrestricted' sinkings by U-Boats in the war zone. However, the *Lusitania* was carrying munitions and Germany did not violate international law in sinking the ship. Only American sensitivity was violated.

As the blockade bit deeper, German prudence wilted. The hardships it caused led to a resurgence of left-wing opposition to the war to which the right and the government reacted to by hardening their war aims. What had been started as a war for national self-interest was increasingly seen by the directing class of the German Empire as a war for national survival in which the stakes justified the taking of higher and higher risks. Effective power passed, with the approval of the industrial, commercial and

Right: US call to the colors in 1917.

Below right: A consignment of Americans arrives in Lorraine as newsreel cameras record the event.

Below: A doughboy befriends some French children.

WAKE UP, AMERICA!

CIVILIZATION CALLS
EVERY MAN WOMAN AND CHILD!

MAYOR'S COMMITTEE 50 EAST 42ND ST

Beat back the **HUN** *with* **LIBERTY BONDS**

Above: The call to arms was especially virulent once America entered the war.

Above: President Wilson and his wife, who took over many of his duties when he was stricken in 1919.

Top: The drive to buy Liberty Bonds raised billions from American citizens.

professional sections of society from civilian politicians to the High Command. Where Ludendorff enthusiastically pursued a total war policy, Holzendorff, the chief of the Naval Staff, had easily persuaded him at the beginning of 1917 that a return to unrestricted sinkings was essential and that by those means Germany would make British sue for peace before the autumn harvest 'even taking into account a break with America.' Accordingly the step was decided upon, and a note declaring it delivered to the American Secretary of State, Robert Lansing, on 31 January, only 24 hours before it was to be put into effect. President Wilson naturally regarded the discourtesy as insulting. On 3 February he announced the severing of diplomatic relations with Germany. A week later the staff of the American Embassy in Berlin left for home:

'The train which left Berlin on the night of 10 February carried the happiest group of Americans who had been in Europe since the war began,' wrote an American journalist who accompanied the party. 'When the Swiss border was reached the Stars and Stripes was hung from the car windows and Americans breathed again in a free land. They felt like prisoners escaping from a penitentiary. Most of them had been under suspicion or surveillance for months. They were delighted to escape the land, where everything is "verboten" except hatred and militarism.'

Many Americans remained steadfastly opposed to any further move toward war. The transmission to the American government by the British Secret Service of secret communications between Germany and Mexico further converted public opinion to the inevitability of intervention. The key document was the Zimmermann Telegram, made public by Wilson on 1 March. In it the German Foreign Secretary promised the Mexican government an alliance in the event of further American violations —

undertaken in response to raids into the United States by the Mexican patriot, bandit Pancho Villa — plus large financial support and the mutual restoration of its former territory of Texas, New Mexico and Arizona. This cleverly unveiled threat to American sovereignty turned the tide and on 2 April 1917 Wilson visited Congress to announce the momentous 'change of policy' for which he felt his people now to be ready:

'With a profound sense of the solemn and even tragic character of the step I am taking and of the grave responsibilities which it involves,' he said, 'I advise that the Congress declare the recent course of the Imperial German Government to be in fact nothing less than war against the Government and people of the

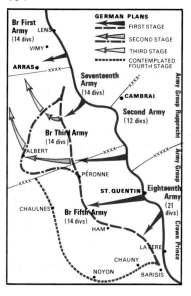

Above: The German offensive of March–July 1918.

Above right: Mule teams bring up American supplies to the Argonne Front.

United States . . . (and) to exert all its power and employ all its resources to bring the Government of the German Empire to terms and to end the war. . . . It is a fearful thing to lead this great, peaceful people into war – into the most terrible and disastrous of all wars, civilization itself seeming to be in the balance. But the right is more precious than peace and we shall fight for the things which we have always carried nearest our hearts – for democracy, for the right of those who submit to authority to have a voice in their own government, for the rights and liberties of small nations, for a universal dominion of right by such a concert of free people as shall bring peace and safety to all nations and make the world itself at last free.'

Four days later Congress formalized a state of hostilities between the United States and the Central Powers.

Enormously heartening though the news was to Britain and France, it could not at first bring anything more than moral comfort to the Alliance (which America did not technically join, remaining an Associated Power). The United States army was only 150,000 strong and without trained reserves. The United States Navy, the world's second largest, could and did at once play a major part in the antisubmarine war. By 5 June 1917 34 American destroyers were based at Queenstown, Ireland, to help with convoying Allied ships. Until the vast reserves of American manpower had been conscripted and trained, there would be no appreciable American military effort in France to make good the weakening physical and moral strength of Britain and France.

That factor was nowhere more strongly appreciated than in Germany. Indeed by the autumn of 1917, when the failure of the U-Boat campaign to starve the British to the peace table had become undisguisedly apparent, it formed the chief element in strategic planning. With the effective collapse of Russia as a military force in September 1917, the way stood open to achieve for the first time an actual superiority in numbers on the Western Front. In January 1918 there were 56 British divisions in France, but Lloyd George's policy of denying Haig reinforcements, which he suspected would be thrown away, had necessitated the reduction of the infantry battalions in each from 12 to nine (a step the French and Germans had taken a year earlier). The French were losing 40,000 men a month, whom Pétain declared himself unable to replace, and could field only 100 divisions. At that time the Germans had 124 divisions in the West and

the number was increasing. By March 1918 it had reached 194, with more still to come from the Russian Front. To offset the growing preponderance, the Allies could expect as a first installment of American help only nine divisions, which were to be in place in April.

By October, however, there would be 42. American divisions were large, almost twice the size of German divisions, and were filled with enthusiastic and physically-robust patriots, longing to do their bit. 'Lafayette, we are here' may not have been the words which their commander, General John 'Black Jack' Pershing, pronounced on setting foot on French soil, but the idea was in the American doughboys' hearts. They were coming to fight on the side of liberty, which Lafayette had helped their ancestors to win, and they intended to fight with the mythical fervor of Washington's embattled farmers.

Ludendorff – for it was he, rather than the 'wooden titan' Hindenburg, who now more and more openly directed German strategy as secretly as he did domestic policy – had therefore to win the war with his new superiority of numbers quickly, before it was eroded by the arrival of Americans en masse. A calculation suggested that he had until midsummer. However to win decisive results in that time required either new weapons or new methods. Of new weapons he had none. Foolishly the German High Command had formed a low opinion of the tank when it had first appeared and had not, until too late, embarked upon the construction of a model of their own, the A7V. The few which had appeared were even slower than the first British tanks and the Germans eagerly pressed the later British models into service whenever captured. From both sources Ludendorff had only dozens of tanks at his disposal, instead of hundreds like the British and French.

He had therefore to trust in new methods – unless he was to subject his own infantry to the pointless martyrdom suffered by their enemies on the Somme and the Chemin des Dames. As it had happened, the German army did have new methods. They principally concerned the artillery, and were the work of Bruchmüller (now nicknamed *Durchbruch* Müller – Breakthrough Müller), who had organized the successful surprise attack at Riga against the Russians in September 1917. What he had overcome was the weakness which had hitherto always robbed

Top center: American conscripts leave New York.

Top right: Georg Bruchmüller, the artillery expert.

Right: Doughboys off to the front in French railroad cars.

Right: American convoy enters British waters to the cheers of fishermen in the Western Approaches.

Below: American convoys broke the back of the German U-Boat campaign by mid-1917.

silent until the opening of the bombardment, which was to be very short. Bruchmüller took the view that the shock effect of a sudden, intense unheralded earthquake of shells would 'open' a front just as certainly as a long, heavy pulverization. The enemy infantry, in brutal terms, would be terrorized into inactivity. All who had experienced a bombardment testified that the first hours were the worst, when the noise and concussion temporarily robbed men

Left: Germans take up their mortar positions during the spring breakthrough of 1918.

Below: Storm troops advance across open fields as the French retreated to cover Paris.

great artillery bombardments of the element of the unexpected. It arose from the need to 'register' the guns when they arrived on a new front by firing trial shots so that their future fire would be accurate. Sound-ranging and flash-spotting techniques, now very refined, were always translated by an alert enemy into signals that the opposing artillery was being reinforced and therefore that an attack might be expected. In view of this expectation, artillery chiefs had always previously thought it better to make bombardments very long, thereby hoping to make up in terms of physical destruction what was lost in moral surprise. A big bombardment

also gave the enemy time to assemble his reserves close to the front of attack — but of course not in it — so that even if the attacking infantry should be able to capture the destroyed area they would be unable to break out of it.

Bruchmüller's achievement was to find ways of measuring a gun's accuracy before it arrived on a chosen front of attack, details which were then entered on a graduated list. It was subsequently necessary to fire only a few guns to establish the data from which the fire of all might be corrected to 'register' an entire artillery force, however large. Once assembled — which was done at night — the guns were to remain

of the power to control their nerves, while indeed their nerves were not yet accustomed to the unremitting racket. His bombardments were planned to last no more than four hours, to be unprecedently heavy – 7000 guns firing together – and to 'neutralize' rather than kill the defenders.

As it lifted, no man's land would be crossed first by specially picked squads of storm troops (*Stosstruppen* or *Sturmabteilungen* – Adolf Hitler would later appropriate both terms for his personal bodyguard, some of whose members had served in such units in 1918). Their task would be, like the Panzers of *Blitzkrieg* 20 years later, to pass through weak spots in the enemy's

defenses and to keep on going, without stopping to fight pockets of resistance. 'Infiltration' was the key word of these infantry tactics, the corollary of 'neutralization.' The elite storm units had been given special light equipment for their role and were allowed to dress and behave with a freedom not accorded the ordinary infantry of the line:

'He did not march with shouldered rifle,' wrote a propagandist of the *Sturmtruppen*, 'but with unslung carbine. His knees and elbows are protected with leather patches. He no longer wears a cartridge belt, but sticks his cartridges in his pockets. Crossed over his shoulders are two sacks for hand grenades. Thus he moves from shell hole to shell hole, through searing

fire, shot and attack, creeping, crawling like a robber, hugging the ground like an animal never daunted, never surprised, always shifting, cunning, always full of confidence in himself and his ability to handle any situation.'

Their officers were especially chosen for their pitiless bravery:

'The turmoil of our feelings,' one of them wrote, 'was called forth by rage, alcohol and the thirst for blood. As we advanced heavily but irresistibly toward the enemy lines, I was boiling over with a fury which

Below: Germans move their 28cm rail gun into position during the Ludendorff offensive.

Below: British field guns in action during the German Somme offensive, 28 March 1918. For the first time since 1914 a war of movement had reopened on the Western Front.

Above: Germans storm through Bailleul in March 1918, for whom rudimentary barricades proved no barrier.

gripped me. The overpowering desire to kill gave me wings. Rage squeezed bitter tears from my eyes. Only the spell of primeval instinct remained.' Officially the stormtroopers were hailed as 'the New Man, the storm soldier, the elite of *Mittel Europa*, a completely new race, cunning, strong and packed with purpose.'

Behind the storm troopers would march the massed columns of the ordinary infantry. They too had been trained to move in small groups, seeking cover and following the trail of the storm troopers to find the gaps in the enemy's lines and press onward deep into his rear. Overhead, the ground-attack squadrons (*Schlastas*) of the air force would patrol, to bomb and machine gun surviving enemy points of resistance.

During February the reinforcements of infantry and guns were moved forward close to the front. Ludendorff, after much thought, had decided on 21 January where the first strike was to be made. It was to be against the British, because they were still the Germans' toughest if not largest enemy and because, as one of his staff officers put it, 'the French will be in no hurry to run to the help of their Entente comrades,' a cynical but accurate judgment, as events were to show. The place he had selected was on the Somme, in a sector the British had recently taken over from the French, where the line was consequently in a poor state of repair and, most important, where a split could be made along the seam of the Anglo-French Front. Once through, the Germans were to turn northward and 'roll up' the British line. Subsequently he planned to attack in the north toward the railroad junction of Hazebrouck, from which all British supplies and reinforcements moved to Ypres. A blow there would split the British Front in two. This double stroke should, he calculated, be sufficient to end the war, if not victoriously then on terms acceptable to Germany. Beyond the putative success of this strategy he did not yet think.

The British Fifth Army on the Somme was in an even worse state than Ludendorff had supposed. Lloyd George's policy of keeping reinforcements in Britain so that Haig could not use them in a new offensive had hit it particularly hard and it was the weakest of the four British armies in France. It had only 12 divisions, dis-

posed on a front of 42 miles. Its trenches had been reorganized in imitation of the system which the Germans had used so successfully to keep the British out of their positions the year before, but the staff had misunderstood the German theory and crowded the infantry far forward in exactly the zone which Bruchmüller's 'neutralizing' bombardment was planned to hit. It was commanded by Hubert Gough, the slap-dash cavalryman whose tactics had been so disastrous at Ypres the previous autumn.

The Germans, by contrast, were able to mass 43 divisions on Gough's front, a superiority of nearly 4:1, and had a superiority of 5:2 in heavy guns. They also planned to attack General Sir Julian Byng's Third Army at the same time, though there the superiority was less. Whatever the proportion of attackers, all were supremely self-confident. Whether old Western Front hands or new arrivals from the East, they had been told, and believed, that this was the *Kaiserschlacht*, the Emperor's Battle, which would end the war. At 0440 hours on 21 March when mist lay thickly all over the valley and plain of the Somme, they heard their guns open up, and tensed themselves to push forward into

the curtain of explosions and gas. They knew that the bombardment was to last for exactly four hours and that then all would depend upon their courage and dash.

On the other side of the front, a colonel of the Royal Scots Fusiliers was asleep in his dugout when:

'a tremendous roll of fire brought us to our feet; even in the depths of the shaft we could distinguish the thunder of gas projectors being fired in enormous quantities. . . . At first only projectors were being fired, and we thought it might betoken merely a big-scale raid. Then our uncertainty was dispersed by the instantaneous crash, the like of which has never been heard before by land or sea, from thousands upon thousands of guns roaring on a front of 30 miles, and we knew that the hurricane had broken on us at last. The noise transcended anything I had ever conceived. . . . . We were stunned by the concussions of literally thousands of bursting shells, and although the light was uncertain, for there hung a mist, we could see that all our front stood wrapped in a sea of smoke, and flame, and the earth heaved and twisted under our feet.'

Below: The Monterail-Château-Thierry Road: refugees passing troops going to the front, by George Harding.

The German general, Oskar von Hutier, commanding the spearhead Eighteenth Army, recorded the immediate results of this tremendous bombardment:

'The enemy's first position was quickly captured at all points. By the evening the infantry of the divisions of the first wave, closely followed by their escort batteries had penetrated to an average depth of six kilometers into the enemy's defensive system. The English suffered terribly heavy losses, both in men and prisoners, guns and war materiel. With ruthless energy the Eighteenth Army's attack was continued during the night of 21–22 March, and on the following day along the whole line. The impetus and enthusiasm of the troops were such that they did not need the Army Order I issued on the evening of 21 March enjoining them to keep up the pursuit. I shall never forget the scenes I witnessed in those days. For the first time after more than two years of heavy defense in the waste of trenches in the West, the hour of liberation had struck and the command had gone forth to Germany's

Right: General Hubert Gough was one of those blamed for the German breakthrough in 1918.

Far right: President Woodrow Wilson.

Below: The German Big Bertha could hit Paris.

sons to strike for final victory in the open field. As if shaking off some horrible nightmare my infantry had risen from its trenches and crushing all resistance with unexampled vigor had broken through the enemy's defensive system.'

Von Hutier did not exaggerate. In two days' fighting, the Germans had captured the whole of the British defended zone on either side of the Somme and were poised to push out into open country. By 24 March they won through and had advanced 14 miles in four days, the greatest gain of territory since 1914, better even than the British had done at Cambrai with massed tanks. Before them the British Fifth Army was in full retreat. The Third Army to its north was being drawn into the rout:

'The journey seemed endless,' wrote a gunner officer, who was evacuating his heavy battery. 'It soon grew dark. The road was flanked by great trees which loomed up and faded away in endless succession. Dust and petrol vapour were everywhere. It filled ears and eyes, nose and mouth. Kilometre stone after kilometre stone went by. It was impossible to grasp the fact that we were in flight.'

Haig was seized by panic at the sight of the way his front was collapsing. He had earlier agreed with Pétain that each should come to the other's assistance if the promised German offensive should provoke a crisis. He had shrunk from a more formal arrangement, his fierce isolationism warning with proper military prudence even at this late stage of the war. Pétain had, in earnest of his promise, sent a single division to stand behind the crumbling British right flank on 22 March, but no more. The German gibe that the 'French would not hurry to help' was proving all too true in practice. On 24 March Haig received unequivocal evidence that such was the case. Pétain came to his headquarters at 1100 hours, revealed that he did not feel able to help the British more than he had

Above: A doughboy explains how his Lee-Enfield rifle operates.

Below: British 60-pounder in action near La Boisselle in the First Battle of Bapaume in March 1918.

Above: The Americans move forward in one of their first actions near Coutigny in late May 1918.

Top left: General Oskar von Hutier.

Above left: General Hubert Gough, Fifth Army Commander.

Top: 6-inch howitzers in action near Boues, April 1918.

Over There

Over there, over there,
Spread the word, send the word, over there,
That the Yanks are coming, the Yanks are coming,
The drums drum drumming everywhere.

So prepare say a Prayer,
Send the word, spread the word to beware
We'll be over, we're coming over,
And we won't come back, till it's over over there.

Right: Poilus return to an abandoned mine shaft near Riffencourt which became their trench in April 1918.

Below: A doughboy surveys the ruins of the town square of Château-Thierry.

Above: A new German tank, the monstrous A7V in action in April 1918, one of the spearheads of the breakthrough.

already and handed him an order, just issued to the French armies, which revealed that he accepted the probability of the Germans' dividing the Allied front, in which case his troops would fall back to cover Paris. When asked if that was his .policy, Pétain merely nodded his head.

In an instant, all Haig's objections to sub-ordinating British troops to foreign command dissolved. He at once signalled London, asking that Lord Milner, the war minister, or General Sir Henry Wilson, the Chief of the General Staff, should at once come to France and make it clear to the French government that 'unless General Foch or some other determined general were given supreme command, there would be a disaster.' On 26 March the two arrived at the little town of Doullens, a little north of the great bulge the Germans had pushed into the Western Front where Haig was waiting. From Paris, which for the last three days had been under bombardment from a range of 75 miles by a gigantic German gun, already nicknamed Big Bertha, came President Poincaré, Clemenceau and Foch. Pétain arrived from his headquarters. As he entered, Foch whispered to a neighbor that he had the look of a man who was preparing himself for defeat in the open field. His obvious defeatism spurred all present toward a decision. The necessary formula was quickly arrived at:

Below: German heavy tanks plow through open country as the way to Paris seemed clear. Germany hoped to win the war before the effect of a million fresh American troops was felt.

'General Foch is charged by the British and French governments with the co-ordination of the action of the Allied Armies on the Western Front. He will make arrangements to this effect with the two Generals in Chief, who are invited to furnish him with the necessary information.'

This was sufficient to give him power over their reserves, which could now be switched wherever danger threatened most. Clemenceau remarked to Foch as the document was distributed 'Well, you've got what you want.' Foch answered 'A fine present. You give me a lost battle and tell me to win it.' However, his real feelings were not so pessimistic. As he sat down to lunch with the party, his mind was already turning on victory. Haig did not join them. The humiliations of the last few days, culminating in subordination to a Frenchman, had robbed him of appetite both for company and food. 'Lunched from sandwich box,' his diary gloomily recorded. Humble pie was on the menu.

As Foch already detected from the situation reports, the worst of the crisis was already over. The Germans had already begun to experience the phenomenon Clausewitz had recognized a hundred years before and termed 'the diminishing power of the offensive,' brought about in this case partly by their lack of tanks and other mechanical means to sustain the speed of their advance, partly by the obstacles of the old Somme battlefield of 1916, which now lay before them, and partly by the temptations of the British supply dumps which their troops were now capturing. These supplies should have fuelled their onward progress. Rather than fill their knapsacks and press on, the German infantry, after three years of blockade, preferred to fill their stomachs:

'Today,' recorded Rudolf Binding on 28 March, 'the advance of our infantry suddenly stopped near Albert. Nobody could understand why. Our airmen had reported no enemy between Albert and Amiens. . . . I jumped into a car with orders to find out what was causing the stoppage in front. . . . As soon as I got near Albert I began to see curious sights. Strange figures which looked very little like soldiers, and certainly showed no sign of advancing, were making their way back out of the town. There were men driving cows,

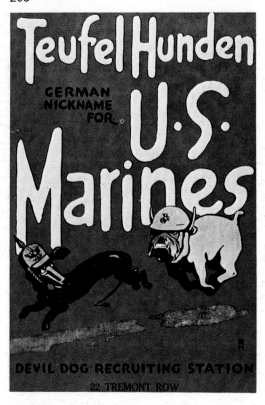

Above: A US Marine recruiting poster. The Germans called them 'devil dogs.'

Below and below right: The German breakthrough and the five major drives which were stopped short of Paris.

another who carried a hen under one arm and a box of notepaper under the other, a man carrying a bottle of wine under his arm and another one open in his hand. . . . More men with writing-paper and colored notebooks. Evidently they had found it desirable to sack a stationer's shop. Men dressed up in comic disguise. Men with top hats on their heads. Men staggering. Men who could hardly walk. When I got into the town the streets were running in wine. Out of a cellar came a lieutenant, helpless and in despair. I asked him "What is going to happen?" It was essential for them to get forward immediately. He replied solemnly and emphatically "I cannot get my men out of this cellar without bloodshed."'

Moreover the static troops of the British rear areas, railroad engineers, tunnellers and transport drivers, were now being collected together as the bases they occupied were threatened and turned into temporary fighting units. One of these held a hastily improvised line of trenches outside Amiens, which Ludendorff was now making his target with great bravery and success. Ground was lost elsewhere. Foch, whose powers were widened to include 'the strategic direction of military operations' on 3 April was manipulating the reserves with great skill. After two attempts at renewal of the advance, on 28 March at Arras and on 4 April in front of Amiens, Ludendorff accepted that the Kaiserschlacht had run into the sand and ordered the attackers to rest. They had lost over 250,000 casualties in two weeks, but so too together had the British and French.

His men's losses did not mean that Luden-

dorff could not still try again elsewhere. His 'battering train' of heavy artillery was intact, and he still had a surplus of infantry. He was also still convinced that he must hurt the British rather than the French, and so moved his attack formations northward to the valley of the River Lys, just below Ypres. Hazebrouck, the railroad junction he had selected as his target, lay only 15 miles from his jumping-off point. Moreover, as luck would have it the center of the 12 miles of front he had chosen was held by a tired division of cold, homesick Portuguese, who had little idea of why their government had sent them to join England's war and little desire to stay and find out when attacked. Under the first breath of German fire on 9 April, they dispersed leaving a hole through which the Stosstruppen pushed hard toward the Channel. The gap was cordoned off by the British who even captured the band behind which the overoptimistic Germans were planning to make a triumphal entry into Béthune, but some of the units used in the cordon had been brought down from the Somme and were still recovering from the battering they had received there. So next day the attack made more ground. By evening it had reached to within five miles of Hazebrouck and Haig saw the fragmentation of his army staring him in the face. He issued an Order of the Day; 'With our backs to the wall and believing in the justice of our cause each one must fight on to the end.'

He appealed to Foch for reinforcements, but that hard and shrewd old warrior did not believe

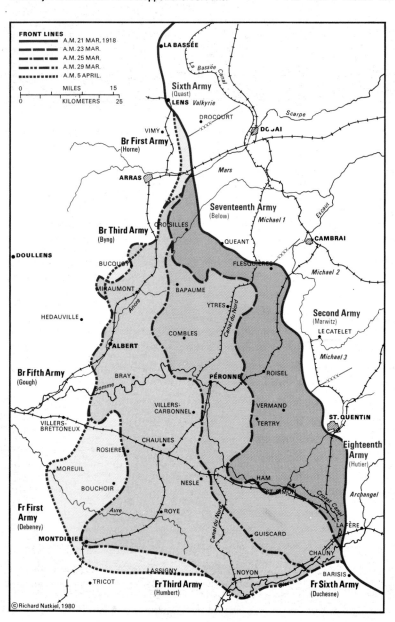

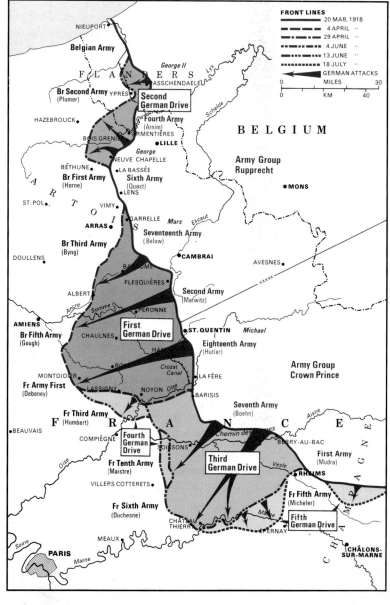

Douglas MacArthur

Douglas MacArthur (1880–1964) was America's greatest war hero both in World War I and II. After his graduation from West Point he served in the Canal Zone and Texas as well as on the General Staff in Washington before he saw his first active service during the American intervention in Mexico. He was appointed Major in 1915 after his return to Washington but when America entered World War I in April 1917, General John J (Black Jack) Pershing was chosen to lead the American Expeditionary Force. MacArthur, who was impressed by Pershing's soldierly bearing and strength of character, was assigned to the Rainbow Division, so-called because it drew its members from all parts of the United States rather than from one state or territorial unit, an innovation at the time. By the end of 1917 only four of the 24 divisions Pershing promised the Allies were complete, and the Rainbow Division was one of them. At this time there were only 175,000 American men in France.

One of the first actions taken by any American unit in World War I was in the Luneville-Baccarat area in February 1918, where the Rainbow Division relieved a French unit. In his first action MacArthur led a raiding party through the barbed wire. For this action MacArthur received the American Silver Star and the French Croix de Guerre, which General de Bazelaire presented to MacArthur, and after pinning it on his tunic, kissed him on both cheeks.

In March 1918 MacArthur led a raiding party into German lines and was decorated with the Distinguished Service Cross, a battle honor second only to the Congressional Medal of Honor. MacArthur was given another DSC later in the War.

The Rainbow Division was withdrawn from action on 19 July, after having suffered over 1500 casualties and MacArthur won his second Silver Star. Thrown back into action on 25 July along the Marne, MacArthur led his 42nd Division from the front during a particularly costly action involving hand-to-hand fighting. MacArthur was given a second Croix de Guerre, a third Silver Star and was made a Commander of the French Legion of Honor.

During the St Mihiel offensive MacArthur's 42nd Division led a breakthrough of a line held by Germans since 1914 which resulted in the capture of almost 15,000 prisoners and 450 guns. Brigadier General MacArthur was awarded two more Silver Stars.

In the Meuse-Argonne campaign, which the 42nd Division entered on 11 October, Major General MacArthur led a successful attack and received his second DSC. Pushing forward to Sedan the 42nd Division was finally withdrawn on the night of 9/10 November. MacArthur was awarded his seventh Silver Star and the next day the Armistice ended the War.

There were some who were jealous of MacArthur's many awards as well as his idiosyncratic methods such as leading from the front and walking around the battlefield unarmed. When Pershing was informed of these criticisms he was said to have replied, 'Stop all this nonsense. MacArthur is the greatest leader of troops we have.' MacArthur's Commanding Officer wrote to Pershing that 'he had filled each day with a loyal and intelligent application to duty such as is . . . without parallel in our army.'

At the age of 38 MacArthur proved his merit as a soldier and as a leader of men and was praised by both his men and his superiors. MacArthur's reputation as America's greatest soldier was secure at the end of World War I.

Above: **An American machine-gun emplacement near the Argonne Forest.**

that things were as dangerous as they looked. He also held to the view that it was better in a crisis to leave tired troops where they were rather than risk their total collapse by the promise of relief. So, while he sent some French troops in the direction of Hazebrouck, he ordered their commanders to make haste slowly. Events proved him right. Many of the German attackers were veterans of the Eastern Front where some shelling and gas usually made the enemy run. When they found the British more stubborn, their will to victory wilted and the offensive began to run out of steam. By 30 April it had petered out altogether.

The most significant incident of its closing stages was the encounter at Villers-Brettoneux on 24 April of British and German tanks. It led to the first tank-versus-tank battle. Four British tanks met three German. Of the British tanks, No 1 tank of No 1 Section, A Company, 1st Battalion, Tank Corps was commanded by 2nd Lieutenant Frank Mitchell. He was warned by a British infantryman that German tanks were about and opened a loophole to keep watch. Some 300 yards away he saw a round, squat-looking monster advancing, behind it came waves of infantry and further away to the left and right crawled two more of these armed tortoises. So the rivals had met at last! For the first time in history tank was encountering tank. Miller's gunner, whose eyes had been badly affected by a barrage of mustard gas through which he had earlier driven, fired two shots at it but missed. It replied with armor-piercing

Above: French tanks in action. They proved less effective than their German or British counterparts.

Right: British tanks on the offensive in September 1918 as German prisoners are rounded up near Bellicourt.

machine-gun bullets which 'filled the interior with a myriad of sparks and flying splinters.' The gunner again fired twice and missed twice. Meanwhile, the German tank was engaging Mitchell's two accompanying tanks and hit them, forcing them to withdraw. Mitchell decided therefore to halt his tank, to give his gunner a steady platform:

'The pause was justified; a well-aimed shot hit the enemy's conning-tower. Another round and yet another white puff at the front of the tank denoted a second hit! Peering with swollen eyes through his narrow slit, the gunner shouted words of triumph that were drowned by the roar of the engine. Then once more he fired with great deliberation and hit for the third time. Through a loophole I saw the tank heel over to one side, then a door opened and out ran the crew.
We had knocked the monster out!'

However, not until the next war would tank duels become of strategic significance. In 1918 Ludendorff still had to win with men – and by May he was running short of reserves. His two 'knock-out' blows against the British having failed, he decided that he would next make a diversionary attack against the French in order to draw Foch's reserves southward and then return to the north for a final stroke at Haig. On 27 May, therefore, after careful preparations, the now familiar 'neutralizing' bombardment fell on the Chemin des Dames. The high ridges and broken terrain, most of which was in German hands, had facilitated the concealment of his troops – he could still find 41 divisions – and Bruchmüller's fire plan was more hellishly refined than ever before. Defending were only

four French and three British divisions which had actually been sent thither as a 'rest' from the battering they had taken in Flanders. The central French division disappeared under a flood of five German divisions, which pounded over their positions and downhill to the Aisne. There they found the bridges unblown, so complete was the surprise, they crossed them and set off into open country. By the second day they had gone 15 miles and by 3 June, while French reserves were still struggling down from the north, were at Château-Thierry, only 56 miles from Paris.

There the Germans received the first ominous warning note of a timetable in trouble. Among the hastily-assembled reserves into which they eventually ran were Americans, United States regulars of the 3rd Division and Marines of the 2nd. At Belleau Wood on 6 June the Marines counterattacked. The place has become one of the Corps' most cherished battle honors and an officer who was present explains why:

'It was a beautiful deployment, lines all dressed and guiding true. Such matters were of deep concern to this outfit. The day was without a cloud promising heat later but now it was pleasant in the wheat and the woods around looked blue and cool. Pretty country, these rolling wheatlands northwest of Château-Thierry, with copses of trees and tidy little forests where French sportsmen maintained hunting lodges and game preserves. Since the first Marne there had been no fighting here. . . . The platoons, assailed now by a fury of small-arms fire, narrowed their eyes and inclined their bodies forward, like men in heavy rain and went on. Second waves reinforced the first, fourth waves the third, as prescribed. Officers yelled, "Battle-sight – fire at will" – and the leaders, making out green-gray clumsy uniforms and round pot-helmets in the gloom of the woods, took it up with Springfields, aimed shots. . . . Men crawled forward; the wheat was agitated and the Boche, directing his fire by observers in treetops, browsed the slope industriously. Men were

wounded, wounded again as the lines of fire swept back and forth, and finally killed. It helped to bag the *feldwebels* in the trees; there were men in that line who could hit at 750 yards three times out of five. Sweating, hot and angry . . . the Marines worked forward. They were there and the Germans, and there was nothing else in the clanging world.'

The French reserves which had been hurried to the front here fought as well as the Americans, no doubt under the stimulus of the cry, not heard since 1914, of 'Paris in danger.' The Germans for a moment did actually get a foothold across the Marne. Clemenceau had to calm the Chamber of Deputies by dismissing some subordinate generals, just as Joffre had done in the terrible August of four years before, but the crisis quickly passed. The German offensive outran its transport and came to a halt at the end of the first week of June. A small subsidiary offensive on the River Matz, a tributary of the Oise, was launched on 9 June, with the same diversionary object of drawing reserves away from Flanders, where Ludendorff still hoped to launch a knockout against the British, but was contained within a week.

The war was now moving to a supreme crisis, foreseen by both sides. Foch, Haig and Pétain sensed that if they could but ride the storm for another month or two at most, the gathering weight of American manpower would crush the life out of the German army. Ludendorff knew that he had strength enough for only one more

Right: What might have happened had two tanks collided head-on.

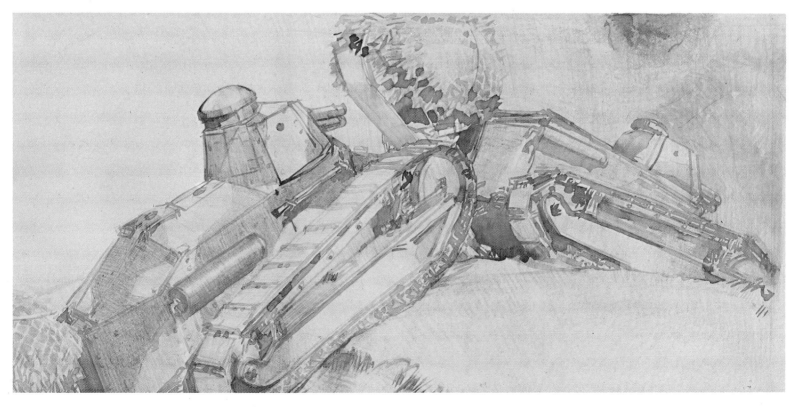

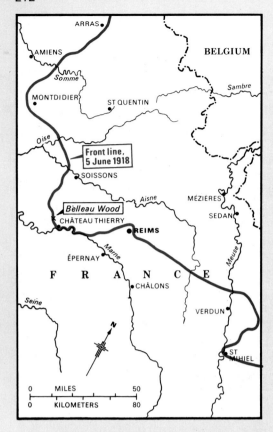

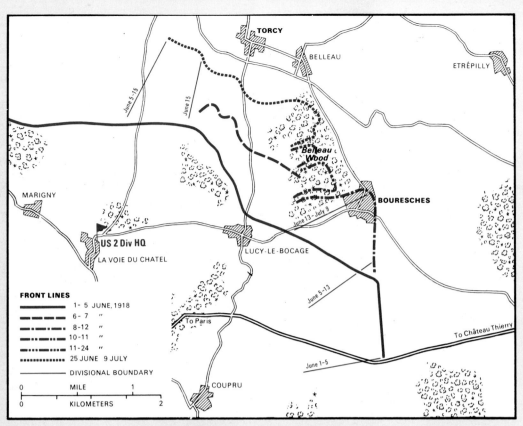

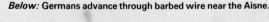

Above: The situation as the Americans entered the fray at Belleau Wood in June 1918, their first major action in the war.

great throw. So stretched were his nerves that he even tinkered with the temptation of playing politics, discussing the desirability of offering the Allies the possibility of a compromise peace in order to confuse them and weaken their will to resist. However, when von Kühlmann, the foreign minister, outraged the Reichstag by airing this suggestion on 24 June Ludendorff threw him to the wolves. The Kaiser, speaking at the Headquarters at Spa on 15 June, at a dinner to celebrate the 30th year of his reign, revealed the mind of the German governing class more accurately. Renouncing any idea of surrendering the conquests made by Germany since 1914, then at their greatest extent, he went on:

'Either the Prusso-German-Teutonic world philosophy – justice, freedom, honor, moral – persists in honor, or the Anglo-Saxon – which means succumbing to the worship of the golden calf. In this struggle, one or the other philosophy must go under. We are fighting for the victory of the German philosophy.'

His characterization of what 'the German philosophy' stood for might have surprised Western liberals, who believed that their way of life enshrined justice and freedom, but the naked combatitiveness of his outlook would not. There spoke the voice of the militarism they feared.

It was supremely still Ludendorff's voice. After much reflection, he decided that before risking all on *Hagen*, the code name (that of the sinister dwarf of the Nibelungen) for the culminating offensive against the British in Flanders, he would give Foch and the French one more bad fright on the Marne, thus ensuring

that the Allied reserves were irretrievably in the wrong place at the hour of decision. Once more the 'battering train' was wheeled forward to prepare the attack. Gas and high explosives were poured into the makeshift French positions on the morning of 15 July and, as day broke, 52 divisions moved forward in two groups, between Soissons and Reims. The more northerly was to aim for the Marne, 15 miles distant, the other to cross the Marne, which was close at hand and join up with the first in a large pincer movement.

Initially the Germans had some success. At a point held by the Italian divisions, sent to France in exchange for Allied divisions moved to the Italian front after Caporetto, they cracked the front and were held only by the hasty arrival of some British troops. Above Reims they reached and crossed the Marne. The steadfast defense of

Top right: German morale showed no sign of slacking as the men marched to the front in April 1918.

Above right: Germans storm into Embermesnil in the Champagne country in May 1918.

Below: Germans advance through barbed wire near the Aisne.

John Joseph Pershing

John Joseph Pershing was born in Laclede, Missouri on 13 September 1860, to a family of modest means in the rural Middle West. He graduated from the United States Military Academy at West Point in 1886 as president of his class.

His first active service was in the last series of Indian wars fought in the American West, when Pershing served in the cavalry. He received a Bachelor of Laws degree in 1893 while teaching at the University of Nebraska, and later taught military tactics at West Point. His academic career was interrupted by the outbreak of the Spanish-American War in 1898, when Pershing went to Cuba and won a Silver Star. Soon afterward he was transferred to the Philippines where he joined the hard campaign the Americans waged against the Moros in Mindanao, winning the praise of the then-President Theodore Roosevelt. He was sent by Roosevelt to act as an observer in the Russo-Japanese War of 1904–05. Roosevelt rewarded him for his work in Manchuria by elevating Captain Pershing to the rank of brigadier general in 1906 over the heads of hundreds of senior officers, an act which created considerable bitterness against Pershing among his fellow officers for many years. After another tour in the Philippines Pershing was rushed back to the United States in 1916 to lead a military expedition into Mexico to pursue Pancho Villa, the Mexican revolutionary who had recently made a surprise attack on the town of Columbus, New Mexico. Arriving at El Paso, Texas, to join his troops, Pershing received the news that his wife and three small daughters had burned to death in San Francisco, his son Warren, being the only survivor. Grimly Pershing led his punitive expedition across the border on 15 March 1916, and his troops plunged deep into Mexican territory. Although the Mexican troops which attempted to repel the Americans were easily swept aside, Pershing was unable to capture Villa after 10 months of wandering through the hostile countryside of northern Mexico. But President Wilson appeared satisfied and made him a major general.

Pershing's expedition was recalled in February 1917, and three months later, after the United States had entered World War I, Pershing was sent to France with a hand-picked staff to command the American Expeditionary Force (AEF) which, at the time, did not yet exist. Pershing was given a free hand by Wilson to organize his forces, although he was cautioned by a Presidential directive to maintain his troops intact and not to allow them to be merged into a combined Allied unit. When he arrived in France Pershing discovered that the Allies wanted no untested American army; they preferred to have American manpower slowly fill their own depleted ranks. Pershing insisted on training a separate American force and on keeping them aloof from the fighting until they were prepared to wage an offensive. He was determined to prevent the Americans being dragged into the wastefulness of trench warfare, and envisioned an army of 1,000,000 men under his own command by spring 1918. Supported by the Secretary of War, Newton D Baker, Pershing achieved his ends, much to the consternation of the Supreme War Council, composed of Lloyd George, Clemenceau and Orlando. Severe pressure was put on the Americans by the Allies to relieve Pershing, but Baker protected him.

When the German threat became increasingly serious during their massive offensive in 1918, Pershing volunteered some reinforcements to Foch, and American action at Château-Thierry and Belleau Wood stopped the Germans on the Marne and opened the eyes of both the Germans and the Allies to the combat readiness of the American divisions. In mid-August 1918 the newly-formed American First Army, with the approval of Foch, was concentrating on the St Mihiel offensive. At the last minute Foch called off the attack, arguing that American reinforcements were needed elsewhere along the front. Pershing refused to break up his unit, and the struggle between Foch and Pershing was settled only through the mediation of Marshal Pétain. The AEF eliminated the St Mihiel salient and a few days later almost 600,000 men were shifted to the Meuse-Argonne area, where they advanced against fierce German opposition. In 47 days of continuous fighting the American forces had pushed forward to Sedan, chewing up German divisions as fast as they were thrown in. The armistice came three days after the AEF reached the outskirts of Sedan.

Pershing's organization of the American forces from scratch was one of the greatest feats of World War I. Starting from nothing Pershing produced an army of 2,000,000 men within 18 months. The entry of the Americans on the Western Front was decisive in the winning of the war. The iron discipline and stern military bearing which he maintained earned him the nickname of 'Black Jack,' and he won respect, if not affection, from his comrades. On 3 September 1919 Pershing was made General of the Armies, a rank unique in American military history. He was made Chief of Staff in 1921, a post which he held until his retirement in 1924. He died in 1948 at the age of 88, honored by most of the European nations as well as his own; his body rests at Arlington National Cemetery.

the American 3rd Division prevented them from enlarging their bridgehead. Other things went wrong. All the observation balloons on which his artillery depended were shot down by Allied 'balloon-busting' airmen and a force of 20 tanks which he had painstakingly assembled was knocked out by gunners firing over open sights.

Worse was to come. Pétain, who had come close to dismissal by Clemenceau during the crisis of the May offensive of the Aisne, had heeded the urgings of Foch and prepared a counterattack force. Its command was given to Mangin, his trap-jawed, fire-eating subordinate of Verdun days. Mangin was irrepressibly aggressive, a veteran of the French Colonial wars in Africa and a ferocious patriot who had never wavered, unlike Pétain, in his belief in French victory. He now had 25 divisions, positioned west of the German break-in. He also had a large force of tanks, and he was to enjoy the supreme tactical advantage of surprise. The Germans, who believed they held the initiative, were not prepared for what now struck them, a well-planned drive into their flank by rested troops under a commander determined on success and ready to dismiss any subordinate who would not carry out his orders.

On that critical morning Ludendorff was driving north to plan the offensive in Flanders, where his heavy artillery was already on its way. Isolated in his motor car, he did not hear the news of his forward infantry collapsing under the thrusts of aggressive French tank-infantry columns, moving concealed among the woods and wheat fields of countryside untouched by war for four years. By the time he arrived at Mons for his conference, the damage had been done. Four miles of territory had been lost and the bridgeheads over the Marne threatened. A steady retirement was in progress which would not end until the Germans had reached the line of the Chemin des Dames. On 6 August, Clemenceau, in recognition of success in what would be called the Second Battle of the Marne, promoted Foch to be Marshal of France.

Top left: **General Pershing arrives at Boulogne to take command of the AEF.**

Right: **US troops in action in Villers-sur-Fère, July 1918.**

Below right: **Men of the 62nd Division advance near Reims, 24 July 1918.**

Below: **General Haig greets Premier Clemenceau at Doullens.**

Doughboys of the 7th Division celebrate the Armistice, 11 November 1918.

Germany's peril at the end of July 1918 could not be measured by the naked eye. Unlike Hitler's Reich in the last four months of its power before defeat, both the Empire's territory and conquests stood almost intact. The coastline of the Baltic as far as Riga, the whole of the Ukraine and much of Russia proper, the line of the Caucasus and the northern shores of the Black Sea were garrisoned by German troops. All her allies remained at her side, and their troops generally stood beyond their own frontiers and still in active contention with the forces of the Alliance. In Italy the Austrians were still on the Piave, a little above Venice. In Macedonia the Bulgarians overlooked the 'Gardeners of Salonika' in their entrenched camp on the River Varda. Rumania, Serbia and Montenegro were occupied. So too was most of Belgium and as much of France as had been captured in the first campaign of 1914. The Russian Bolsheviks, who could be counted as Germany's reluctant collaborators were preparing a campaign of extirpation against the Whites, who represented all that was left of Allied might east of Moscow. Only in the Ottoman lands had British troops pushed any distance toward the center of power. There the Anatolian heartland, recruiting ground of the peasantry who manned the ranks of the Turkish army, still stood far from Allenby's vanguards.

Yet Ludendorff, and the group around him who now manipulated imperial power in Germany, knew that the hands of the clock stood at five minutes to midnight. The U-Boat campaign, which should have starved Britain to the conference table the year before, had been defeated. The young Austrian emperor, Karl I, remained as anxious to make peace as he had shown himself to be the year before, with the difference that he heard his throne creaking beneath him; the subject nationalities — Serbs, Czechs, Slovaks, Poles — would now be satisfied only by independence, not internal autonomy. The opposition to the war within Germany had become bolder and more vociferous. In February there had been a wave of large-scale strikes, when 250,000 workers had come out in demand for larger food rations (in June the potato ration stood at one pound a week), amnesty for

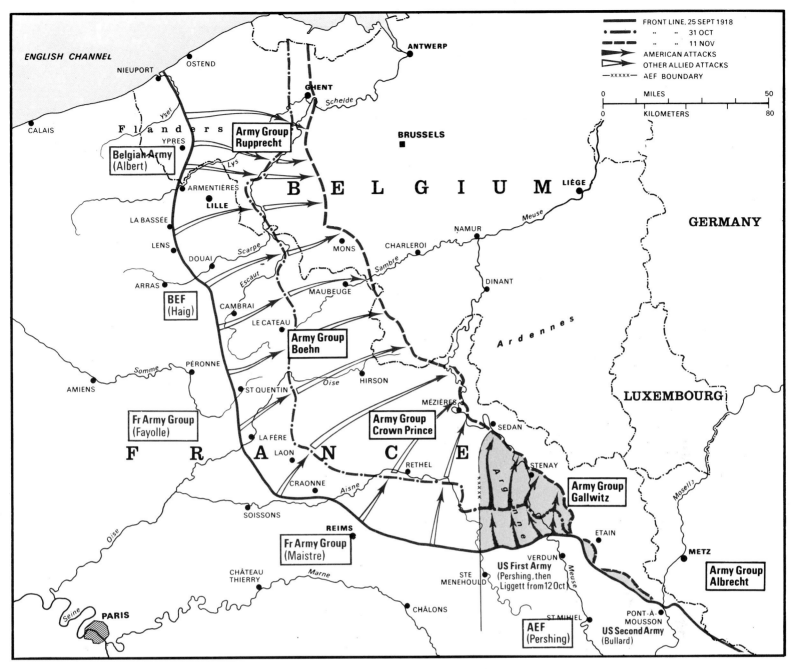

Above: The final Allied advances.

Above left: Irish Rifles in action in Belgium in August 1918.

Left: British Whippet tanks pass a column of New Zealand troops at Maillet Mailly.

Right: Hindenburg and Ludendorff, who in September 1918 were forced to tell the Kaiser that the war was lost.

political offenders, restoration of civil rights, democratization of the government and peace on the basis of 'no annexations and no indemnities.' Worst of all, there was the American menace:

'People here may well look grave,' Princess Blücher wrote in mid-July from Berlin. 'The meaning of America is coming home to them at last. They comprehend now that it means an increase of the French reserves at a rate of 300,000 fresh, well-equipped men (that is, Americans) per month, while Germany can bring up no fresh reserves.'

In fact by the end of July, the Americans had 27 divisions in France, each 28,000 strong and so twice the size of a French or German division. Their very inexperience added to their for-midability. British and French officers who had found American dead lying in long rows in the open wheat fields at Château-Thierry had whispered to each other that the newcomers had a great deal to learn. Precisely because they

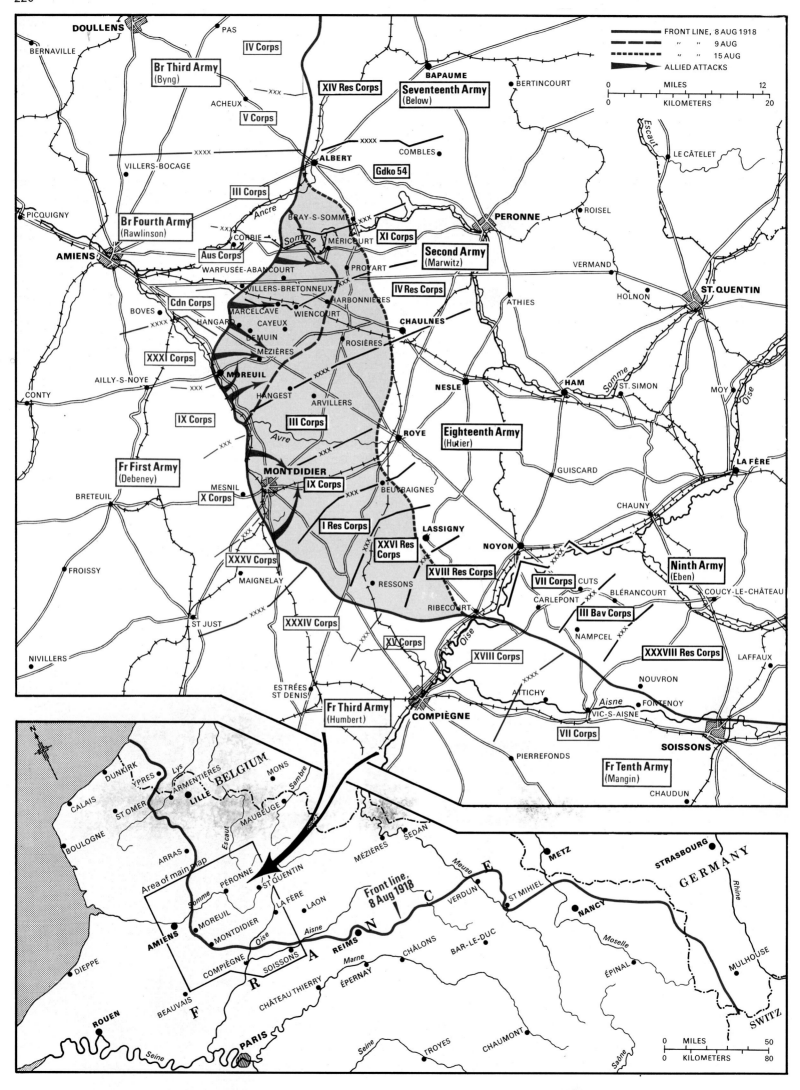

DOULLENS
PAS
BERNAVILLE
IV Corps
Br Third Army (Byng)
XIV Res Corps
BAPAUME
BERTINCOURT
Seventeenth Army (Below)
ACHEUX
V Corps
XXX
ALBERT
COMBLES
VILLERS-BOCAGE
XXXX
LE CÂTELET
Gdko 54
III Corps
Ancre
BRAY-S-SOMME
PICQUIGNY
Br Fourth Army (Rawlinson)
CORBIE
MÉRICOURT
Somme
XI Corps
PERONNE
ROISEL
AMIENS
Aus Corps
PROYART
Second Army (Marwitz)
VERMAND
WARFUSÉE-ABANCOURT
VILLERS-BRETONNEUX
IV Res Corps
ST. QUENTIN
BOVES
Cdn Corps
HARBONNIÈRES
HOLNON
MARCELCAVE
WIENCOURT
ATHIES
HANGARD
CAYEUX
CHAULNES
XXXI Corps
DEMUIN
ROSIÈRES
HAM
Somme
ST. SIMON
MÉZIÈRES
MOY
AILLY-S-NOYE
MOREUIL
Oise
CONTY
HANGEST
ARVILLERS
IX Corps
III Corps
ROYE
Eighteenth Army (Hutier)
GUISCARD
Avre
LA FÈRE
Fr First Army (Debeney)
MONTDIDIER
IX Corps
BEUVRAIGNES
CHAUNY
BRETEUIL
MESNIL
X Corps
LASSIGNY
NOYON
Ninth Army (Eben)
I Res Corps
VII Corps
CUTS
COUCY-LE-CHÂTEAU
FROISSY
XXXV Corps
XXVI Res Corps
XVIII Res Corps
CARLEPONT
BLÉRANCOURT
MAIGNELAY
RESSONS
RIBECOURT
III Bav Corps
XXXVIII Res Corps
LAFFAUX
ST JUST
XXXIV Corps
XV Corps
Oise
NAMPCEL
NIVILLERS
XVIII Corps
NOUVRON
ESTRÉES ST DENIS
ATTICHY
Aisne
FONTENOY
Fr Third Army (Humbert)
COMPIÈGNE
VIC-S-AISNE
VII Corps
PIERREFONDS
SOISSONS
Fr Tenth Army (Mangin)
CHAUDUN

FRONT LINE, 8 AUG 1918
"   "   9 AUG
"   "   15 AUG
ALLIED ATTACKS
0   MILES   12
0   KILOMETERS   20

DUNKIRK
YPRES
Lys
ARMENTIÈRES
LILLE
BELGIUM
MONS
Sambre
CALAIS
ST OMER
MAUBEUGE
BOULOGNE
Escaut
ARRAS
Area of main map
PÉRONNE
ST QUENTIN
MÉZIÈRES
SEDAN
METZ
STRASBOURG
GERMANY
Somme
LA FÈRE
LAON
Meuse
VERDUN
ST MIHIEL
Rhine
AMIENS
MOREUIL
MONTDIDIER
Oise
Aisne
REIMS
NANCY
DIEPPE
COMPIÈGNE
SOISSONS
Front line, 8 Aug 1918
CHÂLONS
BAR-LE-DUC
Marne
Moselle
BEAUVAIS
CHÂTEAU THIERRY
ÉPERNAY
MULHOUSE
ROUEN
Seine
PARIS
TROYES
CHAUMONT
ÉPINAL
Saône
SWITZ
0   MILES   50
0   KILOMETERS   80

were ready to attack with a disregard for danger no German had seen since the early days of the war, they inspired a fearful respect which the more cautious British and French did not.

Recollecting his thoughts of late July, Ludendorff later wrote:

'the attempt to make the Entente peoples ready for peace by defeating them before the arrival of the American reinforcements had failed. The impetus of the army had been insufficient to deal the enemy a decisive blow. I realized clearly that this made our general situation very serious.'

How serious was shortly to be brought home to him, not, however, by the Americans but by the British. At the beginning of August Pershing's divisions were still scattered about the Western Front, where he had lent them as reserves during the worst of the spring and summer crisis. He was now urgently reassembling them for 'an American offensive.' Meanwhile Haig had found a surplus of troops of his own and, more important, a surplus of tanks. He had also been given a clear brief as to where they were to be used. On 24 July Foch had held a meeting with the British and American commanders at which he laid down a scheme to free certain strategic railroad lines whose possession would

Left: The Allied breakthrough on the Black Day, 8 August 1918, which ended all German hopes of victory.

Right: German field artillery in action on the Black Day.

Below: Following the Battle of Amiens German POWs are escorted to the rear, 8 August 1918.

Above: British troops storm forward on the Black Day. The horse-drawn artillery had trouble keeping pace with the British advance.

Above left: British troops fire into a German dugout to roust any German stragglers during the retreat from Delbar Wood near Roye, 29 August 1918.

Below: New Zealanders fire a captured German gun as they advance on the Black Day.

Below: Australian field artillery in action in open country on the same day.

ease the rapid transfer of force about the front. One was the Paris–Verdun line, in fact cleared by Mangin's counteroffensive of July. Another was the Verdun–Avricourt line at St Mihiel, which was eventually to be Pershing's objective; the third was the Paris–Amiens line, from which Haig was now to drive away the Germans.

His tactical plan mimicked that of the German spring offensives in every respect; short 'neutralizing' bombardment, infantry infiltration and aerial ground attack, to which was added the special ingredient of a massed tank vanguard. In all he had 554 tanks, of which 72 were the new 'Whippets,' light and fast enough to move at a cavalry pace into the German lines once the front had been broken. The bulk of his infantry were 'Colonials,' Canadians and Australians whose spirits had never been depressed as those of the home divisions had been by the trauma of March and April.

The ground favored the enterprise. It was a large plain called the Santerre, without hedges or large waterways, across which the tanks could advance at a uniform speed. The German defenses, having been dug only since April, were thin and poorly protected. Their occupants were taken completely by surprise on the morning of 8 August. Some had reported earlier hearing the sound of tank tracks, but higher authority had dismissed the reports as 'phantoms of the imagination or nervousness.' This may have been correct, for extraordinary trouble had been taken to disguise tank noise, special flights of airplanes had been employed to drown it by low-flying exercises. Whether alerted or not, the German infantry were overwhelmed by the tank armada when it emerged from the British lines:

Left: Australian troops rest in an abandoned German trench near a German field gun left behind in their retreat, 10 August 1918.

'The barrage had lifted,' a tank commander remembered, 'and moved on, so had the smoke curtain; the blanket of fog breaks up into wraiths, and these drift away over the undulating ground. The sun comes out through the mist, and before us is waving corn and figures disappearing in the distance, brandishing rifles as they run. The hunt is up!'

As they ran, the German infantry abandoned not only their front but also their support and reserve lines, quickly exposing their artillery to direct attack. A German gunner, deserted in this way, suddenly heard his battery sergeant major shout 'a tank, straight ahead':

'A light tank was roaring toward us at great speed, plunging into craters and climbing over trenches while his machine guns kept firing at our battery. Our men feverishly set the sights and fired one, two shells in rapid succession. Before us, there was a shattering roar followed by a dark cloud the size of a house; the tank had been destroyed. But this was only the beginning. Two more tanks appeared and were knocked out, then three more, the third of which was hit only 300 yards from the gun line. Only two German guns had survived the action and the battery officers were preparing to evacuate the position when one more warning cry rang out. "Tank on the right." A large gun tank, the seventh in a matter of minutes, came speeding straight toward us and opened a murderous fire when only 200 yards distant. Sergeant Wesel's gun was disabled while being trained on this new enemy. Its commander was badly wounded, its crew either wounded or killed. Our last gun's shield and sights were seriously damaged in the attack, but the crew did not give up the fight. Crouched behind the steel shield under a hail of bullets they turned the gun-carriage. The cool-headed pointer took aim and, at the very instant the tank plunged into the sunken path ahead of us, the fatal shell crashed through its side. Nothing but dense smoke and flying pieces of iron could be seen. The tank's destruction was our last-minute salvation. Now it was high time to fall back. The British assault troops behind the tanks were surging in all directions in small groups. Machine guns began rattling, bullets whizzed all round us. We dashed away from shell hole to shell hole.'

By evening, the tanks were seven miles beyond their start lines. Of the German defenders, 15,000 had been taken prisoner, many without having fired a shot. Four hundred guns had been captured. Six out of the 10 German divisions in line had ceased to exist. 'As the sun set on the battlefield of 8 August,' the German official history recorded, 'the greatest defeat which the German army had suffered since the beginning of the war was an accomplished fact.' Ludendorff himself called it 'the Black Day of the German army.' It marked the first moral collapse of the men under his command. Some reinforcements going up to the front even experienced being bleated at like sheep by those coming down, with cries of 'sheep to the slaughter' and 'war-prolongers!' There was more to come. The French also had a large force of tanks now, light models of Renault design, and during 9–11 August they pushed abreast of the British advance on the right, recapturing Montdidier. Then the whole line north of the Marne began to move. The salient above the Somme, on the flank of the gains of 8 August was retaken by the British in the last week of August. The French armies south of the Oise pushed steadily forward to reoccupy all the ground lost to the Germans in the May retreat until they were back on their original line. The Germans recorded this time as one of 'days spent in bloody fighting against an ever onstorming enemy and nights passed without sleep in retirement to new lines.'

On 14 August the Kaiser held a conference at Spa to consider the implications of these alarming events. It was attended by all Germany's military and political leaders and they now revealed a reluctant unanimity to seek an early peace: 'We have reached the limits of our endurance.' Ludendorff did not yet believe that this entailed asking for an armistice. Although his offensives had failed, and he had squandered

The ruins of the Cloth Hall at Ypres after the last Germans had been driven from the area which had been under siege for almost four years.

Above far left: Flame throwers in action by the Czech legionnaires of the Italian Army, 21 September 1918.

Above left: Czech legionnaires with their flame throwers on 3 August.

Above: The Austro–Hungarian *Sankt Stefan* sinks in the Adriatic, 10 June 1918.

Left: British cavalry pass the ruined basilica in Albert, Belgium in September 1918.

in them all the reserves with which to retain the initiative, he still believed that Germany was powerful enough to maintain a long defensive and so to 'gradually paralyze the enemy's will to fight.' He was thus thinking of a war which would last into 1919 at least. Paul von Hintze, the Foreign Secretary, was authorized to put out peace feelers. They were not to be direct — Spain and Holland were to be the intermediaries — and they were to be tried only at 'a suitable moment,' that is, when the military situation had stabilized. Moreover, no one present — Kaiser, the Chancellor Georg von Hertling, Hindenburg, Ludendorff and Hintze to name only the most prominent — was ready to relent from the war aims stated at the last headquarters conference which again were little different from those Germany had held throughout the war: protectorate over Belgium, annexation of the French iron fields, occupation of Liège and maintenance of the war frontier in the east.

On the same day, however, Emperor Karl I of Austria, his foreign minister, Count Burian, and his Chief of Staff, General Arz von Straussenburg, arrived at Spa with demands that the Central Powers make an immediate appeal for an end of the war to all belligerents without waiting for 'a suitable moment.' The Austrians had recently tried and failed in a last offensive on the Piave against Italy, the one enemy whom all the subjects of the empire were enthusiastic to fight, and the evidence of the declining power and unity of the Habsburg army had frightened its leaders into a desire for an immediate peace. Their visit began weeks of wrangling between the two empires over diplomatic policy. Not until 10 September did German headquarters — now the seat of all power — agree to 'arrange a conversation' with a neutral power.

By then events were moving faster than Ludendorff could control. On 12 September Pershing, who had at last succeeded in his aim of assembling an independent American army, launched his own offensive against the St Mihiel salient, which had been in German hands since September 1914. In fact, Ludendorff had decided to evacuate it four days before, but the

local commander was slow to carry out his instructions and the Americans' 12 divisions caught the defenders in the act of retirement. The offensive was thus a complete success, bringing 15,000 prisoners and great kudos for little cost. In the next two weeks the British army pressed forward along the whole length of the Hindenburg line, gradually penetrating the outworks and winning positions from which to make a final breakthrough. The French army reconstituted its forces to provide a reserve for a similar breakthrough battle on its part of the line. If and when the Hindenburg line was broken the situation of the German army in the West would be insupportable.

The breakthrough was now planned for 26 September and its key action was to be a drive by the American army into the Argonne, north of Verdun, a tangled wilderness of forest and streams. The Americans attacked with the panache that had now become their trademark, but were quickly impeded by the fallen trees and patches of marsh. Only outside the forest did their progress meet the timetable. On the next day the British First and Third Armies attacked north of Arras, on 28 September the British, French and Belgians attacked in Flanders and on 29 September the British Fourth and French First Armies advanced on the Somme. In all 160 Allied divisions moved to the attack and though the Germans counted 113 in the front line, Allied intelligence reckoned only 51 as fit for combat. All were well below strength, some with only 3000 infantry instead of the 9000 required by establishment.

The attack of the Fourth Army was decisive. At the end of the day's fighting it had cracked the Hindenburg position, the infantry crossing the huge, deep trenches via brushwood bundles dropped into them by tanks which led the attack. This bad news for German headquarters was reinforced by worse from the Balkans. On 29 September the Bulgarian government, whose army had been under continuous pressure by the Allied Salonika force throughout the month, sued for an armistice. Its defection laid open the way to the Danube and so to the back door of the Austrian empire, whose leaders were now frantic to make peace on almost any terms they could get. Under this double assault from front and rear, Ludendorff's nerve cracked. Taking Hindenburg with him for support, he sought an interview with the Kaiser and announced that President Wilson must be asked to arrange an armistice, 'at once, as early as at all possible.' Hintze, the Admiral who had recently been made Foreign Minister to replace the more moderate Kuhlmann, revealed how this maneuver was to be used to gain time without surrendering concrete strategic advantages. The High Command would impose a 'revolution from above' by appointing ministers from the ranks of the liberals, thus persuading Wilson that Germany had been democratized and so become a legitimate partner in his search for peace based on the Fourteen Points he had enunciated in January as a basis for a just and lasting settlement. While appropriate negotiations proceeded, the High Command would 'concentrate all the nation's resources for a final defensive struggle.' Next day Hertling, the High Command's nominee as Chancellor, was replaced by the liberal Prince Max of Baden. Matthias Erzberger and Gustav Stresemann, liberals from the parliamentary group, were also admitted to the Cabinet.

Wilson's Fourteen Points, which by no means carried the full support of his British and French cobelligerents, were a statement of high diplomatic and political idealism. Their aim was to reorder Europe so that the rights of small nations should henceforth be respected by large ones and to reform the practice of diplomacy so that secret agreements should not suddenly overwhelm the world in war as had happened in 1914. The freedom of the seas was to be guaranteed, armament to be reduced, colonial questions to be settled with regard to the interests of the peoples concerned, free trade to be fostered and an international body to safeguard peace established. None of that disfavored Germany. Those points which did, and they required the evacuation of all Germany's conquests, the re-arrangement of the Austrian and Turkish empires by 'self-determination' of the minority peoples and the creation of an independent Poland, might, it was hoped, be deferred until Germany had sufficiently recovered her military strength to oppose their application.

Curiously, during October the German army's strength did revive. Civilian labor had been used to construct a new defensive line toward which the armies fell back in easy stages. Bad weather and shortage of transport heightened among the Allies the 'diminishing power of the offensive,' which had now set in. The soldiers also seemed to have rediscovered the will to fight as the frontiers of the homeland appeared to be threatened. Certainly all Allied generals reported a stiffening of enemy resistance as they bumped up against the 'Flanders Position' in mid-October. By then, however, peace negotiations were in full swing. Ludendorff had instructed Prince Max to request an armistice and he had done so on 4 October, though of President Wilson not Marshal Foch. In his request he announced that Germany accepted the Fourteen

Above right: Americans advance near the Somme in September 1918.

Below: American troops in French tanks in the Argonne Forest.

Above: Tommies have a sing-song in a ruined church in Exermont.

Above left: Doughboys on the march in the Argonne.

Above: American wounded watch German POWs march into captivity in October 1918 in the Argonne campaign.

Left: The ruins of Cambrai on 19 October 1918.

Right: The British enter Lille, October 1918.

Points, which France and Britain had not yet done. Delighted, Wilson replied that he was ready to negotiate an armistice provided the acceptance was genuine and that Germany evacuated all occupied territory. Before Prince Max could clinch the deal a stroke of bad luck deflated his trial balloon. On 12 October a U-Boat sank a passenger ferry in the Irish Sea, drowning 450 civilians, some of them Americans. Public outrage, and his own anger, forced Wilson to adopt a firmer line. On 16 October he told the German Chancellor that submarine warfare must stop at once, that an armistice would have to be arranged with the Allied military commanders, and that there must be firmer evidence shown of Germany's democratization. Next day the German government and High Command debated these demands. Ludendorff, encouraged by the improving situation at the front, was for rejection and fighting on. Prince Max, after hearing all views, overruled him and announced accep-

Above: Generals Rawlinson, Byng, Horne, Lawrence and Birdwood surround their C in C, Field Marshal Sir Douglas Haig in Cambrai, 31 October 1918.

Above: Marshal Ferdinand Foch, C in C of the French army.

Right: Americans pause in the remains of the Argonne Forest.

Below: Americans press forward into the St Mihiel salient in early October 1918.

tance of Wilson's terms. He assured the President that Germany had indeed become democratized and on that basis Wilson asked the Allied generals on 23 October to draft armistice terms. At the same time he invited their governments to accept the Fourteen Points.

Both invitations prompted inter-Allied bargaining. Pershing, curiously, was against granting an armistice at all, since he believed he could win full victory with his fresh and untested army. Haig wanted no more than the Germans' withdrawal from occupied territory since he felt that his own army was flagging before the Germans' renewed strength. Foch was determined to get a French army into the Rhineland, which it had long been a secret French war aim to annex, and he persuaded the British to accept the condition in return for agreeing with their admirals that the High Seas Fleet should be interned in British waters. All parties agreed that the enemy must hand over large numbers of guns, machine guns and aircraft to prevent them renewing the struggle.

The Allied politicians also differed among themselves. They eventually accepted the Fourteen Points but rejected, on British insistence, the freedom of the seas. Clemenceau persuaded Lloyd George to demand German reparation of the war's cost, which was not in the Wilsonian spirit. Wilson would no doubt have argued the point, since he was still committed to a 'peace without victors or vanquished,' but his power to do so almost instantly evaporated as a result of the current congressional elections which promised to return a Republican and therefore Hun-hating but isolationist majority. The Republicans wanted no part of the League of Nations which was Wilson's dearest ideal. His potential role as protector of a 'democratized' Germany was further undermined by the sudden and progressive collapse of the Kaiser's allies. The 'easterners' who had always believed in 'knocking away the props' now saw their policy bearing fruit; the 'westerners,' who had believed in grinding away in France, would have said that it was the result of their policy. Certainly it seems to have been the spectacle of the great pillar of the Central Powers, Germany seeking a way out of the war which prompted her weaker partners to beat her to the post. On 30 October Turkey signed a local armistice with the British

in the Middle East, which allowed the Royal Navy to steam up the Dardanelles and a British garrison to occupy Constantinople.

In Austria a stranger turn of events began. The Habsburg Government, following Germany's example, asked Wilson to arrange an armistice on its fronts, which principally meant with Italy. Since enunciating the Fourteen Points Wilson had been persuaded by representatives of the Polish and Czech nationalists to promise his support for their independence as well as that of the Rumanians and Serbs within the empire. That being the case, he said it was for the representatives of those peoples to make their own terms with the Allies. Glimpsing the chance not merely to become independent but to end up on the winning side, Czechs and Poles immediately set up provisional governments of their own. The Hungarians, though a ruling not a subject people of the empire, tried the same trick, leaving only Austria proper as a combatant. Totally disoriented, the government in Vienna made no further move to disengage from the war until, on 23 October, the Italians took advantage of the empire's internal collapse to launch an offensive from the Piave. It was spectacularly successful, if chiefly because the Poles, Czechs and Slavs took the attack as an excuse to run for their new homelands as hard as they could. Shocked into sense, Vienna hastily begged an armistice, which was signed on 2 November, to come into effect 24 hours later. In the interval the Italians took 300,000 prisoners, many of whom would starve to death or die of disease in the coming winter.

In Germany, things were moving the other way. The spectacle of collapse in the East and suspicion of how harsh an armistice the Allies would impose had further hardened Ludendorff's determination to fight on. On 24 October he attempted a direct appeal to the army over the head of Prince Max, who immediately presented the Kaiser with a demand for Ludendorff's resignation against the threat of his own. The Kaiser, who knew that the Socialists in the Reichstag were calling for a republic, swiftly chose Max against Ludendorff, whose resignation he accepted in person on 26 October. He was now to experience identical trouble from his admirals. Knowing that the High Seas Fleet was to become a pawn of the armistice, they had begun to urge each other toward one last sortie into the North Sea, where by battle they might just improve the chance of settling the war on terms of equality. 'Better an honorable death than a shameful peace' was the nub of their argument.

American and French troops celebrate their victory in the streets of Paris, 11 November 1918.

Above: WACs and tanks behind the lines in June 1918.

Above left: British troops celebrate the end of their long war.

Below: Soldiers are carried aloft in the joyous frenzy of Armistice Day in Paris.

Left: Londoners celebrate their victory.

Below left: Presidents Wilson and Poincaré salute the Parisian crowd upon Wilson's triumphal arrival in the capital.

It did not appeal to their crews, who had not been out of harbor for two years and among whom trade unionism and socialism were strongly established. At the rumor of this 'death ride' on 29 October, the stokers of the Third Battle Squadron extinguished boiler fires and many of the other crew men announced that they would not raise anchor. Loyal sailors and marines removed the mutineers and took them ashore. That step merely transferred the trouble from the comparative isolation of the fleet to a more fertile seedbed. On 3 November the streets of Kiel filled with sailors and their allies among the dockyard workers, demanding the release of the prisoners. There was firing outside the prison, some demonstrators were killed and next day Kiel was in the hands of a Sailors' Soviet.

The disturbances at Kiel convinced the Berlin government that it had a revolution on its hands, which could only be checked by securing an immediate armistice. It would pacify popular opinion and also bring home the army in whose absence the government was without means to quell disorder. On 7 November, therefore, the German armistice Commission radioed Foch with an appeal for an immediate meeting and that evening sent its two civilian members, Erzberger and Oberndorff, to meet the Generalissimo at Rethondes in the forest of Compiègne. There Foch read them the terms next day, but by the time they returned to Berlin, revolution had caught fire. The Socialists, both radical and moderate, were demanding the Kaiser's abdication and the declaration of a republic. Prince Max himself was now convinced that only abdication could stave off disaster. That evening on the telephone, he advised, speaking:

'as a relative; your abdication has become necessary to save Germany from civil war. The great majority of the people believe you are responsible for the present situation. The troops are not to be depended upon. This is the last possible moment.'

The Kaiser, at his HQ in Spa, still refused.

He had gone to Spa from Berlin on the day he had dismissed Ludendorff, in order to be with his troops, the ultimate protectors of the House of Hohenzollern. Now even they were weighing their devotion to the All-Highest against the survival of more substantial things, not only domestic peace but the life of the army itself. On the night of 8 November Hindenburg — his old authority restored by the departure of Ludendorff — and General Wilhelm Gröner, the latter's successor, decided that they too felt as Prince Max did. Gröner immediately took the precaution of summoning to Spa 50 senior officers from the fighting line. Each was asked in strict secrecy if the Emperor at the head of his troops could 'reconquer the Fatherland by force' and if the troops would 'fight the Bolsheviks on the home front?' Only one answered yes to both questions, the others either no or an equivocation. Armed with this evidence, the two most senior officers of his army confronted the Kaiser in his office at Spa on the morning of 9 November and intimated to him that the war was lost and he must go. A prolonged and painful argument ensued, in which Crown Prince Wilhelm joined to challenge the evidence of the army's disaffection. Ultimately the Kaiser rounded on Gröner — the sacrilege of the proceedings had reduced Hindenburg to suffering silence — and demanded 'What of the oath on the Colors.' The

Right: Lloyd George, General Sir Henry Wilson and Marshal Foch in Paris.

Below right: Austrian Kaiser Karl I visits Kaiser Wilhelm's HQ at Spa in the last days of the war.

Oath (*Fahneneide*) was the personal word of loyalty until death sworn by every one of the Kaiser's officers on commissioning. Gröner shrugged and answered with exasperation, 'Today the Oath on the Colors is just words.

This shaft of appalling truth reduced the Kaiser first to silence and then to an offer to abdicate as Emperor but not as King of Prussia. Almost immediately word was brought that Prince Max had anticipated him and proclaimed the republic in Berlin. The officers now went on to warn that they could not guarantee the Kaiser's personal safety even at Imperial Headquarters and that he must at once go into exile. Holland was the obvious place of refuge as the nearest neutral country. He took his private train there the next morning. He was never to set foot on German soil again.

In Berlin, where socialists, disaffected soldiers, the hungry and the merely feckless were busy throwing down the symbols of monarchy from public buildings, the new republican government was so occupied with the business of asserting its authority that it scarcely had time to consider negotiating the armistice. Despite the harshness of the terms — surrender of Alsace-Lorraine, occupation of the Rhineland, annulment of the treaties of Brest-Litovsk with Russia and Bucharest with Rumania, transfer of main war stocks to the Allies and internment of the High Seas Fleet — Frederich Ebert, the new socialist Chancellor, simply instructed Erzberger to return to Compiègne and sign. There at 0500 hours on 11 November, in a railroad carriage parked in a siding in the forest, he did so. The armistice came into effect six hours later.

'On the morning of 11 November, remembered a British cavalryman, 'there were rumors of an armistice, but we did not take much notice of them.' It is not surprising that the British troops did not, for the German High Command had kept its rearguards full of the best, loyal troops who continued to fight even though giving ground throughout the first weeks of November:

'At about 1045 we were in action against the Germans east of Mons, and one of our troops had just charged some German machine guns. A private soldier came galloping toward us. He was much excited, had lost his cap, and could not stop his horse. As he passed us he shouted. 'The war's over! The war's over!' We thought undoubtedly the poor fellow was suffering from shell-shock.'

In the Vosges, a French officer still in the trenches noticed that his own men:

'retained their composure and self-control in these solemn moments. The attitude of our conquered armies was quite different. At 1100 hours sharp they surged out of their trenches, shouting and flourishing a red flag, and carrying big signs with the word 'Republic' written on them. Many Germans wore republican cockades in their caps. They were all eager to engage in conversation with our soldiers but, to their intense surprise, were disdainfully ignored by them. Having been rebuffed, they began celebrating the armistice in their own trenches; they threw grenades, blew up the ammunition dumps and in the evening fired all their star shells, illuminating the sky with an incomparable fireworks display. They also began to sing merry songs and played instruments, apparently not realizing that the armistice meant their country's complete collapse, the deepest humiliation ever suffered by Germany.'

Curiously the crowds celebrated too in the great German cities, welcoming back the first soldiers

from the front as if they were victors; and, like victors, the soldiers came home with flowers in their buttonholes and rifle-muzzles, just as they had done when the regiments marched away in that distant August of 1914. In the cities of the Allies, celebrations were more unrestrained:

'There was great liveliness, calls, cries, whistles and hooters sounding, noise and crowds grew as we proceeded' a traveller from the suburbs to inner London recorded. 'Chancery Lane was very lively. Going out for lunch about one o'clock, great excitement prevailed. Every vehicle going along the Strand was being boarded by people, most of whom waved flags. Boys and girls flung themselves on anywhere and boarded as best they might. One scene was more unusual than others. A stout policeman on point duty was surrounded by girls all clamouring to dance with him. The London bobby rose to the occasion — without a word he took on one after another for a turn round on the narrow pavement as they stood, while his countenance remained absolutely impassive. Custom and convention melted away as if a new world had indeed dawned. Officers and privates mixed in equal comradeship. Privates drilled officers, munitionettes commanded platoons made up of both. The spirit of militarism turned into comedy. Never in history perhaps have such great multitudes, experienced such restoration of joyousness in the twinkling of an eye.'

Was there to be 'a new world' of which this Londoner had glimpsed the dawning in the rejoicing crowds? Wilson was determined that there should be. Lloyd George had promised one ('A land fit for heroes'), while far away in Russia Lenin believed he had begun to build one. In the lands between the leaders of the new independent nations — Poland, Czechoslovakia, the Kingdom of the Serbs, Croats and Slovenes (Yugoslavia) — were disputing with the old and with each other the exact shape each of their people's new worlds should take. While peace broke out in the West, war continued or found new outlets in the East. The leaders of the Baltic minorities, Latvians, Lithuanians and Estonians, whose independence the Bolsheviks had recognized along with Finland's, were soon at war with their own Reds, through whom the Bolsheviks hoped to work a widening of the Revolution. In Hungary there shortly was to be a new Bolshevik government, under the leadership of Bela Kun. Poland had begun or was on the point of fighting three enemies, the Ukrainians for the possession of eastern Galicia, the Germans for Lower Silesia, Posen and West Prussia, the Russians for an eastern border — and eventually for the survival of their new state. Italian patriots, under the leadership of the poet-demagogue Gabriele d'Annunzio, had staked their kingdom's claim to the head of the Adriatic, while the Greeks were set on pushing the boundaries of the Kingdom of the Hellenes, deep into Anatolia. In its remote fortresses, Kemal, the defender of Gallipoli, was gathering some scraps of the broken Ottoman army to oppose them. Strangest of all the wars were those of 'intervention' against Russia. The Allies' decision to support the Whites against the Reds, while the latter seemed to be co-operating in Germany's war effort, had led to the landing of some British, French, American and even Japanese troops at the Whites' supply ports, Archangel, the Crimea and Vladivostok, while British naval flotillas operated in the eastern Baltic.

This sea of confusion was too wide and too troubled for the peacemakers to make their concern. They could not even yet begin to consider what peace they should offer Turkey or Austria (what remained of it) or Hungary. During December and January of 1918–19, it was as much as they could do to agree on a policy for peace-making with Germany. That

country had more or less restored internal order by 18 January 1919, when the Peace Conference was convoked at Versailles. The Spartakist revolt in Berlin had been put down. The German army, which had dissolved itself overnight as soon as its columns had marched into their home barracks, had been replaced with a makeshift but efficient stopgap, recruited from right-wing *Freikorps* raised to buttress the authority of the republican government. Without an army capable of defending the national frontiers, the republic was at the mercy of the victors' goodwill when it came to meeting them at the Conference table, and there was to be little goodwill at Versailles.

France, who had suffered most, insisted on extortionate terms. She wanted the permanent and almost total disarmament of Germany, long-term occupation of the Rhineland, which she actually hoped to establish as a separate state under her influence, and reparations of a size calculated not merely to make good the devastation of her territory but also the expense she had incurred in defending it. The British were almost equally as demanding. They were

Left: Italian patriot Gabriele d'Annunzio (right) seized Fiume for Italy in a daring coup after the war.

Below: Austrian President Carl Renner replies to the peace terms offered by Clemenceau and Wilson (background).

determined to keep the High Seas Fleet (which, in a sense, they did when its crews scuttled their ships in the anchorage of Scapa Flow on 21 June 1919). Their dominions — Australia and South Africa — were also anxious to possess the adjoining German Colonies, New Guinea and Southwest Africa, so Westminster chummily offered to annex the rest in East and West Africa. A device, known as a League of Nations Mandate, was invented to regularize this imperialism, and the French made use of it to divide the Turkish Middle East with the British. They took Syria and the Lebanon, their ally Iraq (Mesopotamia) and Palestine, where thousands of European Jews had now begun to settle under the provision of the Balfour Declaration. The Americans, whose foreign policy was still determined by Wilson, demanded nothing for themselves, not even reparations, but were intent on all parties accepting their League of Nations, even Germany who was not to be admitted to it.

When Wilson was satisfied that his fellow peacemakers — Lloyd George, the Italian Vittorio Orlando and Clemenceau (who at 79 survived the wound of a would-be assassin while the Conference was in progress) — would form the League he readily agreed to their individual demands. The Germans were scarcely consulted. Democratized or not, they were regarded and treated by the Allies as enemies, and the blockade was maintained throughout the spring of 1919 to ensure that they would accept the Allied terms. In May these terms were presented. France had reduced her financial demands to the indemnification of war damage, as long as Germany admitted 'war guilt.' The Rhineland was to be occupied for 15 years and thereafter permanently 'demilitarized.' The frontier with Poland was fixed very much where the Poles asked for it, though a plebiscite was allowed in Silesia. Austria, against the wishes of its German-speaking population, was forbidden to unite with Germany. Above all, Germany was disarmed. The air force was abolished, the navy forbidden submarines or heavy ships, the army

Below: Thomas Masaryk, President of the new Czech Republic.

forbidden tanks or heavy artillery and reduced to a strength of 100,000 men, who must all be 12-year volunteers. There was to be no chance of building up hidden reserves with rapidly-trained conscripts. Allied inspectors, with wide powers of entry, were to police these provisions.

German opinion was outraged by the treaty. It seemed to make a mockery of the sacrifice each social group had made in ending the war; that of the monarchy by the traditional right and center, that of self-defense by the threatened peasants and landowners of the eastern frontier, that of political popularity by the socialists and liberals who had created the republic. Reparations threatened the pockets of all classes, the confession of 'war guilt' stuck in the throats of all patriots — and Versailles made every German a patriot. Even the peace-loving Ebert, now President, was driven to ask Hindenburg what chance there was of resuming the war as an act of protest. Through Gröner, his spokesman in every awkward moment, Hindenburg replied that 'the Army might hold its own against the Poles in the East. It could not resist an Allied advance in the West.' On 28 June 1919, a silent and embittered German delegation signed the treaty in the Hall of Mirrors at Versailles.

So ended the First World War. Men had already begun an attempt to reckon its cost in lives. Men still continue today. The British Empire had lost 1,000,000 dead; indeed, a tablet placed in every French cathedral records that fact: 'To the Glory of God and in memory of One Million men of the British Empire who fell in the Great War, and of whom the greater part rest in France.' About 750,000 were British and Irish, the rest Australians, Canadians, South Africans, New Zealanders, Indians and Africans. The French, with a smaller population, had suffered worse. About 1,700,000 Frenchmen had died. German casualties were usually recorded at the same figure, but may have exceeded 2,000,000. The Americans had suffered only about 125,000 casualties, quite enough considering how short their active war had been. Russia's losses were counted at over 1,000,000 before the February

Below: Bela Kun, who headed a Communist government in Hungary for four months in 1919.

Revolution, but were certainly many more, perhaps three times that. The peoples of Austria-Hungary suffered over 1,000,000 deaths, the Italians over 600,000. Turkish losses were never counted. In total there were probably 10,000,000 battle deaths in the First World War. Civilian casualties by privation, atrocity and disease, in particular through the great 'Spanish' flu epidemic which swept through the under-nourished populations of Europe in the winter of 1918, were higher. In all the war caused directly or indirectly the deaths of at least 20,000,000 people.

It had also transformed the map of Europe, inaugurated revolutionary regimes in new and old states which would never have come to power in the settled days of pre-1914, and shaken the industrial and financial world to its foundations. Grievances and rancors far more bitter than those which had animated the selfish and aggressive foreign policies of the powers in the last years of Imperial Europe had taken deep root and would fester on. The Bolsheviks, mis-used by the Germans, attacked by the Allies and then made a diplomatic pariah, would feed their belief in eventual ideological triumph on the discharge of these wounds. The Balkan peoples and their Turkish neighbors would each resent either what they had lost by the war or the bigger prizes of which they had been cheated. The Italians above all would see in its outcome a frustration of their 'divine selfishness,' and look to dictatorship for a chance to indulge it again. The Germans were not yet thinking of dictator-ship. Their belief in the unreality of defeat, in the 'crime' of Versailles, in their right to primacy in continental Europe was absolute and they would use any means to achieve them. Their provinces teemed with violent men who had

Right: Renner at St Germain during the peace talks.

Far right: The victory parade down the Avenue de la Grande Armée in Paris.

Below: Orlando, Lloyd George, Clemenceau and Wilson.

learned the philosophy of struggle in the trenches, applied it in the Civil Wars of 1918–19 and were ready to use it again against Germany's foreign neighbors, to east or west, north or south, if struggle would make Germany great once more. One of them was an ex-corporal of the 16th Bavarian Reserve Infantry Regiment, thrice wounded on the Western Front, called Adolf Hitler.

The war had changed more than people's nationalities, political status and economic expectations. It had also changed their way of looking at the world. The Europe which died on 31 July 1914 was not a fairyland. Its peoples knew inequality, oppression, exploitation and injustice. They also knew peace and order and expected to die in their beds. The First World War had carried violent death into every family circle. To those who had fought, it had shown the skull beneath the skin, often by direct and unforgettable confrontation. The men of the trenches might seek to obliterate from their minds the horrors but few ever managed, some chose not to and none could ever feel again an

absolute respect for the sanctity of human life. A terrible ugliness had been born on the Somme, at Verdun, on the vast nameless battlefields of the Carpathians and the Ukraine, along the choked stream beds of the Argonne and Ypres, which lent a dreadful and profane irony to the most beautiful and best-loved of all First World War poems by John McRae.

In Flanders fields the poppies blow
Beneath the crosses, row on row
That mark our place; and in the sky
The larks, still bravely singing, fly
Scarce heard amid the guns below.

We are the Dead. Short days ago
We lived, felt dawn, saw sunset glow,
Loved and were loved, and now we lie
In Flanders Fields.

Take up our quarrel with the foe;
To you from failing hands we throw
The torch; be yours to hold it high.
If ye break faith with us who die
We shall not sleep, though poppies grow
In Flanders Fields.

A victorious Tommy on his way home.

Casualty Figures

Balance of Casualties 1914-1918
Allies

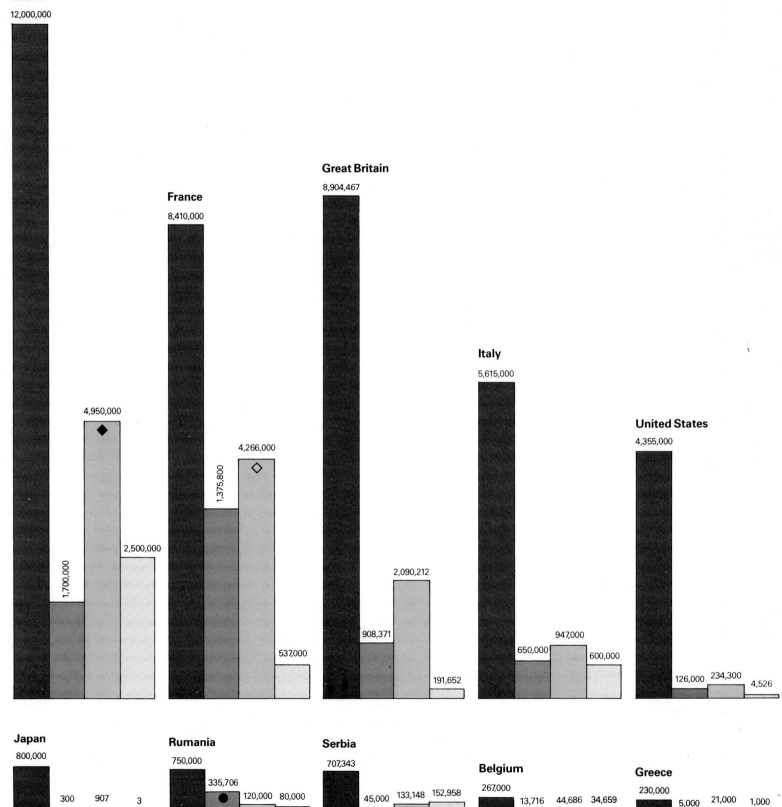

Russia
12,000,000

France
8,410,000

Great Britain
8,904,467

Italy
5,615,000

United States
4,355,000

4,950,000
1,700,000
2,500,000

1,375,800
4,266,000
537,000

908,371
2,090,212
191,652

650,000
947,000
600,000

126,000
234,300
4,526

Japan
800,000
300   907   3

Rumania
750,000
335,706
120,000   80,000

Serbia
707,343
45,000   133,148   152,958

Belgium
267,000
13,716   44,686   34,659

Greece
230,000
5,000   21,000   1,000

Portugal
100,000   7,222   13,751   12,318

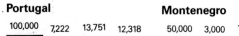

Montenegro
50,000   3,000   10,000   7,000

Central Powers

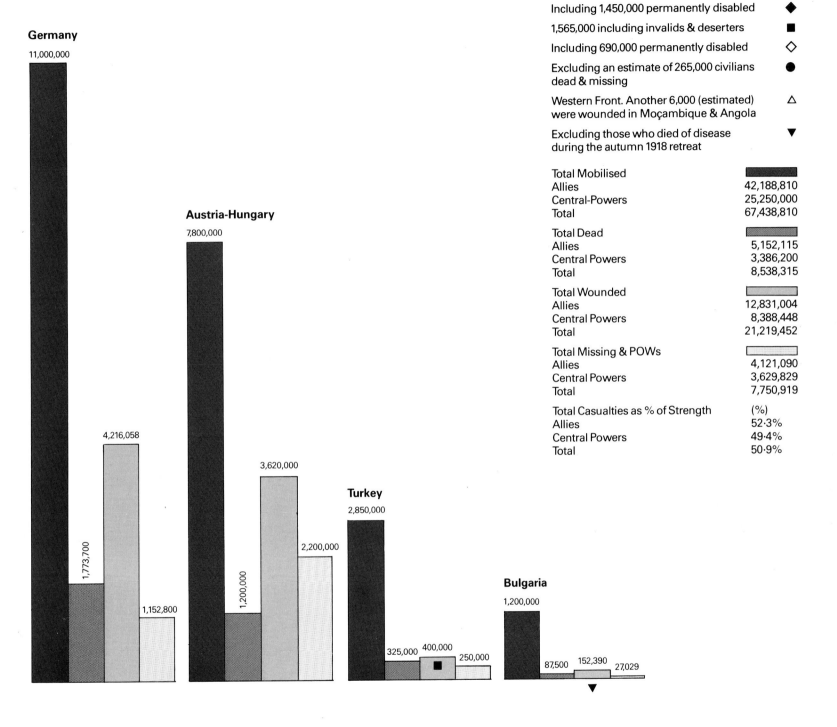

Germany

11,000,000

1,773,700

4,216,058

1,152,800

Austria-Hungary

7,800,000

1,200,000

3,620,000

2,200,000

Turkey

2,850,000

325,000

400,000

250,000

Bulgaria

1,200,000

87,500

152,390

27,029

Including 1,450,000 permanently disabled ◆

1,565,000 including invalids & deserters ■

Including 690,000 permanently disabled ◇

Excluding an estimate of 265,000 civilians ●
dead & missing

Western Front. Another 6,000 (estimated) △
were wounded in Moçambique & Angola

Excluding those who died of disease ▼
during the autumn 1918 retreat

Total Mobilised	
Allies	42,188,810
Central-Powers	25,250,000
Total	67,438,810

Total Dead	
Allies	5,152,115
Central Powers	3,386,200
Total	8,538,315

Total Wounded	
Allies	12,831,004
Central Powers	8,388,448
Total	21,219,452

Total Missing & POWs	
Allies	4,121,090
Central Powers	3,629,829
Total	7,750,919

Total Casualties as % of Strength	(%)
Allies	52·3%
Central Powers	49·4%
Total	50·9%

Index

Acknowledgments

The author would like to thank the Robert Hunt Library for supplying most of the pictures used in this book. The author would also like to thank the agencies listed below for allowing the reproduction of the following pictures:

BBC Hulton Picture Library: pp 16 (bottom left and right), 100 (center), 142 (top right), 145 (top), 157 (top), 165 (bottom right), 243 (bottom right).
Bundesarchiv: pp 21 (bottom right), 22 (top left), 23 (top right), 64–65, 64 (bottom left), 88 (top), 98 (bottom), 100 (top left), 138–139, 146 (top), 148–149 (top), 160–161, 162–163, 180–181 (top), 182 (bottom), 188–189, 189 (top right), 199 (center right), 203 (top left), 206–207, 221 (bottom).
Imperial War Museum: pp 8–9, 14 (top), 15 (main picture), 20 (top right), 27 (bottom), 34, 38 (top right), 38 (center), 40 (top left), 40–41, 41 (bottom right), 43 (both), 46–47, 46 (top both), 48 (top right), 49 (top left, bottom left and center right), 54 (center), 55 (center), 56 (top), 57 (top), 58–59, 59 (center), 60 (center), 61 (center), 62–63, 63 (top), 65 (top left), 66 (top), 67 (top right), 69

(top both), 70 (center), 71 (top right and center), 72–73, 88 (bottom), 89 (all three), 90–91 (all five), 92–93, 92 (top), 94–95 (all four), 99 (bottom), 100–101, 101 (top three), 102–103, 102 (center), 103 (top left), 104 (bottom right), 105 (top left and bottom right), 106–107, 107 (center), 108–109, 110–111, 111 (center), 112–113, 113 (top), 114–115, 121 (top both), 123 (center and bottom right), 124, 125 (bottom both), 126–127, 128 (bottom right), 129 (top left and bottom both), 130 (top), 133 (center), 136, 149 (top), 150–151, 156 (top right), 158–159 (top), 163 (top), 164 (bottom left), 168 (top and center left), 170–171, 172 (top), 172–173, 174–175, 176–177, 178–179 (all five), 180 (top), 181, 182–183 (top), 196–197, 198–199 (top and bottom), 202 (top), 203 (top right and center left), 212–213, 214–215 (bottom), 215 (bottom), 218 (both), 219 (bottom), 221 (top), 222–223, 222 (top), 224–225, 226–227, 228 (bottom), 233 (bottom), 234 (top), 242–243 (bottom), 244 (center), 246–247.
National Archives: pp 194 (top), 195 (top left), 198 (top), 200 (top), 206 (top), 213 (top), 215

(top), 230–231, 235 (bottom), 236–237, 238–239, 240 (bottom).
National Maritime Museum: pp 98 (top), 99 (top), 106 (top both), 107 (top).
Novosti: pp 18 (bottom), 21 (bottom left), 140 (bottom), 154–155.
Ullstein: pp 74–75, 75 (top left), 77 (bottom), 78–79, 79 (center), 80 (top right), 81 (top both), 96–97, 100 (top right).
USAF: pp 119 (top both), 120 (bottom), 133 (top right), 134 (bottom).
US Army: p 235 (top left).
USIS: pp 190–191, 216–217.
US Navy: pp 196–197.

The author would like to thank the following people who helped prepare this book:
David Eldred, who designed it; Catherine Bradley and Jane Laslett, who edited the text; Richard Natkiel, who prepared the maps; Mike Badrocke, who drew the technical illustration on p 130; Peter Endsleigh Castle, who drew the technical illustration on p 135; and Donald Slater, who prepared the index.